Natural Law

The Library of Conservative Thought
Milton Hindus, Series Editor

Natural Law

An Introduction to Legal Philosophy

Alexander Passerin
d'Entrèves

With a new introduction
by Cary J. Nederman

Transaction Publishers
New Brunswick (U.S.A.) and London (U.K.)

Second printing 1996
New material this edition copyright © 1994 by Transaction
Publishers, New Brunswick, New Jersey 08903.
Originally published in 1951 by Hutchinson & Co, Ltd.

This book is printed on acid-free paper that meets the American National
Standard for Permanence of Paper for Printed Library Materials.

Library of Congress Catalog Number: 92-37171
ISBN: 1-56000-673-0
Printed in the United States of America

Library of Congress Cataloging-in-Publication Data

Passerin d'Entrèves, Alessandro, 1902–
    Natural law : an introduction to legal philosophy / Alexander
Passerin d'Entrèves : with a new introduction by Cary J. Nederman.
      p. cm.
    Originally published: Hutchinson & Co., 1951.
    Includes bibliographical references and index.
    ISBN 1-56000-673-0
    1. Natural law. 2. Law—Philosophy. I. Title.
K460.P37   1993
340'.112—dc20   92-37171
                                           CIP

CONTENTS

INTRODUCTION TO THE TRANSACTION EDITION

The doctrine of natural law is perhaps as ancient as the very notion of law itself in Western thought. Inseparable from the early Greek discussion of *nomos*, human law or convention, was the recognition of its inherent connection with *physis*, nature in a specifically human as well as a broader cosmological sense. For the Greeks, the salient problem was the appropriate relation between nature and human laws and ways of life. Did law hinder or promote the realization of a truly human existence? Was it possible to establish any absolute or general standards of human conduct beyond the conventions and legislation that specific communities adopted? Such questions stimulated answers formulated according to the notion of the law of nature, construed as a principle of conduct accessible to every rational being.

Despite its continuing appeal even at the close of the twentieth century,[1] the history of natural law thinking has never really been untroubled. That loose grouping of legal philosophers who are today associated with the so-called "positivist" conception of law are in many ways the inheritors of an on-going critique of natural law that can be traced back through Jeremy Bentham, Thomas Hobbes, Marsiglio of Padua, St. Augustine and Protagoras, among others. Politically, natural law ideas have been judged both revolutionary and reactionary: the latter, because they have been employed to justify or support religious and cultural intolerance, racism, classism, sexism, and a variety of other attitudes that are by no means universal or necessary; the former, because such teachings have provided the groundwork for the withdrawal of allegiance from, and even violent resistance to, tyrants and authoritarian regimes in many ages (ranging from Cicero and John of Salisbury to John Locke and the Declarations of Independence and of the Rights of Man).

The doubts evinced by modern as well as ancient critics remain.

Is the attraction of natural law a result of its arbitrariness or ideological elasticity? Are there any substantial and valid lessons to be learnt from the study of natural law theory? Has the very notion of the law of nature been exhausted? One of the most thoughtful and nondogmatic attempts to take up the challenge of defending natural law in recent times was a comparatively slender volume by Alexander (or Alessandro) Passerin d'Entrèves, entitled *Natural Law: An Introduction to Legal Philosophy*, published in 1951. Through eight reprintings, and the publication of a second edition in 1970, as well as translation into Spanish and Italian, d'Entrèves' little book served as a standard work on its topic for a generation of political, social, and legal philosophers and theorists. Although long out of print, *Natural Law* is still required reading in some educational institutions even today. Thus, *Natural Law* deserves our attention as much for its continuing philosophical value as for its influence during the latter half of the twentieth century.

A.P. D'ENTRÈVES

In spite of its popularity among students and teachers, *Natural Law* is in some ways an intensely personal book, in style as well as in substance, as its author himself admitted (d'Entrèves 1970, 11). It reflects not only the academic interests of d'Entrèves in political theory and jurisprudence, but also his cultural, religious, and political experiences in Italy and Britain during the 1930s and 1940s. Thus, a full appreciation of *Natural Law* properly requires some anterior familiarity with d'Entrèves himself.

Throughout his life, d'Entrèves remained closely tied to his native Piedmont, and especially to the Val d'Aosta. He was born in 1902, the fourth son of Count Hector Passerin d'Entrèves et Courmayeur. His early environment in the family castle near the southern slopes of Mt. Blanc was at once provincial and cosmopolitan: growing up on the frontier on which Italy borders both France and Switzerland, he was exposed to a broad range of cultural experiences; yet his devotion to his region and its autonomy was so deeply felt as to claim his first loyalty during his entire life. As late as 1979, d'Entrèves published in Italian a collection of essays on the local history of the Val d'Aosta. Nor was his dedication to his native locale exceptional: it was shared, for instance, with his nephew, Ettore Passerin d'Entrèves, and with Federico Chabod, both prominent Italian historians with strong roots in the valley (see d'Entrèves 1960 and Traniello 1988, 9–10 and note 4).

D'Entrèves completed initial training in law at the University of Turin, receiving his Doctor of Law degree in 1922. The award of a Rockefeller Foundation travelling fellowship brought him to Balliol College, Oxford in 1926 for advanced studies. This crystallized a lifelong admiration of England and, especially, Oxford. Indeed, d'Entrèves soon came to affect the sort of rigorous adherence to the English manner at which non-English Anglophiles are so adept. This quality was captured quite incisively in a description of him by George Morton, an English army officer who encountered d'Entrèves in the Val d'Aosta at the close of the Second World War. Morton reports that d'Entrèves greeted him with the words: " 'Were you by any chance at Oxford or Cambridge?' When I said I was at Cambridge he replied: 'Oh, alas, I was at the other place' . . . It was astonishing to meet this charming cultured figure speaking perfect English and wearing very English clothes" (Morton 1986).

D'Entrèves' love for England extended to his choice of thesis topic. He elected to study the work of the enigmatic but influential English political theorist and churchman Richard Hooker, whose name is closely associated with the Anglican church in the age of Elizabeth I. D'Entrèves' research was conducted under the guidance of some of the best historians of the day, including A.J. Carlyle, A.D. Lindsay, and R.H. Tawney. The central theme of the dissertation revolved around Hooker's relation to his medieval antecedents. D'Entrèves concluded that Hooker's conception of law (particularly natural law) constituted a significant departure from the preceding tradition, despite certain evident debts. Hooker appeared in the thesis as a "transitional" figure, midway between Aquinas and Locke. In this regard, as in so much of his scholarship, d'Entrèves articulated a balanced and nondogmatic interpretation of his topic.

Although the dissertation was not submitted for the doctorate until 1932, d'Entrèves returned to Italy in 1929 to take up a lectureship in the Faculty of Law at his alma mater. He rose steadily up the academic ladder, accepting in rapid succession chairs at Messina and Pavia. During the 1930s, he published an Italian version of his dissertation and a more general study of medieval political philosophy, also in Italian. This research he consolidated into a series of lectures delivered at Oxford during the summer term of 1938 and published the following year under the title, *The Medieval Contribution to Political Thought*.

The rise of fascism was not congenial to d'Entrèves' liberal temper, and he became an increasingly outspoken figure in his native land. Although he was appointed to a chair at Turin in 1938, he soon chose to withdraw from academic life entirely. Returning to his ancestral home, he involved himself actively in the resistance movement, joining his wife, Nina, whom he had married in 1931, and other family members. The cause of the partisans made a profound intellectual as well as personal impact on d'Entrèves. For it seemed to him that the "real heroes" who emerged during the Resistance were the embodiment of the principles of natural law that he had already begun to address in his prewar writings (d'Entrèves 1970, 202). It was not simply the recollection of the physical courage of fallen comrades that led him to dedicate *Natural Law* "to the memory of many a friend of later and darker days"; it was instead his view that their "deeds bear witness to the existence of the Law which alone deserves ultimate allegiance" (1970, 12). D'Entrèves contended that the vitality of natural law (as the intersection between morality and legal statute) was confirmed by the actions of "men and women who, rather than submit to injustice and tyranny, took the bitter road into exile, or actually staked their lives for the sake of the cause of humanity. Shall we not say that good old natural law took its revenge?" (1970, 144).

The period immediately following the liberation, d'Entrèves devoted to the service of his native region. He acted briefly as the Podesta of Aosta prior to the arrival of staff from the Allied Military Government, and he was selected in December 1945 to sit as a member of the Council of the Val d'Aosta. The opportunity for a renewal of academic pursuits came during 1946 in the form of an invitation from Oxford to take up a fellowship at Magdalen College and the Serena Chair of Italian Studies. He was reluctant to accept the position since, as he told George Morton, he felt a strong responsibility to contribute to the rebuilding of postwar Italy. Morton advised d'Entrèves that "he would be helping Italy more by going to Oxford" (1986, 14). D'Entrèves seems to have taken this counsel to heart, judged by the direction of his research interests upon his return to Oxford: he published a set of reflections on Italian history in 1947; he delivered the 1949 annual Italian lecture to the British Academy on the topic of the nineteenth-century Italian poet and novelist Alessandro Manzoni; and he released a study of Dante's thought in 1952.

D'Entrèves did not, however, abandon his work on legal and political philosophy. In 1948, the Committee on Social Thought at the University of Chicago, a haven for many exiled European intellectuals such as Leo Strauss and Hannah Arendt, invited him to deliver a lecture series on the topic of natural law. This permitted him "the opportunity . . . to return to a subject which has been on my mind for many years" (1970, 11). In revised and polished form, the Chicago lectures were published three years later as *Natural Law*.

LEGAL PHILOSOPHY AT MID-CENTURY

D'Entrèves constructed his remarks in Chicago, as well as the book to which they gave rise, mindful of the highly polarized state of legal philosophy at the time. The prevalent approach—one which had indeed nearly achieved hegemony within jurisprudence by 1950— may be broadly classified as legal positivism. The origins of the positivist school, while perhaps traceable to Bentham and Hobbes, lay directly in the writings of the nineteenth-century English jurist John Austin, who held that the essential characteristic of law was its capacity to command obedience. Adherence to some version of the Austinian thesis united the main body of jurisprudential thinking at the middle of the twentieth century, including such major figures in the field as H.L.A. Hart, Hans Kelsen, Alf Ross, and Noberto Bobbio. The goal of responding to the legal theory enunciated by these thinkers guided d'Entrèves' arguments in *Natural Law*.

It would be a mistake, however, to view legal positivism as a single, unified movement. Rather, the term more accurately denotes a range of efforts to work out the consequences for the theory and practice of law of the adoption of several related claims.[2] Specifically, legal positivists would seem logically committed to at least four propositions:

1. Law constitutes a domain of inquiry separate from morality in a manner analogous to the distinction between fact and value.
2. The validity of law is "external" rather than "internal" in the sense that the command of a law—not the contents of the law itself—render its observance obligatory.
3. Resolution of all questions arising in regard to the dictates and requirements of law is a wholly empirical matter the determination of which falls to the expertise of the legal practitioner.
4. The primary (if not sole) consideration for whether a law should be enacted is its consistency with the preexisting legal frame work.

Thus, for legal positivism, as for scientific positivism, the role of the philosopher is severely diminished. At best, the legal philosopher becomes a sort of gatekeeper, halting and repulsing attempts to insinuate moral or value-laden issues into the study and practice of law. But this effectively abolishes legal philosophy itself. Traditional philosophical questions regarding the essence of law or ideal legal standards are excluded from jurisprudence. This does not, of course, imply that the positivist must uphold the meaninglessness of such questions per se. The concern of legal positivism is instead to ensure that problems of that kind remain wholly within the realm of moral and political philosophy and do not intrude into and confuse issues of jurisprudence.

Legal positivism is thus overtly hostile to theories of natural law, inasmuch as they seek to establish independent or external criteria for the legitimation of statutory legislation (see Shiner 1992). The very expression "*natural* law," positivists charge, misuses the word "nature," since it denotes not the physical world at all but instead a universal moral code the tenets of which are rational rather than empirical (see Hart 1961, 182–83). This fundamental confusion in the use of the term "nature" leads to the more damaging accusation that natural law theory ultimately proves to be either arbitrary or vacuous. For to the extent that the natural law theorist maintains that there exist definite universal precepts to which any positive law deserving of the name must conform, he is committed to the specification of these precepts. When such principles have been stated in the past, they have tended to be not especially universal at all, but on the contrary extremely contingent and often linked to the justification of forms of oppression or subordination (for example, the alleged "natural" inferiority of women, racial or ethnic groups, socioeconomic classes, and so on). In other words, the appeal to natural law commonly turns out to be the mere universalization of particular historical beliefs and prejudices; natural law confuses values for facts, it is a reification.

Some natural law thinkers—starting perhaps as early as Cicero—have attempted to allay this objection by treating natural law in a more formalized manner. The formalistic approach holds that the status of natural law is to be accorded to whatever laws are conducive to the maintenance of the bonds of human society. Thus, for instance, the institution of private property may not be strictly dictated by the content of natural law, but once it is seen to be necessary for the perpetuation of stable association (else conflicts over scarce resources could not be settled peacefully), it acquires the authorization of natural law. In this sense, then, natural law is not a permanent set of moral doctrines; it is a flexible system of justice whose standard of judgment is the conduciveness of human law to social life. While this conception indeed avoids the charge of arbitrariness, it does so, as positivists have pointed out, only at the price of trivializing the very idea of the law of nature. For at the core of natural law thinking has been the claim that moral precepts of universal force can be translated into a basis for ascertaining the vitality of human law. The formalized interpretation of natural law, however, reduces this judgment to an essentially utilitarian process. In principle, natural law construed formally could authorize any statute whatsoever provided only that it was consistent with the maintenance of human association. Hence, the moral limits which natural law purports to establish are emptied of content.

The main challenge to the dominance of legal positivism during the first half of the century arose from the neo-Thomist school of philosophy pioneered by such Roman Catholic luminaries as Jacques Maritain and Etienne Gilson. Once again, it must be emphasized that neo-Thomism admits of a great deal of variation. Yet the gist of the neo-Thomist approach can nevertheless be stated: it aims at the revival of the Christianized teleology pioneered by Aquinas. The basic neo-Thomist principle is perhaps summarized by the equation "*natura, id est Deus.*" God as creator of all nature endowed the human species with its own ends which may be ascertained through both reason and revelation. The object of rational reflection regarding the good is, in effect, natural law; but natural law must be strictly consonant with divine law decreed directly by God through revelatory experience. The neo-Thomists thus appropriate the conceptual matrix propounded by Aquinas, according to which human beings, on account of their dual natures, may legitimately seek both earthly and eternal goods, yet always with the eternal as the ultimate or final goal. This permits all rational creatures to discover for themselves the dictates of justice that are central to the law of nature. Yet insofar as such dictates must conform to God's own law, individual conclusions about the content of natural law are always subject to evaluation by those who are especially trained and spiritually qualified to understand and apply divine law, namely, the priesthood and its leadership. Hence, natural law cannot be equated with a simple appeal to individual conscience or reason. The fact that God stands behind and warrants natural law means that the Church enjoys special authority to determine and pronounce on the tenets of that law. This affords the Church and its minions a unique responsibility for judging and criticizing positive human legislation when it does not accord with the terms set out by the law of nature.

There is little doubt that the attraction of the neo-Thomist position

was directly related to the perceived moral bankruptcy of legal positivism. Adherence to positivism on the part of jurists under fascist,
Nazi, and collaborating governments has often been adduced to explain their readiness to acquiesce to the decrees of those regimes
without regard for broader considerations of right.[3] Yet the impact of
neo-Thomism was largely confined to jurisprudence and philosophy
in Catholic academic institutions in France and sections of North
America. Consequently, the wartime and immediate postwar period
saw virtually no direct dialogue between positivists and neo-Thomists.
Each position flourished in a state of relative geographic, disciplinary
and/or institutional isolation from the other. It seems unlikely that
much constructive discussion between the two perspectives would
have been possible in any case, given the vast gulf separating the
theological underpinnings of neo-Thomism from the skeptical value-
freedom of the positivist stance.

D'ENTRÈVES AS NATURAL LAW THEORIST

In many ways, *Natural Law* represents an attempt to make a fresh
start at the study of the philosophy of law from a standpoint outside
and beyond the prevalent positivist and neo-Thomist models. Readers
should not be deterred by the subtitle of the book—*An Introduction to
Legal Philosophy*—or by the author's apology in his first forward
for the "tertiary" character of his scholarship and the "foreign" quality of his philosophical language. However genuine the modesty
expressed by d'Entrèves, *Natural Law* is no simple textbook for the
uninitiated. Although its survey of natural law theory is plainly stated,
balanced, and accessible, the volume's overriding purpose is the
presentation of a sustained and independent defense of natural law
as the foundation for any coherent philosophy of law. At the same
time, d'Entrèves wished to recover the law of nature as a viable and
useful component of liberal social and political theory. These are not
inconsiderable tasks and it is to d'Entrèves' credit that he performed
them so successfully in the mere 116 pages that the text of the first
edition of *Natural Law* occupied.

D'Entrèves ostensibly divides his book between historical narrative
and philosophical inquiry. But this division is somewhat misleading,
since his allegedly historical account in fact serves a powerful theoretical purpose. Critics of natural law thinking have argued for its
inherently conservative character, implicit in an unbroken tradition
running from the ancient Greeks and Romans through the medieval
canonists and schoolmen and into various modern aristocratic and

religious teachings. Neo-Thomists and other twentieth-century advocates of natural law have certainly reinforced this impression of continuity (see Delhaye 1967). By contrast, d'Entrèves insists that, similarities of terminology aside, the idea of natural law has undergone a series of profound transformations during the past two-and-a-half millenia. In a manner reminiscent of the strictures of interpretation proposed more recently by so-called "new historians" such as Quentin Skinner, d'Entrèves argued in *Natural Law*:

There can be no greater delusion than to believe that the history of these [political] notions may be written by simply drawing up a list, as careful and complete as possible, of all the references to them which can be found in political writers. The formal continuity of certain expressions is not the decisive factor: the same notion may have had very different meanings and have served entirely different purposes. (1970, 15)

In the case of natural law, d'Entrèves believed it possible to distinguish pronounced differences of meaning and purpose within classical, medieval, and modern usages of the doctrine. There is no history of a single, unified natural law tradition to be written; rather, one should properly speak of a multiplicity of traditions that are not necessarily even commensurable.

The basis for this distinction, according to d'Entrèves, rests upon the shifting intellectual and historical matrix within which the doctrine of natural law was applied. Changing attitudes towards human and physical nature, and indeed towards the function of law, as well as social, economic, and political disjunctions, meant that the signification of "natural law" depended upon a wider context of experience. Thus, natural law conceived within the framework of Roman law served to unite humankind into a universal community under a single legislative standard. Regardless of apparent differences, human beings could be demonstrated to share the rational faculty necessary for acquiescing to law, which in turn qualified them for the status of citizenship. In this sense, d'Entrèves points out, the function of natural law was not to generate an external measure against which to judge positive statute so much as to explain why the human race could be placed under an obligation to obey an identical set of human laws without regard for geographic, cultural, linguistic, or racial differences. The bearing of natural law within the Roman legal tradition is hence primarily formal and external.

By contrast, the function of natural law for medieval canonists and schoolmen was inward and moral. In Gratian as in Aquinas, natural law represented a binding principle of moral conduct, guaranteed by its divine ordination, which could be employed in the evaluation of human institutions. The grounding of natural law in the will of God was central to the medieval conception of natural law, in d'Entrèves' view. It was the direct association of the law of nature with a divine source that permitted medieval thinkers to repeat endlessly the dictum that no dictate has the force of law unless it conforms to the rational principles of justice established by natural law. Since submission to God, and hence to the natural moral order that He created, was the primary goal of the faithful Christian, the law of nature might even be invoked (as it was by John of Salisbury [see Nederman 1988]) to justify a duty to oppose actively a government which persists in imposing its will contrary to the terms fixed by justice. Unlike its classical predecessor, medieval natural law permitted (indeed, sometimes encouraged) individuals to judge the contents of human law for themselves insofar as its proponents insisted upon the inferiority of what is purely man-made to that which emanates from God Himself.

So long as Western society as a whole remained committed to a belief in an omnipotent Christian deity, and furthermore to a single authoritative interpretation of the will of that God, the medieval account of natural law was readily sustained. But d'Entrèves asserts that the function of the natural law doctrine shifted again in modern times once unchallenged faith in the medieval worldview began to erode. Specifically, as nature came to be seen as a force independent of the immanent guidance of a revealed God, the validation of natural law was transferred from the divine will to the faculty of human reason itself. Hence, in the work of modern natural law theorists—even those who retained their Christian convictions—d'Entrèves detects a marked change in the foundations and consequences of the law of nature. He observes that the doctrine of natural law became rationalistic, individualistic and radical. The rationalistic element stems from the claim (attributable to Grotius) that human reason is adequate in itself to discern the precepts of the law of nature, irrespective of whether such tenets are supported by either institutional arrangements or divine decree. Modern natural law is individualistic inasmuch as it construes human beings to be bearers of personal or subjective rights (rather than merely duties) deriving from correlative rational law, and hence to be free of any political encumbrance to which they have not previously agreed to submit. Finally, the radicalism of modern natural law is entailed by the vindication of those rights which reason demonstrates to be self-evidently human, in opposition to governments or social institutions that would seek to suppress such rights: it is this impulse which guided the revolutionary sentiments of Americans as well as Europeans. D'Entrèves is anxious to remind his readers that rationalism, individualism, and radicalism were not, as many scholars have argued, antithetical to natural law in early modern thought. In general, the theorists who promoted the modern doctrine of individual rights self-evident to reason regarded themselves to be adherents of natural law teaching. Yet this was an entirely novel version of the law of nature: "Rationalism, individualism and radicalism combined to give the old word an entirely new meaning" (d'Entrèves 1970, 62). The very bases of modern liberal philosophy, in sum, were embedded in natural law theory.

The point of d'Entrèves' historical excursus was not, however, to undermine or trivialize natural law's claim to universality by illustrating the linguistic and conceptual ruptures that have marked the evolution of the concept. Rather, his aim was to demonstrate that the usefulness of natural law transcends any given intellectual framework within which it is employed. Thus, natural law is not (*pace* both its friends and its foes) inherently hierarchical, conservative, or authoritative; only by virtue of certain definitions of nature and law, and certain connected beliefs and assumptions, does natural law take on such characteristics. But does this not merely confirm the legal positivist suspicion that the principle of natural law is devoid of real content? To answer in the affirmative is to miss the force of d'Entrèves' argument. For he emphasizes that despite the diversity of interpretations attached to natural law, there has always been a basic agreement among its advocates up to the eighteenth century that the creation and enforcement of law presumed a minimum common morality accessible to all rational minds. Throughout its history, "natural law" was a sort of shorthand expression for the moral boundaries within which law functions. This is, philosophically, the heart of the case in *Natural Law*. While we may dispute the terms of the morality to which we subscribe, we recognize that the existence of law logically supposes *some* moral standards and limits: it is this recognition that the phrase "natural law" embodies.

In light of the assertions of legal positivists, the claim that law inevitably runs up against certain moral constraints, even if the definition of those constraints is variable according to a broader intellectual matrix, is hardly vacuous. Indeed, it yields the basis for the detailed appraisal of and reply to the positivist perspective with which the second half of the main body of *Natural Law* is occupied. D'Entrèves identifies three claims with regard to which the positivist conception of law is vulnerable: (1) the essence of law is constituted by command; (2) law adopts a neutral stance in regard to moral values; (3) law is not subordinate to any ideal standard against which it may be measured. He proceeds to critique each proposition in its own terms, revealing that none can be sustained according to the internal principles of positivist legal philosophy. Only then does he suggest how appeal to natural law thinking—and more specifically to the modern liberal account of the law of nature—resolves the difficulties which plague positivism. This immanent method of analysis reflects the spirit of *Natural Law*: d'Entrèves sought to identify the areas where dialogue among legal thinkers of various persuasions was possible, rather than to reinforce the already polarized state of the discipline.

D'Entrèves' own vision of how natural law can fruitfully contribute to contemporary legal debate flows directly from his critique of positivism. Positivism takes its inspiration from a literalist interpretation of law as that which is written in statute books. By contrast, d'Entrèves desires to broaden the scope of legal experience. For him, human beings are profoundly nomological, in the sense that their obedience to law is not confined to conscious submission to human legislation. Indeed, positive law is only really the tip of the iceberg; it is the externalization of the law-abiding tendency within human beings whose stimulus is the law-like character of moral reason. In this regard, d'Entrèves is Kantian in his attitude towards the structure of morality. Human beings generally frame the answer to the question "How ought I to act?" in a nomological fashion; the outward codification of such responses, compliance with which may be required of individuals on threat of punishment, is the distinguishing token of positive law. Statute should enjoin us to act in essentially the same fashion as our moral reason demands of us. Indeed, one might argue that citizens of modern societies, while largely ignorant of the technicalities of statutory law, still succeed in negotiating a law-abiding path most of the time. If law were merely command and obedience occurred purely out of fear (as the so-called "bad man theory of law" has it), then one would expect modern citizens to apprise themselves with far more care of the details of legislation, lest they inadvertently step out of bounds. While the congruence between moral reason and positive law is not perfect, the former still serves as an effective guide for the requirements of the latter.

To some extent, the reverse statement is also true for d'Entrèves. That is, he remarks that positive law can and ought to be regarded as a valid source of moral education. For if it is generally the case that people find in statute a confirmation of the conclusions of their own moral reasoning, then such human law can act as a powerful aid in instructing us in matters of moral rectitude. "The purpose of law," he remarks, "is not only to make men obedient, but to help them be virtuous" (d'Entrèves 1970, 82). There is clearly an Aristotelian tinge to his conception of law. But he does not wish to say that virtue can be coerced through external command. D'Entrèves in fact accepts the liberal's concern that "we may have good reason for fearing any doctrine which is based on the assumption that it is the purpose of law to make men 'virtuous.'" Yet he immediately adds that this legitimate fear should not be used to conceal the moral dimension of positive law: "But are we so sure that we can, even at the present day, draw a clear line between the precepts which can and cannot, or should and should not, be enforced by positive legislation?" (1970, 89). Law for d'Entrèves is inescapably embedded in the realm of moral values. This is a lesson that we ignore at our peril, inasmuch as respect for law itself erodes when law ceases to reflect the moral reason of citizens. Positive law that deviates too greatly from the moral judgments of individuals, no matter how forcefully it is commanded, is sure to meet with derision and (where possible) resistance.

In this connection, d'Entrèves' commitment to a specifically modern account of the law of nature comes to the fore. Without a universal human fraternity or the spiritual authority of the Church to fall back on, natural law today must endorse the sovereignty of individual reason supported by the structure of subjective rights as the bulwark against commands of evil by the state. This position correlates with his observations about the heroic actions of resistance fighters: they captured the spirit of rationalism, individualism, and radicalism inherited from the French and American revolutionaries of the eighteenth century. The events of the war and its aftermath demonstrate that the moral reason at the core of natural law theory cannot be so readily dismissed by the philosopher of law. Not only in the resistance, but also in the statutory declarations of governments-in-exile and in the trial of war criminals, "natural law seems to have taken its revenge upon the very champions of the pernicious doctrine that there is no law but positive law, or that might equals right" (d'Entrèves 1970, 107). D'Entrèves in effect issues a challenge to legal philosophers to take cognizance of and adjust themselves to the historical vindication of natural law. The failure of jurisprudence to begin addressing the questions posed by natural law only compounds its near-criminal complicity in legitimating the decrees of totalitarian regimes.

The immediate reception of *Natural Law* was muted, quite possibly because it charted a course through legal theory that had never enjoyed great popularity in Britain while at the same time it adopted a mode of inquiry very distant from the analytic philosophy favored by d'Entrèves' contemporaries. Yet the main thrust of the book—confronting the shortcomings of legal positivism with the practical and philosophical strengths of a modern conception of natural law—touched several important chords in postwar jurisprudence. The most pronounced of these was a serious self-evaluation on the part of positivists, led by H.L.A. Hart in England and Noberto Bobbio in Italy. In particular, Hart produced an influential series of lectures, articles and books during the 1950s which acknowledged that classic positivism had a serious blind spot with regard to the moral dimension of law. Part of Hart's attempt to rectify this limitation involved a direct appropriation of naturalistic norms. In his famous 1955 essay, "Are There any Natural Rights?", he argued that logically there must be at least one natural right, namely, a right to personal freedom in the absence of some self-imposed constraint on that right. In *The Concept of Law* (1961), Hart lauded the "core of good sense" that existed in the moral framework which stands at the center of natural law theory. He defended a valid "minimum content" of natural law arising from "universally recognized principles of conduct which have a basis in elementary truths concerning human beings, their natural environment, and aims" (Hart 1961, 189). Just how much Hart was prepared to concede to the substance of natural law may be debated. But his acknowledgment of such "minimum content" meant that, for the first time in many decades, mainstream jurisprudence on both sides of the Atlantic had begun to take stock of the idea of a law of nature.

D'Entrèves certainly applauded Hart's attempt to define a role for natural law (see 1970, 185–203). But we should resist the temptation to imagine that *Natural Law* played any direct role in the process of Hart's rethinking. While the two were Oxford colleagues, and Hart spoke early on with d'Entrèves about his new interest in natural law (d'Entrèves 1970, 185), these facts prove little. Hart's dispute with American legal theorist Lon Fuller during the late 1950s probably had a more direct impact on his reflections regarding the relation between law and morality (see the resumé of the debate in Fuller 1969, 188).

Yet d'Entrèves did immediately stimulate the process of positivist self-reflection and self-criticism in other ways. Choosing for personal reasons to leave Oxford, he returned to the University of Turin in 1958 to take up a chair in political theory, and soon thereafter began to organize (with Bobbio) an international conference on legal positivism, which ultimately convened for two weeks at the Rockefeller Foundation's Bellagio estate in September 1960. The meeting brought together some of the most eminent figures among the legal philosophers of the day (Hart, Bobbio, Alf Ross), as well as a number of younger European and North American scholars whose names have since become familiar (including Brian Barry, now professor of government at the London School of Economics, and Martin Golding, currently professor of philosophy and law at Duke University). D'Entrèves' actual contribution at the conference seems to have been twofold. First, he upheld the banner of natural law as a corrective and supplement to the positivist case (although consciously distancing his account of the law of nature from the neo-Thomist version which in Italy has been insinuated as a method of ecclesiastical interference in secular judicial affairs[4]). Second, at a conference where differences of culture and philosophical background were apt to distort understanding, d'Entrèves (with his highly cosmopolitan experience and conciliatory demeanor) served to facilitate communication and to harmonize needless dissonance.

D'Entrèves also took a central part in the revitalization of natural law theory during the same era. It is perhaps somewhat ironic that the non-Thomist d'Entrèves was invited by the University of Notre Dame to deliver a lecture series on natural law in the autumn of 1954 pursuant to a discussion of the establishment of a journal devoted to the study of that topic. His lectures, delivered under the title "The Case for Natural Law Re-examined" (reprinted in 1970, 119–72), became the cornerstone for the 1956 founding of *Natural Law Forum* (renamed *American Journal of Jurisprudence* in 1970). From its inception, the *Forum* became an important voice in non-positivist philosophy of law and a major resource for the study of the history of legal theory.

Although the 1960s saw some reorientation in the focus of d'Entrèves' writing (reflected in his *The Notion of the State* [1967] and his essays on political obligation [cited in 1970, 7 note 3]), he nevertheless agreed to supervise publication of a new edition of *Natural Law*, which appeared in 1970. Rather than alter the original text, the second edition simply appended three further essays: an article on Hart's naturalistic turn that had originally been published in French, a reprinting of his Notre Dame lectures, and a short paper entitled "Two Questions about Law." The effect was nearly to double the length of the book. Whether such a substantial increase in size was warranted may be left to the judgement of the reader. But the later essays added by d'Entrèves do reflect a significant evolution in his thought. Two points in particular stand out. First, d'Entrèves seems to set aside the historical classification of natural law theories into the categories of "ancient," "medieval," and "modern" in favor of a purely conceptual set of labels. Commencing with his Notre Dame lectures, he began to speak in terms of "technological," "ontological," and "deontological" theories of natural law: the first entails knowledge of how to derive the right rule from the "nature of things"; the second depends upon recognition of a purposeful metaphysical order, usually guaranteed by a divine will; the third involves a clear aware-ness of the *good reasons* that exist for the law we obey, that is, a law is rational because there are morally compelling reasons for it. These three models overlap with but do not precisely parallel his previous historical categories. How might we account for this change? One important factor may have been d'Entrèves' realization that a purely historical framework distorted the continuing application of all three interpretations of natural law. Romanist and neo-Thomist ideas of natural law could not be so easily relegated entirely to the past, as was implied in the main text of *Natural Law*: they remained in com-petition with d'Entrèves' own preferred deontological model. The vitality of alternate theories of natural law meant that he had to contend not merely with positivists and others who dismissed natural law altogether, but also with those who sought to push the doctrine in significantly different directions.

Moreover, one of the main strengths of his own deontological position, d'Entrèves felt, was its ability to give the most satisfactory answer to the question: "Why should I obey this law (or any law)?" The problem of the basis of obligation to law became increasingly central to his thought during the 1950s. All three of the essays ap-pended to the revised edition of *Natural Law* revolve around this is-sue to some extent. The Notre Dame lectures criticize both the tech-nological and ontological approaches on this score: the former is held wanting because it relies too heavily on the specialist knowledge of the professional jurist, while the latter demands too great a com-mitment to a single and indisputable cosmological and/or theological doctrine. Deontology, by comparison, appeals directly to the moral intellect of individual persons. In "Two Questions about Law," d'Entrèves expands this argument and also relates it to a second concern—political obligation towards the state—that was to become his main focus during the 1960s. And in his discussion of Hart, his most trenchant criticism of *The Concept of Law* stems precisely from the inadequacy of its treatment of the limits to moral obligation and of the political consequences of respecting those limits. In sum, it appears that d'Entrèves came in the years after the initial publication of *Natural Law* to view the law of nature as essentially a theory (perhaps the only viable theory) of the obligation of individuals and of citizens to obey law.

THE FUTURE OF NATURAL LAW

By the time of A.P. d'Entrèves' death in December 1985, natural law theory had reentered the discourse of main stream legal and political philosophy. This process crystallized in the works of such thinkers as John Finnis, Joseph Raz, Ronald Dworkin, and Germain Griesez, who participated in reviving awareness of the moral foundations of law.[5] Perhaps the most prominent recent defense of the natural law tradition is to be found in Finnis' *Natural Law and Natural Rights,* which has already spawned at least one book length critique and many critical studies (for example, Hittinger 1987 and the essays by George, Maccormick, Moore, and Weinreb in George 1992). Finnis offers an extended defense of natural law couched in a language and argumentative style acceptable to contemporary analytic philosophers and structured according to current debates within Anglo-American legal and political theory. D'Entrèves had always felt at a loss when dealing with this mode of philosophical discourse (1970, 9); for him it was as inscrutable as the game of cricket on which so many English philosophers relied for their metaphors (1970, 126–27). Indeed, to the extent that *Natural Law* failed to make an immediate impact commensurate with the significance of its arguments, the blame may lie primarily with the divergent intellectual assumptions and expectations of the continental scholar and his English audience.

The same fact may also explain the absence of attention to d'Entrèves' thought among the most recent wave of natural law theorists. For example, except for a single, dismissive reference, Finnis does not mention *Natural Law* or d'Entrèves anywhere in *Natural Law and Natural Rights* (1980, 25 note 1). Yet the interpretation of natural law which Finnis articulates is self-consciously deontological in orientation, in the sense that he has sought to strip away the teleological implications of "nature" that typify the Thomistic position. Moreover, Finnis frames his doctrine in a manner intended to reinforce and promote many of the central tenets of liberal political thought, such as individual rights and political obligation derived from consent. This is terrain that had already been explored in *Natural Law*, and it reflects no credit on more recent theorists that they have stinted in their recognition of d'Entrèves' earlier accomplishments.

There is no exaggeration in saying that *Natural Law* broke ground that was not only virgin but also extremely fertile. This is not to classify the book, however, as a mere forerunner or anticipation of later philosophical trends. Rather, the way in which d'Entrèves constructs his case in favor of natural law can still be usefully contrasted with current writing. In particular, *Natural Law* offers a powerful corrective to the disturbingly ahistorical cast of succeeding natural law theorists. Where Finnis and his cohorts seem intent on the discovery of a "pure" theory of natural law, d'Entrèves teaches us that we must take seriously the philosophical significance of the historical functions which the doctrine has played. Thus, *pace* Finnis (1980, vi), St. Thomas' Christian context is not irrelevant or extraneous to an appreciation of the content of his conception of the law of nature. It is naive to believe otherwise. D'Entrèves attempts to bridge the apparent gap between intellectual history and philosophical analysis by revealing how the different accounts of natural law theory are constrained by the intellectual frameworks within which they were articulated. This does not reduce them to a mere reflection of their historical conditions, but it does require us to attend to the limitations arising from the assumptions built into their mode of philosophical discourse. Whether we ultimately choose to accept, reject or revise d'Entrèves' actual account of the historical traditions of natural law theory, some insight into history is sorely needed to supplement contemporary literature on the topic. Thus, *Natural Law* is a book which repays careful reading not only to those who wish to understand how legal philosophy has evolved during the twentieth century, but also to those who would hope to contribute to the philosophy of law (or indeed political philosophy) in the future.

The stimulus to republish *Natural Law* after nearly two decades came from Paul Roazen who, along with Gordon Schochet and Martin Golding, convinced me of the work's importance as a contribution to legal and political philosophy. The initial drafting of the new introduction was undertaken during my affiliation with Siena College in Loudonville, New York; I am grateful to Sean Maloney of the Siena Library Reference Department for his aid in identifying and obtaining useful source material. Professor Roazen, as well as a former colleague, Paul Santilli, read versions of the new introduction and offered many valuable suggestions.

NOTES

1. One important recent example of this is the reliance by U.S. Supreme Court nominee Clarence Thomas upon natural law in order to explain his beliefs about the role of the judiciary during his Senate confirmation hearings in 1991. It should be noted, however, that the way in which Thomas put "natural law" to use appears to confirm the legitimate suspicions which philosophers have sometimes properly evinced about the doctrine.
2. See Falk and Shuman 1961, 219–21 regarding the complexities of defining legal positivism.
3. Of course, the relative passivity of Rome in opposing the Nazis and their ilk does not speak well for the claims of neo-Thomism on behalf of the Church as a preeminent spokesman for moral restraint.
4. This concern on the part of all the Italian participants is noted by Falk and Shuman 1961, 217–18. Professor Golding in a personal conversation recollects that d'Entrèves, because of his attachment to natural law, was especially careful to dissociate his position from the claims of the official church.
5. Of course, not all of these thinkers couch their analysis of the moral dimension of law in natural law terms. For instance, neither Raz nor Dworkin should be strictly regarded as proponents of the law of nature as a standard for legal judgement; see Raz 1979 and Altman 1992, 173 note 1.

REFERENCES

Altman, Andrew. 1992. "Fissures in the Integrity of *Law's Empire*: Dworkin and the Rule of Law." In Alan Hunt, ed., *Reading Dworkin Critically*. New York: Berg Publishers.

Delhaye, Phillippe. 1967. *Permanence du droit naturel*. 2nd ed. Louvain: Nauwelaerts.

d'Entrèves, Alexander P. 1932. *Riccardo Hooker*. Turin: G. Giappichelli.

———. 1934. *La filosophia politica medioevale*. Turin: G. Giappichelli.

———. 1939. *The Medieval Contribution to Political Thought*. Oxford: Oxford University.

———. 1947. *Reflections on the History of Italy*. Oxford: Clarendon Press.

———. 1950. "Alessandro Manzoni," *Proceedings of the British Academy* 36: 23–49.

———. 1952. *Dante as a Political Thinker*. Oxford: Clarendon Press.

———. 1960. "Federico Chabod e la Valle d'Aosta," *Rivista storica italiana* (1960): 793–810.

———. 1967. *The Notion of the State*. Oxford: Clarendon Press.

———. 1970. *Natural Law: An Introduction to Legal Philosophy*. 2nd ed. [1st ed. 1951]. London: Hutchison.

———. 1979. *Scritti sul Valle d'Aosta*. Bologna: M. Boni.

Falk, Richard A. and Samuel I. Shuman. 1961. "The Bellagio Conference on Legal Positivism," *Journal of Legal Education* 14: 213–28.

Figgis, John. 1980. *Natural Law and Natural Rights*. Oxford: Clarendon Press.

Fuller, Lon. 1969. *The Morality of Law*. Rev. ed [1st ed. 1964]. New Haven. CT: Yale University Press.

George, Robert P., ed. 1992. *Natural Law Theory: Contemporary Essays*. Oxford: Clarendon Press.

Hart, H.L.A. 1955. "Are There Any Natural Rights?", *Philosophical Review* 64: 175–91.

———. 1961. *The Concept of Law*. Oxford: Oxford University Press.

Hittinger, Russell. 1987. *A Critique of the New Natural Law Theory*. Notre Dame, IN: University of Notre Dame Press.

Morton, George. 1986. "Prof Alexander d'Entreves." *The Times of London* 17 January: 14.

Nederman, Cary J. 1988. "A Duty to Kill: John of Salisbury's Theory of Tyrannicide." *Review of Politics* 50: 365–98.

Raz, Joseph. 1979. *The Authority of Law*. Oxford: Clarendon Press.

Shiner, Roger. 1992. *Norm and Nature: The Movements of Legal Thought*. Oxford: Clarendon Press.

Traniello, Francesco, ed. 1988. *Dai Quaccheri a Gandhi: studi di storia religiosa in onore di Ettore Passerin d'Entreves*. Bologna: Il Mulino.

It is odd, when one thinks of it, that there are people in the world who, having renounced all the laws of God and nature, have themselves made laws which they rigorously obey . . .

PASCAL

FOREWORD TO THE SECOND EDITION

I am most grateful to the Editors of Hutchinson University Library for agreeing to include in this ninth reprint of my little book on *Natural Law* three additional essays[1] in which I have returned to the subject I first broached in English as long ago as 1950. This seems in fact a much better way for clarifying my thought than attempting to revise the book itself—which would have implied re-writing it completely after all these years. Yet, however much I may have modified some of the views which are here presented, the problem of natural law has continued to be very much in my mind. Indeed, that problem has come more and more to appear to me as central not only to legal philosophy, but to political theory as well. I can therefore only refer the reader, for a more complete appraisal of my thought, to my recent book on the subject[2] and to some other articles which I have published of late on political obligation—a question with which the notion of natural law used to be closely associated in past days.[3]

Turin, September 1969

[1] Essay (A), 'The Case for Natural Law re-examined', is reprinted from *Natural Law Forum* (1956) of the Notre Dame Law School, Indiana; Essay (B), 'Two questions about law', from *Existenz und Ordnung: Festschrift für Erik Wolf* (1962), Essay (C), 'A core of good sense: reflections on Hart's theory of natural law', from *Philosophy Today*, translated from the original in *Revue internationale de Philosophie* (1963).
[2] *The Notion of the State. An Introduction to Political Theory*, Oxford, Clarendon Press, 1967.
[3] 'Legality and Legitimacy' in *The Review of Metaphysics*, vol. XVI, no. 4, June 1963; 'Obeying Whom' in *Political Studies*, vol. XIII, no. 1, February 1964; 'On the Nature of Political Obligation' in *Philosophy*, vol. XLIII, no. 166, October 1968.

FOREWORD TO 1952 REPRINT

In revising this book for its first reprint, I have not been able to make more than a few corrections and additions to the text. Most of these have been suggested by readers and reviewers—and there have been friends and foes among them. I have taken care to meet the complaints of my critic in *Mind* regarding the initials of the authors cited in the bibliographies; but I have made no attempt to better what he calls my 'elusive prose'. As I pointed out in the Foreword, I was well aware that to many my language would seem 'ambiguous' and obsolete.

Since this essay was written, however, I have come across a sentence by the editor of *Mind* which I would like to quote here at length, not only as an example of the language which I have so far been unable to master, but also as conveying a thought which (if I understand it correctly) is not very dissimilar from that which forms the main contention of this book.

Ethical statements, (writes Professor Ryle in *The Concept of Mind*) as distinct from particular *ad hominem* behests and reproaches, should be regarded as warrants addressed to any potential givers of behests and reproaches, i.e. not as personal action-tickets but as impersonal injunction-tickets; not imperatives but 'laws' that only such things as imperatives and punishments can satisfy. Like statute laws they are to be constructed not as orders, but as licences to give and enforce orders.

I am not sure that I would meet the objections of my critic and make my argument more clear and convincing if I now hinted that my own notion of law somewhat corresponds to Professor Ryle's

'personal action-tickets' and my notion of morals to his 'impersonal injunction-tickets'. But I am sure that the distinction to
which Professor Ryle lends the weight of his authority—viz. that
it is a different thing 'to give and enforce orders', and to provide a
'licence' for doing so—is one which will make the old natural law
theorists rejoice in their graves. 'Laws' that are not 'imperatives'
but 'warrants' for 'potential givers of behests and reproaches'
seem to me to bear less resemblance to statute laws than to the
'natural law' that fills so many volumes now lying dusty and
neglected on the shelves of our libraries.

Oxford, May 1952

FOREWORD TO FIRST EDITION

This book is the outcome of eight lectures delivered at the University of Chicago in April 1948. I wish to thank the Committee on Social Thought and its Chairman, Professor J. U. Nef, for the opportunity they gave me to return to a subject which has been in my mind for many years. I also wish to thank the editor of this series, Professor H. J. Paton, for allowing me to state, in a concise and straightforward manner, my own very personal views and conclusions about the 'nature of natural law'. I wish further to thank him, as well as Professor D. A. Binchy, Mrs I. Henderson and especially Mr C. G. Hardie, for many helpful suggestions with regard to language and style.

Yet, on the point of releasing this short essay, I cannot avoid some misgivings. I am well aware that the language in which I have tried to express my thoughts is altogether a different one from that which prevails among present-day philosophers and political theorists. I am not sure that I have always succeeded in avoiding the over-emphasis which is the great temptation for a Latin. Above all, I have no claims to make as to the novelty of my material. The book is a good example of what supercilious scholars here in Oxford call 'tertiary writing'. The results of my own work in the field of legal and political philosophy I have published in a number of books and articles both in English and in my native Italian. I have had little scruple in drawing heavily upon them. But neither have I hesitated to avail myself of the conclusions of better scholars than I am, wherever they seemed to me to carry weight and final authority. What little originality the book may possess must therefore lie in the statement of a case rather than in the production of the evidence. That case may or may not be accepted. It is my hope that I may at least have succeeded in making it worth hearing.

To account for the themes that have inspired me would require a separate volume. I have no doubt that they will be sufficiently apparent to the attentive reader. I would like to recall in this connection my lasting attachment to the Law Faculty of my old University in Turin, where I received my first training *in utroque iure*, as well as in that *vera non simulata philosophia* which has remained an essential part of a great legal tradition. But, if so short an essay allowed of a dedication, I would not hesitate to inscribe it to the memory of many a friend of later and darker days, whose deeds bear witness to the existence of the Law which alone deserves ultimate allegiance.

Oxford, March 1950

I

INTRODUCTION

For over two thousand years the idea of natural law has played a prominent part in thought and in history. It was conceived as the ultimate measure of right and wrong, as the pattern of the good life or 'life according to nature'. It provided a potent incentive to reflection, the touchstone of existing institutions, the justification of conservatism as well as of revolution. But recourse to natural law was never entirely unchallenged. The notion was laden with ambiguity even in the days when it was considered self-evident. In the last century and a half it has been assailed from many sides as critically unsound and as historically pernicious. It was declared to be dead, never to rise again from its ashes. Yet natural law has survived and still calls for discussion. It is the purpose of this book to examine the reasons for that vitality and the claim of natural law to have served the cause of humanity well.

But how is natural law best approached and how should it be handled? This is a serious difficulty to the modern student. There is no doubt that, for a number of reasons, we have grown unfamiliar with the whole body of doctrine and with its terminology. We find ourselves confronted with a variety of definitions, and we can see no reason why we should make our start from one rather than from another. There is, however, one important restriction which must be laid down from the outset, to circumscribe the ground which this book proposes to cover. The notion of natural law which it discusses is a notion which refers to human behaviour, not to physical phenomena. Our concern is with ethics and politics, not with the natural sciences. The word *nature* is the cause of the equivocation. The failure to distinguish clearly between its different meanings was the source of all the ambiguities in the doctrine of natural law.[1]

Prima facie, there seem to be two possible lines of approach to our subject. I would call the one historical, the other philosophical. We may consider the doctrine of natural law as an historical product. A recurrent motif in Western thought and history, we may attempt to retrace its development and to stress its importance in shaping the destinies of the West—and our own. But we may, on the other hand, consider natural law as a philosophical doctrine. An ideal or a deception, it claims to have a value which is not merely historical, but universal. It can be stressed as a positive or negative contribution to man's knowledge of himself and of his place in the universe.

Neither line of approach seems entirely satisfactory. Not the historical, because a history of natural law is a formidable undertaking, however confidently eminent scholars may have thought and felt about it. 'The Law of Nature has a perfectly continuous history,' wrote Sir Frederick Pollock in an admirable little essay on 'The History of the Law of Nature'. This view was accepted and emphasised by almost all modern historians of political thought. They have all stressed, and rightly, the tenacity with which natural law terminology has held its ground in ethics and politics ever since the Greeks first coined it at the dawn of our civilisation. A quotation from Sir Ernest Barker's recent book, *Traditions of Civility*, will provide a good illustration of the manner in which the process is viewed by one of the greatest English students of the subject:

> The origin of the idea of natural law may be ascribed to an old and indefeasible movement of the human mind (we may trace it already in the *Antigone* of Sophocles) which impels it towards the notion of an eternal and immutable justice; a justice which human authority expresses, or ought to express—but does not make; a justice which human authority may fail to express—and must pay the penalty for failing to express by the diminution, or even the forfeiture, of its power to command. This justice is conceived as being the higher or ultimate law, proceeding from the nature of the universe—from the Being of God and the reason of man. It follows that law—in the sense of the law of the last resort—is somehow above law-making. It follows that lawmakers, after all, are somehow under and subject to law.

[1] For an analysis of the notion of the law of nature in scientific thought see A. N. Whitehead, *Adventures of Ideas*, 1935, ch. vii.

The movement of the mind of man towards these conceptions and their consequences is already apparent in the *Ethics* and the *Rhetoric* of Aristotle. But it was among the Stoic thinkers of the Hellenistic age that the movement first attained a large and general expression; and that expression . . . became a tradition of human civility which runs continuously from the Stoic teachers of the Porch to the American Revolution of 1776 and the French Revolution of 1789. Allied to theology for many centuries—adopted by the Catholic Church, and forming part of the general teaching of the Schoolmen and the Canonists—the theory of Natural Law had become in the sixteenth century, and continued to remain during the seventeenth and the eighteenth, an independent and rationalist system, professed and expounded by the philosophers of the secular school of natural law.

This is a grandiose picture, but it leaves out many details and raises more questions than it purports to solve. Surely the mere fact that an identical expression recurs in different writers is no proof of the continuity of thought from one to the other. That Cicero and Locke should both have defined natural law in a very similar manner is no evidence of the uninterrupted acceptance of that notion during the eighteen odd centuries which separate them. The philosophers of the 'secular school', to whom Sir Ernest Barker refers, would probably have denied the continuity which he outlines so effectively. They had different views from ours about the losses which the 'dark ages' inflicted upon mankind. They would have denounced Schoolmen and Canonists alike for obscuring the true doctrine of natural law which they claimed to restore to its purity.[1] Except for the name, the medieval and the modern notions of natural law have little in common.

This is the sort of difficulty which we would certainly encounter if we were ever to entertain the ambitious programme of writing a history of natural law. It is a difficulty inherent in the history of political ideas, perhaps in *Ideengeschichte* altogether. What I have said of natural law can be said of other famous political concepts, such as the social contract or democracy. There can be no greater delusion than to believe that the history of these notions may be written by simply drawing up a list, as careful and complete as possible, of all the references to them which can be found in political writers. The formal continuity of certain expressions is not the decisive factor: the same notion may have had very different meanings and have served entirely different purposes. The history

[1] This point was significantly stressed by Pufendorf, the most celebrated and influential of all seventeenth-century writers on natural law.

of ideas is an internal history; it is from within, not from without that the value of a doctrine must be assessed—as when new wine is poured into old bottles, it is the new wine that matters and sometimes causes the old bottle to burst.

I remember that Dr A. J. Carlyle used to say that there is very little that is really new in political theory. Men have kept repeating the old slogans over and over again. The novelty is very often only a question of accent. Democracy, Social Contract, Natural Law may well be traced back to the Greeks. But Aristotle's notion of democracy is not that of Jefferson; nor does the fact that the Sophists came very near the idea of a social contract give us much help to a better understanding of Rousseau. As far as natural law is concerned, it was Lord Bryce who remarked that, at a given moment, 'that which had been for nearly two thousand years a harmless maxim, almost a commonplace of morality', was converted into 'a mass of dynamite which shattered an ancient monarchy and shook the European continent'. We should not pretend to know much about natural law unless we are able to solve this historical riddle.

What I have called the philosophical approach brings us undoubtedly much nearer the answer. I have already noted that many of the ambiguities of the concept of natural law must be ascribed to the ambiguity of the concept of nature that underlies it. But it is not enough to point out that, notwithstanding the similar words which are used to denote them, the notion of natural law which has played so prominent a part in ethics and politics is something intrinsically different from the notion of the law of nature which is elaborated by the scientist. It is necessary further to account both for the similarity and for the difference.

Now it is easy enough to understand the reason which prompted men to indicate by a similar name the measure of their actions and the rules that govern a reality which escapes their control. It is the quest after some immutable standard or pattern, independent of their choice and capable of carrying conviction. The contrast between 'nature' and 'convention' is only one aspect of a deeper antithesis. As Pascal pointed out, it may well be that 'nature' is but a 'first custom', as custom is a 'second nature'.[1] What matters is the constant endeavour to place certain principles beyond discusssion, by raising them to a different plane altogether. The nature-metaphor was admirably fitted to express the notion of

[1] 'J'ai grand peur que cette nature ne soit elle-même qu'une première coutume, comme la coutume est une seconde nature.' (*Pensées*, II, 93)

finality and inevitability. It is a curious paradox that this same metaphor should also have been used to indicate a task or a duty. The concept of nature was a double-edged sword which could be employed in two opposite directions.

It was not only double-edged. It was flexible. Nature could have widely different meanings. We cannot fail to be aware of that difference when we read two sentences like 'man is by nature a political animal' and 'men are by nature equal and free'. The different meanings of natural law are but the consequences of the different meanings of nature. Professor Ritchie, himself a declared enemy of natural law, saw this point very clearly in his old but still valuable book on *Natural Rights*. He pointed out that the history of the law of nature is really nothing else than the history of the idea of nature in law and in politics. He therefore attempted to clarify, under different headings, the principal usages of the word 'nature' in political science, and gave this section of his book the significant title 'De Divisione Naturae'.

I think that this is, on the whole, a much more satisfactory approach to the problem of natural law than the purely historical one. For one thing it accounts for the fact that there is really not one tradition of natural law, but many. The medieval and the modern conceptions of natural law are two different doctrines; the continuity between them is mainly a question of words. The philosophical approach also allows for the grouping of different authors on deeper than mere chronological grounds. If Cicero and Locke agree in their definition of natural law, this is an indication of a more intimate link than mere imitation or repetition. Finally, only philosophy can provide the clue to the problems which history lays bare but is unable to solve. If the modern doctrine of natural law proved to be so different from the old both in its implications and in its far-reaching consequences, the reason is that a new conception of man and the universe turned what had been for centuries a harmless and orthodox doctrine into a potent instrument of progress and revolution, which gave an entirely new turn to history and of which we still feel the effects.

There is, however, one serious objection to this manner of handling our subject. Classifications are open to question. They vary according to the conceptions or preconceptions that underlie them. They are very often mere window-dressing for superficial thought. There is no end to the divisions and sub-divisions required to cover and to account for the infinite varieties of natural law. And these in turn provide arguments for the sceptical denial of

B

natural law as one of the great deceptions of ethics. 'The word *natural*,' wrote Hume, 'is commonly taken in so many senses, and is of so loose a signification, that it seems vain to dispute whether justice be natural or not.' It would indeed be lamentable if, having approached natural law from the angle of philosophy, we found ourselves pursuing a will-o'-the-wisp. It is good that history should remind us that this highly controversial doctrine was after all one of the most creative forces, one of the most constructive elements of our culture and of our civilisation.

I can see only one way out of the difficulties which I have outlined and stressed so far. It is to combine history and philosophy in the study of what I have already called the vitality of natural law and its claim to have served the cause of humanity well. In my opinion what really calls for attention on the part of the modern student is the function of natural law rather than the doctrine itself, the issues that lay behind it rather than the controversies about its essence. 'In order to understand the dominance of natural law we must interpret it psychologically, and therefore relate it to the forces that operated through its medium.' I think that we should take as our guide this pregnant remark of a great student of history and of philosophy.[1] We must try to see through the abstract and academic façade of natural law. We must endeavour to understand the causes of its constant recurrence. Surely an undertaking of this kind calls for historical as well as for philosophical assistance.

I shall not attempt in this book to sketch a history, however condensed, of the doctrine of natural law. I shall concentrate on its merits. I have therefore chosen what seemed to me the best illustrations of the part which that doctrine has played in the course of our history. But for natural law the petty laws of a small peasant community of peninsular Italy would never have become the universal law of an international civilisation. But for natural law the great medieval synthesis of godly and of worldly wisdom would not have been possible. But for natural law there would probably have been no American and no French revolution, nor would the great ideals of freedom and equality have found their way into the law-books after having found it into the hearts of men. These three major events provide the substance of the three first chapters of this book. They will certainly need to be revised and implemented by the professional historian.

[1] See note at the end of this chapter.

When we come to our present situation the line of approach must necessarily vary. The author of this study has no particular axe to grind in favour of one notion of natural law or another. He cannot help wondering at the ingenuity with which certain authors still contrive to draw up elaborate treatises on 'natural law and the rights of man' in an age which has grown so sceptical about absolute and immutable values, so hostile to the spirit of hope and optimism which inspired that doctrine in its heyday and ensured its success. But he cannot help feeling that the case for natural law is not usually put forward with the necessary fairness. He would like to draw attention to the fact that, though the terminology has gone and little seems left of natural law thinking in modern jurisprudence and politics, many of the points which are generally accepted as the first elements of those 'sciences' are really nothing else than the points which were traditionally discussed under the heading of natural law.

The essence of law, the delimitation of its province, the conditions of its validity, were problems long known to the student before the invention of positive jurisprudence and political science. They survive, *mutato nomine*, in the text-books of academic teaching. Present-day lawyers and politicians may scorn their benighted forebears. They may declare that they have nothing to do with natural law nor with the ideals which it represented. But they have not succeeded in eliminating the problems which natural law purported to solve. They cannot fail to be faced by these problems the moment they begin to reflect on the results of their labours and on the safety of the ground which they tread.

We have indeed done little more than give a new name to a very old thing. We say that these problems are the domain of legal and political philosophy. I think that legal and political philosophy are nothing else than natural law writ large. And I earnestly hope that I may succeed in the last three chapters of this book in making this statement less paradoxical. That there may be some scope for a re-examination of the problem is after all the tacit assumption which underlies the inclusion of a book on natural law in a series on the main problems of philosophy.

NOTE

I know of only one author who has followed on the lines suggested in the words of Dilthey, which I have quoted on p. 18 of this Introduction. E. Troeltsch was not merely a student of history, but a trained philosopher and theologian. He was thus admirably equipped to survey the complex interplay of forces and ideas which resulted in the formation of European culture. Some of his works have been translated into English, and I wish to refer to them as the best and most stimulating treatment of the problem of natural law from the point of view both of philosophy and of history. It is significant that Troeltsch should never have claimed for his conclusions anything more than a provisional value. He conceived them as a personal contribution towards a better understanding of our spiritual heritage.

He began by outlining the function of natural law in the development of Christian ethics (*The Social Teaching of the Christian Churches*, 1912—transl. by O. Wyon, 2 vols., New York, 1931). Natural law, he pointed out, meant the intrusion of an alien element in Christianity. It represented the inheritance of the ancient world which could be adapted to Christian teaching. It provided the basis for a social and political programme which was entirely lacking in the Gospel. The variations of natural law between the two extremes of rationalism and irrationalism accounted in his view for the different attitude of the Christian Churches towards the 'outer world', and for the variations of their social and political doctrines. The great contrast between the Catholic and the Protestant views on such matters could be reduced, according to Troeltsch, to a fundamental difference in the manner of conceiving the powers and duties of man as expressed in the law of nature.

Later, under the impact of the First World War and of the defeat of his country, Troeltsch was led to recast his views in a new and different pattern. In his lecture on *The Ideas of Natural Law and Humanity* (1922), he puts forward an even more dramatic explanation of the contrasts which divided Europe. The belief in natural law, both as a recognition of a law common to humanity and as an assertion of the fundamental rights of man, was, he pointed out, the distinguishing mark of political thought in Western Europe. From that belief the German world had broken away in the age of Romanticism, perhaps indeed at an earlier date still. From that time onwards German thought had been drifting towards the glorification of force over reason and of the State as the supreme embodiment of moral life.

As Sir Ernest Barker has remarked, the contrast drawn by Troeltsch between German thought and the thought of Western Europe is a contrast which can be accepted only with many qualifications. But, as I have already said, Troeltsch never considered his interpretations as final. It is useless to speculate how he would have recast them had he lived to witness the ideological conflict of the Second World War and that of present-day Europe. The sweeping advance of Marxism would probably have made him aware of the fallacy of linking theoretical attitudes to racial or national characters. But he would not have hesitated, I think, to maintain that it is no use opposing the old doctrine of natural law to the challenge of the economic interpretation of history without reviving the spirit which found in that doctrine its verbal expression.

Sir H. S. Maine, *Ancient Law*, 1861, chs. iii and iv.

D. G. Ritchie, *Natural Rights*, 1895, pt 1, chs. i-iv.

Sir J. W. Salmond, 'The Law of Nature' in *Law Quarterly Review*, 1895.

Sir F. Pollock, 'The History of the Law of Nature', 1900, in *Essays in the Law*, 1922.

Lord Bryce, 'The Law of Nature' in *Studies in History and Jurisprudence*, Vol. II, 1901.

E. Troeltsch, *The Ideas of Natural Law and Humanity in Western Politics*, 1922 (Appendix I to Gierke-Barker, *Natural Law and the Theory of Society*).

J. Dewey, 'Nature and Reason in Law', in *Philosophy and Civilisation*, 1931.

Sir E. Barker, Introduction to Gierke, *Natural Law and the Theory of Society*, 1934.

J. W. Jones, *Historical Introduction to the Theory of Law*, 1940, ch. iv, 'The Law of Nature'.

H. Rommen, *The Natural Law*, trans. T. R. Hanley, 1947.

A German work by J. Sauter, *Die philosophischen Grundlagen des Naturrechts*, 1932, deserves to be mentioned.

General works on the history of political theory, such as Hildebrand, Rehm, Janet, Dunning, Carlyle, McIlwain, Doyle, Sabine and others, should be consulted.

A useful selection of texts will be found in J. Hall, *Readings in Jurisprudence*, ch. i.

2

A UNIVERSAL SYSTEM OF LAWS

The first great achievement of natural law lies in the legal field proper, in the foundation, that is, of a system of laws of universal validity. That system was embodied and transmitted to posterity in the law-books of Justinian.

It is no exaggeration to say that, next to the Bible, no book has left a deeper mark upon the history of mankind than the *Corpus Iuris Civilis*. Much has been written about the impact of Rome upon Western civilisation. Much has been disputed about 'the ghost of the Roman Empire' that still lurks far beyond the shores of the Mediterranean. The heritage of Roman law is not a ghost, but a living reality. It is present in the court as well as in the market-place. It lives on not only in the institutions but even in the language of all civilised nations.

To the pessimist or the sceptic, who too readily accepts the view that ideologies are nothing but a superstructure on facts, the history of that heritage is a reminder of the predominance of the spiritual over the material factor. 'The history of Roman Law during the Middle Ages testifies to the latent vigour and organising power of ideas in the midst of shifting surroundings' (Vinogradoff). The revival of Roman law was a powerful leaven in the trans-formation of the social and political structure of Europe. Those who speak of a *damnosa hereditas* have their eye only on one side of the picture. They overlook what is our greatest debt to the Roman inheritance: the notion that law is the common patrimony of men, a bond that can overcome their differences and reduce them to unity.

The great compilation and codification of legal material which is commonly known by the name of the *Corpus Iuris Civilis*, was completed in the year A.D. 534 by a body of Byzantine lawyers who had been ordered to undertake that task by the Emperor Justinian. It embodied the results of a long and complex development which had begun in the fifth century B.C. with the first written laws of the Romans, the *Twelve Tables*. For many centuries to come Roman law was identified with 'the godly approved laws of Justinian the Emperor'. The mature fruit obscured the process by which the fruit had been ripened.[1]

It is only in comparatively recent times that Roman law has begun to be treated 'historically'. Modern scholars are engaged in painstaking efforts to disentangle the 'classical' element from the Byzantine additions and modifications. But in the eyes of posterity it was Justinian's greatness to have given the laws simplicity and symmetry. Dante reserved a special place in Paradise to the Byzantine Cæsar:

> Who by the will of Primal Love possessed
> Pruned from the Laws the unneeded and the vain.
> (*Paradiso*, vi, 11–12, trans. Binyon)

What impressed later generations, besides the admirable construction of Justinian's law-books, was their claim to universal validity. Little heed was paid to the fact that those books had been compiled in the East, and at a time when the power of Rome had ceased to hold sway in Western Europe. Nor for a time did their composite structure disturb the student with questions of authenticity or 'interpolations'. Our medieval ancestors were perhaps more appreciative than we are of that Byzantine art of the mosaic, to which the *Corpus Iuris* offers a striking parallel. But their historical judgment was after all not entirely inaccurate. It was through her law that Rome reconquered the provinces which she had lost on the battlefield.

Now there is one point about that claim to validity which should not fail to impress even the modern and unprejudiced reader. That claim was not based on force, but on reason. It was an appeal to the intrinsic dignity of the law, rather than to its power

[1] The *Corpus Iuris Civilis* comprises three different works: the *Institutes*, a short educational handbook, published in November 533; the *Digest*, a collection of excerpts or fragments from earlier jurists systematically arranged (published December 533); and the *Codex* or codification of Imperial constitutions, first published in 520, and revised in November 534.

of compulsion. In a resounding proclamation (Const. 'Deo Auctore') Justinian declared that it had been his purpose to erect a temple to Justice, a citadel of Law. 'Of all subjects none is more worthy of study than the authority of Laws, which happily disposes things divine and human, and puts an end to iniquity.'

This idea is taken up and expanded in the opening paragraphs of the *Digest*, where the views of the more famous Roman jurists on the subject are quoted (*Dig.*, liber I, titulus 1, *De Iustitia et Iure*). Law—*Ius*—is an art and a science all in one.[1] As a science, it is a knowledge of human and divine things (*divinarum atque humanarum rerum notitia*), a theory of right and wrong (*iusti atque iniusti scientia*). As an art, it is the furtherance of what is good and equitable (*ars boni et aequi*). So high is the mission of the jurist that it may rightly be compared with that of a priest (*merito quis nos sacerdotes appellet*). He is indeed a minister of justice, for justice and law are correlative (*iustitia est constans et perpetua voluntas ius suum cuique tribuendi*).

Now of laws there are different sorts. There is the law of the State, which expresses the interest of one particular community (*ius civile*). There is a law of nations (*ius gentium*), which men have devised for their mutual intercourse. But there is also a law which expresses a higher and more permanent standard. It is the law of nature (*ius naturale*), which corresponds to 'that which is always good and equitable' (*bonum et aequum*).

I have summarised and condensed what to the scholar is an object of hair-splitting controversy. Every single word in this first chapter of the *Digest* has been weighed and contested. What liberties did the Byzantine compilers take with the texts they were quoting? Is the fundamental distinction between the three categories of law (*ius civile, ius gentium, ius naturale*) a 'classical' Roman conception, or is it a later invention? How can we account for the contradictions which are still apparent between the very authors who are bundled together under the heading *De Iustitia et Iure*? What, behind their rhetorical appeal, is the exact meaning and the real source of such words and concepts as *naturale, aequum et bonum* and others? It is difficult to say whether there is more cause to take pride or to complain that, after more than a hundred years of historical studies, large sections of the *Corpus Iuris* have become a quagmire, or rather a minefield, for the inexperienced reader.

[1] On the different meanings of the Latin word *ius*, and the difficulty of giving its correct English equivalent, see below, p. 61.

I think however, that we should not hesitate to read the opening paragraphs of the *Digest* with the candour of the inexperienced. It is after all the only way we have to try and represent to ourselves the impression that they must have conveyed to generation after generation of students who turned to the *Corpus Iuris* for apprenticeship in the law, and who took its words at their face value. The impression in approaching the temple or citadel of law must have been enhanced rather than diminished by that rhetorical opening—Byzantine or genuinely Roman as the texts may be. Here was a system of laws which purported to fulfil the highest aspirations of men and their needs in all circumstances. The edifice was grandiose enough, and the archway leading to it proportionate to its grandeur. Natural law was its key-stone. No wonder that it should have focussed admiration and attention.

But on the part of the modern student both admiration and attention must be qualified and critical. We are confronted with a problem of interpretation exactly on the lines which have been discussed in the Introduction. Let me recall briefly how the Roman doctrine of natural law is usually viewed by historians and political philosophers. The origin of that doctrine, it is pointed out and correctly, was certainly not Roman. It was a foreign importation. It was borrowed wholesale from Greek philosophy, particularly from Stoicism. Stoic doctrine inspired the definition of Cicero, a good representative of the fashionable eclecticism which prevailed among the Roman well-to-do in the last century before our era.

True law is right reason in agreement with Nature; it is of universal application, unchanging and everlasting; it summons to duty by its commands, and averts from wrong-doing by its prohibitions. And it does not lay its commands or prohibitions upon good men in vain, though neither have any effect on the wicked. It is a sin to try to alter this law, nor is it allowable to attempt to repeal any part of it, and it is impossible to abolish it entirely. We cannot be freed from its obligations by Senate or People, and we need not look outside ourselves for an expounder or interpreter of it. And there will not be different laws at Rome and at Athens, or different laws now and in the future, but one eternal and unchangeable law will be valid for all nations and for all times, and there will be one master and one ruler, that is, God, over us all, for He is the author of this law, its promulgator, and its enforcing judge.   (*De Republica*, III, xxii, 33)

This famous passage from Cicero's *Republic* clearly sets forth the doctrine of the law of nature which had been elaborated by the

Stoics. Mankind is a universal community or cosmopolis. Law is
its expression. Being based upon the common nature of men, it is
truly universal. Being endorsed by the sovereign Lordship of God,
it is eternal and immutable. The doctrine passed into the *ius
naturale* of the Roman jurists as well as into the teaching of the
Christian Church. It is significant that Cicero's definition should
have been preserved for us by a Christian writer, Lactantius. It is
not surprising that Justinian, the Christian law-giver, should have
taken the idea of natural law as the corner-stone of his system. It
could be supported and implemented by the authority of the
jurists who are quoted in the *Digest* as referring to *ius naturale* as
the ultimate principle underlying all legal differences, and as the
infallible means of reducing those differences to unity.

A similar continuity of thought is usually traced also in a number of concepts closely correlated to the doctrine of natural law.
First and foremost the concept of equality. Cicero, following
the Stoics on this point also, had clearly formulated the notion of
the fundamental equality of all men.

No single thing is so like another, so exactly its counterpart, as all of
us are to one another. Nay, if bad habits and false beliefs did not twist
the weaker minds and turn them in whatever direction they are inclined,
no one would be so like his own self as all men would be like all others.
And so, however we may define man, a single definition will apply to
all . . . For those creatures who have received the gift of reason from
Nature have also received right reason, and therefore they have also
received the gift of Law, which is right reason applied to command and
prohibition. And if they have received law, they have received Justice
also. Now all men have received reason; therefore all men have received
justice.   (*De Legibus*, I, x, 29; xii, 33)

The notion that men are equal is here deduced from the very
existence of a bond that unites them. Human equality is the direct
consequence of natural law, its first and essential tenet. This
doctrine, which Dr Carlyle defined as the dividing line between
ancient and modern political theory, was admirably traced by
him down to the Roman jurists—and far beyond. Cicero's
sweeping generalisations about the nature of man and the
dictates of the law of nature recur in Seneca and are the foundation of the dogmatic statements of the lawyers in the *Corpus Iuris*.
'We are indeed at the beginning of a theory of human nature and
society of which the "Liberty, Equality and Fraternity" of the
French Revolution is only the present-day expression.'

Lastly, according to modern interpreters, one common mark of the doctrine of natural law from Cicero to Justinian is a particular attitude to the social and political problem. Here again we must turn for the sources of that attitude to the Greeks rather than to the Romans. It is the idea of a difference or contrast between the ideal pattern of society which is expressed by the law of nature, and the positive legal institutions which confront us in the reality of human interrelations.

This idea can be retraced in Cicero's definition, which I have just quoted. It is implicit in the reference to the laws of Rome and of Athens, of the present and of the future, as contrasting with the eternal and unchangeable law of God and of Nature. It is further enlarged where the fundamental equality of men is contrasted with their actual inequalities, and these are attributed to the impact of 'bad habits and false beliefs'. The notion of natural law clearly refers to that contrast between 'nature' and 'convention', between φύσις and νόμος, which played so great a part in Greek philosophy and in Greek political thought. That contrast had provided the Sophists with the most powerful weapon for their criticism of existing institutions. It had been successfully met by Plato and Aristotle in their discussion of human nature in politics. It was revived in the Stoic gospel of cosmopolitanism and of a 'return to nature'. It is characteristic of Cicero that he should not have drawn all the implications which the contrast implied. But later writers, such as Seneca, were to develop them more fully. And the distinction between the natural and the conventional is the very backbone of the theory of law which is laid down in the *Corpus Iuris Civilis*.

Thus do modern historians and political philosophers tend to attribute a paramount importance to the philosophical element underlying that theory. A further confirmation of that importance is derived from the very opening of the *Digest*, where it is said that the jurist, in order to be a minister of justice, must also be a follower of 'true philosophy'. The great jurists of the golden age of Roman law, says a recent historian (Rommen), were for the most part also philosophers. Under the influence of Stoic philosophy the doctrine of natural law passed into Roman law—to be handed on to later thought. Justinian's law-books afford the confirmation of the 'perfectly continuous history' of that doctrine.

Now it may seem impertinent to raise doubts on what is still the current and commonly accepted interpretation. But it is impossible not to do so when the evidence is more closely examined. For one thing, it is highly perplexing to find that modern students of Roman law take a very different view of the matter.

According to them, the Roman jurists were a singularly un-philosophical breed of men. They were a professional class, and far-reaching speculations (such as Cicero's) about the ideal law or the ultimate nature of justice were not properly within the range of their interest. They may have availed themselves of Greek philosophical notions, but legal philosophy never developed among them. This applies not only to the jurists of the Republican period, the period when Greek influences and modes of thought were beginning to sweep the Roman world. It applies also to the 'classical' period, which stretches from Augustus to Diocletian, the great creative period of Roman law and Roman jurisprudence.

Whatever occasional references can be found in the writings of the jurists to the problem of justice, or to the nature of jurisprudence, or to natural law, should therefore be treated with the greatest suspicion. They should be considered as possible reminiscences of class-room teaching, or as ornamental commonplaces not to be taken too seriously. Or the words may have a technical meaning which can be only obscured by referring them to philosophical currents and influences. Finally, allowance must be made in all cases for post-classical insertions and additions.

Such warnings as these make us realise the importance of what I have called the painstaking efforts of scholars to ascertain the authenticity of the texts which were transmitted to us by Justinian. They make us aware that the high-sounding phrases which are set forth in the opening paragraphs of the *Digest*—and above all the notion of *ius naturale*—conceal the most complex and difficult problems of interpretation. Clearly, our views about the continuity and importance of the natural law tradition cannot fail to be seriously affected if it is proved that all references to it are but rhetorical ornaments of doubtful attribution.

But there is no need to be a specialist in Roman law to feel uneasy about the definition of *ius naturale*. It is indeed very difficult to construct a coherent doctrine from the different views which are expressed on the subject in the passages quoted in the *Digest*. These views appear to contradict one another to an extent which cannot fail to impress even such readers who are unaware of the most up-to-date results of textual criticism. The most characteristic contradiction is that which concerns the relations between natural law (*ius naturale*), the civil law (*ius civile*) and the law of nations (*ius gentium*).

There is no doubt that, in the lawyers whose authority is referred to by Justinian, we find not one but several different views on the matter. Here are the passages which best illustrate this contradiction. The first is given under the name of Ulpian, a jurist of the age of Alexander Severus (first half of the third century A.D.). It is allegedly derived from his book of *Institutes*, a work which has unfortunately been lost; indeed, its very existence has been doubted by scholars. The passage runs as follows:

Dig., I, i, 1 (*ULPIANUS libro primo institutionum*): Private law is threefold; it can be gathered from the precepts of nature, or from those of the nations, or from those of the city. Natural law is that which nature has taught all animals; this law indeed is not peculiar to the human race, but belongs to all animals . . . From this law springs the union of male and female, which we call matrimony, the procreation of children and their education. . . . The law of nations is that law which mankind observes. It is easy to understand that this law should differ from the natural, inasmuch as the latter belongs to all animals, while the former is peculiar to men.

A few paragraphs below this quotation from Ulpian we read one from Gaius, a jurist of an earlier generation. It is taken from his book of *Institutes*, the only classical work which has come down to us in anything like its original state, and which is usually dated A.D. 161. There can therefore be little doubt about the authenticity of the text as given in the *Digest*:

Dig., I, i, 9 (*GAIUS libro primo institutionum*): All peoples who are governed by law and by custom observe laws which in part are their own and in part are common to all mankind. For those laws which each people has given itself are peculiar to each city and are called the civil law (*ius civile*) . . . But what natural reason dictates to all men and is most equally observed among them is called the law of nations, as that law which is practised by all mankind.

Only a few paragraphs further on, we find the definition of Paulus, a contemporary of Ulpian's:

Dig., I, i, 11 (*PAULUS libro quarto decimo ad Sabinum*): We can speak of law in different senses; in one sense, when we call law what is always equitable and good, as is natural law. In another sense, what in each city is profitable to all or to many, as is civil law (*ius civile*).

The divergencies between these three passages are obvious. Ulpian lays down a tripartite division of law; Gaius and Paulus a twofold one. Ulpian sharply asserts the difference between natural law and the other human laws; Gaius the identity of the dictates of natural reason with the law of nations. Finally, Ulpian conceives of natural law as something like the general instinct of animals; while Gaius and Paulus see the reason for the universal validity of certain principles in their rational character and in their acceptance by all mankind, as well as in their inherent utility and goodness.

The difference between these quite opposite ways of approaching the problem of the ultimate foundation of law is further apparent from many other passages referring to natural law, both in the first chapter of the *Digest* and elsewhere. The jurists from whom the Byzantine compilers derived their authorities seem to fall into two groups.

On one side, Ulpian himself, and several other authors, clearly oppose the *ius gentium* to the *ius naturale* or to nature. They seem to conceive of all men as having been born free and equal, bound only by the ties of family relationship, and with an equal right to such things as by natural law are the common patrimony of mankind. One of the jurists of a still later date, Hermogenianus (fourth century A.D.), is quoted as giving a list of the institutions which come under the *ius gentium*; among them are wars, the separation of nations, the foundation of kingdoms, the division of property, in short, all those legal and political institutions which have developed out of the growing complexity of human intercourse and life. It is not said explicitly of these institutions, as it is said of slavery, that they are against nature; but the assumption is clearly that they do not correspond to natural law, and the inspiring motive is a contrast between nature and convention.

Gaius, on the other hand, seems to stand alone in maintaining that the institutions of the law of nations can be rationally justified, inasmuch as men have been led by 'natural reason' to adopt them.

I have tried to sum up as briefly as possible the difficulties which the doctrine of natural law, as it is laid down in the *Digest*, presents to the reader. I have no intention of discussing in detail the many explanations which have been proposed in order to solve these difficulties.

The easiest and most obvious explanation is an historical one. The literature which was used and condensed by order of Justinian, it is pointed out, covers a range of several centuries. Such an extent of time may well account for a change of mind and of attitude. The different views which appear to have been held by the writers of different periods might thus be referred to the impact of different schools of thought, perhaps also to the growth of a new conception of life which was to find its full expression in Christianity.

More radically, many among the most authoritative students of Roman law have suggested that all the general definitions which are contained in the text of the *Digest* should be considered as dubious. When they were not actually the result of direct inter-polation by the Byzantines, these definitions are at any rate—as has already been said—purely ornamental and devoid of any juridical value. In particular, Ulpian's definition of natural law—that unlucky phrase, as Sir Frederick Pollock termed it, entirely alien to the legal tradition (Jolowicz) as well as contrary to the Stoic conception of the law of nature (Schulz)—is now usually considered a post-classical insertion; and so is the trichotomy *ius civile, ius gentium, ius naturale*, as opposed to the dichotomy *ius civile, ius gentium* (= *ius naturale*). All the blame would then rest with the Byzantine compilers. They had been ordered by Justinian to omit, and even to alter, 'everything in the ancient books that ye shall find badly stated, or superfluous, or imperfect' (Const. 'Deo Auctore'). They made the issues only more obscure in their endeavour *de solliciter doucement les textes. . . .*

Such explanations and suggestions carry weight, coming, as they do, from most authoritative quarters. But they do not account for one fact, which impresses itself upon the reader of the *Digest* the moment he forgets the quarrel about the classical and post-classical elements that went into its composition. If there are many contradictions between the texts, surely the Byzantine compilers must have been aware of them. And since they had authority to remove them, why did they not do so? How can it be explained that they should have welded together a number of contradictory authorities, in the deliberate attempt to prefix to their compilation a section dealing with the highest problems of law, *De Iustitia et Iure*? I think that we should fix our attention on the common elements which that section contains rather than on its contradictions.

Let us go back for a moment to that claim to universal validity which, in the eyes of posterity, constituted the greatest appeal of Justinian's law-books and which was so prominently in the mind of their author. The foundation of that universal validity purported to be a rational foundation. It could be provided only by an absolute standard of justice. This standard is *ius naturale*. In the *Digest*, Ulpian's 'natural instinct' could suffice to prove that there are certain institutions which are inherent in all animal life. The universality of law is pegged to nature in its broadest sense. In the *Institutes*, where the Christian Emperor speaks out in his own name, the existence of natural law is attributed to a will superior to that of any law-giver. 'The laws of nature, which are most equally observed by all nations, remain always stable and immutable, enacted as they are by some kind of divine providence' (*Inst.*, I, ii, 11).

But along with the principles which can be traced back to that ultimate foundation, law includes other principles which have been devised by men. Some of them can be shown to be common to all nations. 'The Roman people apply a law which is partly its own, and partly is common to all men.' Gaius' words are quoted in the *Institutes*; both in the *Institutes* and in the *Digest* his definition of *ius gentium* provides the explanation of the cosmopolitan character of Roman law.

Finally, allowance had to be made for the solid core of purely Roman institutions which had become the law of the universal Empire. The *ius civile* derives its name from the *civitas*. There have been many cities and many laws. But 'when we do not specify of what city we are speaking, we mean our law'—the law of the Romans (*Inst.*, I, ii, 2).

There is little incoherence in all this. There is rather an appraisal of the causes of the universal validity of Roman law which closely corresponds to the facts. The trichotomy *ius civile—ius gentium— ius naturale* may have been a post-classical insertion. But it reflects, in a simplified form, what had actually been the different stages in the long process of the universalisation of Roman law, that process which, in Vico's opinion, and in that of many great thinkers after him, represents a sort of ideal pattern of all legal evolution.

The meaning and function *ius gentium* has been described many times. It was certainly the most important factor in that evolution. Under the stress of the growing intercourse with foreign peoples, the Roman jurists found in it the practical means for overcoming the limitations and extending the boundaries of municipal law; until in due time it developed into a theoretical principle expressing the common element in all legislation. But the meaning and function of *ius naturale*, more subtle and less spectacular, requires some further assessment.

It is only by keeping in mind the practical use of such expressions as *ius naturale, naturalis, natura*, that we can hope to understand the part which was played by the corresponding notions in the heyday of Roman legal development. A careful survey of their manifold applications provides convincing evidence that they were invoked in the most different fields. They were invoked to provide a basis of rights and of duties. But that basis was not of a speculative, transcendental kind. It can best be described as a quest for the intrinsic character of a given situation.

Such words as *natura hominis, natura rei*, which recur so often in the texts, seem to indicate nothing more than the 'normal' condition of men and of things. *Contra naturam* means the abnormal; illness is described in one place as the 'unnatural' condition of the body. The word *naturalis* indicates the condition of fact which is the presupposition of legal regulation. Thus there is a *naturalis possessio* at the root of all property. There is a *naturalis obligatio*, which may or may not be legally protected, but which is the necessary prerequisite of all obligations. There is a *cognatio naturalis* which must be distinguished from the *cognatio civilis*, in accordance with the two aspects, the 'biological' and the political, of the Roman family.

Ius naturale played indeed a considerable part in Roman jurisprudence. But it had little to do with legal philosophy; it was rather—as has been suggested—a 'professional construction of lawyers' (Schulz). What the Roman jurists were striving after was to find the rule corresponding to the nature of things, to a concrete situation of fact and of life. In short, *ius naturale* was to them not a complete and ready-made system of rules, but a means of interpretation. Along with *ius gentium*, with which it was certainly connected and possibly for a time even identified, it played a decisive part in the process of adapting positive law to changing conditions and in elaborating the legal system of an international or rather super-national civilisation.

Now it is impossible to believe that the Byzantine compilers should not have been aware of this particular, legal and not philosophical, meaning of the notions which were incorporated in the texts which they preserved, faithfully or not, for posterity. However anxious they may have been to stress the notion of natural law as a moral standard and to give prominence to it as the ultimate foundation of all laws and the expression of divine providence, there is one essential point in which they did not

C

forgo what can well be called the most characteristic feature of the
Roman conception of *ius naturale*. On this point that conception
is as widely different from the medieval and modern, as it is from
the essentially philosophical views which, under the influence of
Stoicism, had been put forward by Cicero in the passage quoted
at the beginning of this chapter. Here we reach possibly the very
heart of the matter, where an explanation might be found of the
difficulties in which so many students of that conception have
become involved.

Nowhere, in fact, do we find in the *Corpus Iuris* an assertion
of the superiority of natural to positive law, in the sense that,
in a case of conflict, the one should overrule the other. The
Roman conception of natural law is anything but a revolutionary
principle. It contains no vindication of the 'rights of man'.
Neither has it much in common with the notion of a 'higher law',
such as is laid down in some modern constitutions. Being in itself
merely 'a reflection upon existing law', it was not meant to give
'legal sanction to what was not otherwise law'. In fact, it 'was
overruled in cases of conflict by what *was* law' (Zulueta). However
contrary to natural law, such institutions as slavery could still
appear, even to the Byzantine lawyers, as perfectly acceptable and
legal. We must indeed divest ourselves, in order to understand the
Roman conception of natural law, not only of the modern conception of natural rights, but of the notion of the subordination of
positive to natural law with which later ages have made us
familiar. If this should be a disappointment to those who expected
too much of the 'perfectly continuous history' of natural law, let
them not forget that the Roman doctrine had some other undeniable merits.

First and foremost is its lasting achievement in founding a
system of law of unequalled completeness and harmony. The
greatness of that achievement cannot be better described than in
the following passage from Maine's *Ancient Law*:

I know no reason why the law of the Romans should be superior to
the laws of the Hindoos, unless the theory of Natural Law had given it a
type of excellence different from the usual one. In this one exceptional
instance, simplicity and symmetry were kept before the eyes of a society
whose influence on mankind was destined to be prodigious from other
causes, as the characteristics of an ideal and absolutely perfect law.

These words offer a striking confirmation of what I suggested in the Introduction, viz., that the real significance of natural law must be sought in its function rather than in the doctrine itself. Because of that very function, the notion of natural law came to be as it were embodied in the Roman tradition, and was able to exert an influence which it would hardly have exerted had it remained in the regions of philosophical abstraction.

A system of law which purported to be grounded on its intrinsic value rather than on its power of compulsion was a unique experiment in the history of mankind. Roman legal tradition has taught the Western world to conceive of law as the common substance of mankind, as an unceasing effort to realise *quod semper aequum ac bonum est*. Let us read the Roman definitions with all necessary caution. *Semper* may have been an interpolation. Unlike the Byzantine Emperor, the classical Roman jurist may not have conceived of natural law as an immutable and eternal standard. There still remains the demand that law should correspond to nature, to equity and justice.

This demand has not been forgotten. In later days, historical circumstances and the very perfection of the Roman system of laws could lead to its veneration as the embodiment of natural justice. It could be hailed as universally valid because of its coincidence with the law of nature. This belief was not the outcome of only medieval credulity. It was maintained down to more recent days. In a letter to Hobbes of July, 1670, Leibniz declared that, in his endeavour to reduce Roman law to its general elements, he had found that a clear half of it consisted of 'pure natural law'.

We may not share that belief any longer. But we cannot be entirely insensitive to the demand which the Roman jurists expressed. It is this demand, more than their actual definitions, which will always make the doctrine of natural law a subject of interest to the student.

R. W. and A. J. CARLYLE, *A History of Medieval Political Theory in the West*, vol. I, 1903, 1 and 2.
The Legacy of Rome, Oxford, 1923: 'The Conception of the Empire', by SIR E. BARKER; 'The Science of Law', by F. DE ZULUETA.
C. H. MCILWAIN, *The Growth of Political Thought in the West*, 1932, ch. iv.
H. F. JOLOWICZ, *Historical Introduction to the Study of Roman Law*, 1932.
F. SCHULZ, *Principles of Roman Law*, 1936; and *History of Roman Legal Science*, 1946.
SIR P. VINOGRADOFF, *Roman Law in Medieval Europe*, 2nd ed., 1929.

The references to the *Institutes* and the *Digest* are from the Berlin edition (Krüger–Mommsen) of 1889; those to Cicero's *De Re Publica* and *De Legibus* from Loeb's Classical Library.

The survey of the references to *ius naturale, naturalis, natura,* is taken from an Italian work by C. A. MASCHI, *La concezione naturalistica del diritto e degli istituti giuridici romani,* 1937.

A useful selection of texts can be found in F. SENN, *De la justice et du droit,* 1927.

Historical and critical study of Roman Law has developed, in the last hundred years, and particularly in Germany and in Italy, into an immense literature which cannot be referred in detail. To the English reader the most inspiring approach to Roman Law and jurisprudence may perhaps still be provided by GIBBON's *Decline and Fall,* ch. xliv.

3

A RATIONAL FOUNDATION OF ETHICS

'Mankind is ruled by two laws: Natural Law and Custom. Natural Law is that which is contained in the Scriptures and the Gospel.' These words are taken from another great law-book, the authority of which for a time evenly balanced that of the *Corpus Iuris Civilis*. They form the opening paragraph of the *Decretum Gratiani* (*c.* 1140), the oldest collection of Church law embodied in the *Corpus Iuris Canonici.*[1] They provide the best introduction to the medieval conception of the law of nature.

Once again that ancient notion was called to play a capital role in the history of thought. In the hands of professional philosophers it became the cornerstone of a complete system of ethics.

But that remarkable achievement would probably not have been possible had not the notion of natural law undergone a thorough transformation. The lawyers of the Church—the Canonists—stand out among medieval lawyers for the freedom and daring with which they recast the whole problem of law and morals. They gave natural law an unprecedented coherence, clearness and force. Canon law has been said, and correctly, to

---

[1] *Corpus Iuris Canonici* was the name adopted by the Council of Basle in 1441 to indicate several collections of Church laws of which the first—the *Concordia discordantium Canonum* is reminiscent of the *Digest*, the others of the *Code*. The *Concordia*, or as it is usually called the *Decretum Gratiani*, was the work of an Italian monk, Gratian, who was active in Bologna, the great medieval centre of law studies, in the first half of the twelfth century.

constitute the principal vehicle, in the Middle Ages, of the doctrine of the law of nature.[1]

It is best to begin by reducing that doctrine to its simplest expression. Natural law goes back to God. Its precepts derive their authority from the fact that they are confirmed and implemented by Revelation. Properly speaking natural law is essentially the concern of man. The old 'legal tradition'—says an early commentator of Gratian referring to Ulpian's definition—defined natural law in the most general terms as that law 'which nature has taught all animals . . . But we shall disregard so general an acceptation and consider the meaning of it essentially in relation to matters which are proper to the human race alone.'

Because of its divine character, natural law is absolutely binding and overrules all other laws. It precedes them in time, 'because it came into existence with the very creation of man as a rational being, nor does it vary in time but remains unchangeable' (*Decr. Grat.*, P.I., dist. v, 1, §1). It also precedes them in dignity. 'Natural law absolutely prevails in dignity over customs and constitutions. Whatever has been recognised by usage, or laid down in writing, if it contradicts natural law, must be considered null and void' (*Decr. Grat.*, I, viii, 2). This statement of Gratian is still further reinforced by his commentator: 'it must be considered null and void because the Lord has said *I am the Truth*, not *I am Custom or Constitution*'.

These are strong and sweeping phrases. They make us aware that we have entered a very different world from that of the Roman lawyers. And yet it is not altogether impossible to trace the process by which the cautious and often ambiguous phrases of the Roman lawyers about natural law came to be modified and extended to provide a platform for the startling assertions of the medieval writers. As far as the 'formal' continuity of the notion is concerned, there is no doubt that medieval natural law is the progeny of the Greeks and the Romans. To medieval eyes the idea of the law of nature appeared surrounded by the glamour of the Roman legal inheritance. It had, however, received as it were the necessary christening by being accepted and embedded in the

---

[1] This, according to Sir Frederick Pollock, is the explanation of the fact that the doctrine of natural law was never popular among English lawyers. *In Anglia minus curatur de iure naturali quam in aliqua regione de mundo*, wrote an early commentator of Bracton. For a further discussion of the relationship between the law of nature and the Common law, see Sir W. Holdsworth, *A History of English Law*, vol. II, app. ii.

teaching of the Christian Fathers. Scholars are still discussing to what extent the Christian notion of natural law is derived from Stoic philosophy or is a native product of Christianity.[1] However closely the Stoic and the Christian notions of the law of nature may resemble each other, there are undoubtedly subtle and far-reaching differences between them, derived from a different ideal and view of life.

There is, at any rate, nothing new nor staggering in Gratian's assertion of the divine and absolute character of the law of nature. That character had been emphatically asserted by Cicero; and Lactantius, in preserving and quoting Cicero's famous definition of natural law, had pointed out that not even a Christian could have given a better one. In the hands of the Fathers, natural law had come to be identified with the law given by God to Adam, the 'general and primitive law of mankind'. Justinian, the Christian law-giver, had stressed in the *Institutes* the immutable character of the laws of nature, based on the providence of God.

Nor is there anything very surprising in the restriction of natural law to essentially human concerns, as against the general instinct of all animals and beings. Cicero's *recta ratio in iubendo et vetando* as well as Gaius' *naturalis ratio* had laid the emphasis on the inherent capacity of man to discover the universal principles of law. However different their conception of man, Christian writers like St Ambrose or St Augustine had developed the notion of a *lex naturalis in corde scripta* and of an *innata vis* to attain to the knowledge of it. There could be little difficulty on the part of Christians in accepting a notion which seemed so pertinently to confirm the Apostle's saying of the Gentiles, 'which shew the work of the Law written in their hearts, their conscience also bearing witness' (*Rom.*, II, 15).

Finally, not even the twofold division of law, which supersedes the tripartite division of the *Digest*, is entirely without precedents. In laying it down at the beginning of his compilation, Gratian could refer to the authority of a Christian writer of the seventh century, whose encyclopaedic work—the *Etymologiae*—exerted a deep influence on medieval literature. It is from St Isidore of Seville that the sweeping generalisation is taken: 'All laws are either divine or human. Divine laws are based on nature, human laws on custom. The reason why these are at variance is that different nations adopt different laws.'

[1] For a full discussion of this problem, see the works of E. Troeltsch, to which I have called attention in a lengthy note to the Introduction.

Thus again it is perfectly possible to build up a strong case for the continuity of the natural law tradition which seems to leave little room for original thinking. But once again that continuity is misleading. The importance of Gratian's definition was not in what lay behind, but in what lay ahead of it. It is no exaggeration to say that in those simple words was contained the whole programme of medieval moral and legal philosophy. The words have a double meaning which must not be overlooked. They mean that the law of nature is embodied in the Scriptures. But they also mean that the Scriptures do not contradict the law of nature. The evidence of reason and that of Revelation are correlative. The Christian religion is no longer a 'folly', a flat contradiction of human nature and the abolition of the old Adam. Worldly and godly wisdom must be reconciled. Reason and faith are not incompatible. Christianity can be implemented and enriched by philosophy.

The spirit of medieval Christianity can alone account for the part which natural law was called upon to play in this new conception of ethics. It is a different spirit from that of primitive Christianity. No doubt the Fathers of the Church had drunk deep at the well of heathen philosophy. They had not hesitated to accept whatever notions could be squared with Christian belief and used as a means of enhancing it. Natural law was one of the most prominent among them. Both St Ambrose and St Augustine could stress the natural capacity of man to attain to the knowledge of what is good and conducive to perfection. But at bottom the contrast between the world and the Kingdom of God remained a capital issue. In the manner of conceiving that contrast, however, there had been oscillations.

The extreme view is that which we still associate with Augustinianism. The fifth book of St Augustine's *City of God* remains the most dramatic illustration of the dilemma which faced Christian ethics. In that book St Augustine had discussed the virtues of the ancient Romans. They had been great and beneficient. The Romans had given the world free institutions and good rulers. They had set the love of their country above their own interest and welfare. Virgil is quoted at length to provide evidence for the greatness of Rome. It was thanks to their virtues that the Romans had achieved 'so many wonderful deeds, worthy of praise and of glory according to the judgment of men'. God had rewarded those virtues by giving them 'the worldly glory of the most excellent Empire'. But what were such virtues other than illusions? What but smoke and vanity is the glory of the Earthly City compared to the glory of the Heavenly? 'What does it matter to man, in this brief mortal life, under whose rule he lives, provided the rulers do not force him to do evil?' (*De Civitate Dei*, V, xvii). In such words all political interest seems to have come to a standstill. One almost hears in them the echo of a crumbling world. They mark the end of an epoch.

Not all Christian writers had gone to such extremes. Social and political institutions could not fail to be a matter of concern to the Christian. A rational explanation of their existence and necessity could be given by welding together the philosophic notion of a contrast between nature and convention and the religious idea of human corruption and sinfulness. Actually the belief in the corruption of human nature could help to explain the hardships and miseries of man's present conditions, while the idea of a divinely appointed remedy could lead men to conceive of the State as an expression of God's inscrutable providence. From such premises a body of political philosophy could be elaborated which dominated the West for many centuries. It is a philosophy of pessimism. With nature corrupt, with an absolute ideal of Christian perfection, little room was left for a natural order of things, for a system of ethics based on man's nature. The function of natural law was narrowly circumscribed. It was called in to express a forsaken ideal, a condition of things irretrievably lost to fallen humanity. It did not provide the rational basis for social and political institutions.[1]

It is this rational basis which natural law was asked to provide by medieval thinkers. The old pessimism has gone. If anything, the Middle Ages seem to have been over-optimistic. The City of God is no longer an unattainable ideal. It is in this world that man is called to achieve it. The rigid alternative which had been stressed by St Augustine has given way to an entirely new view of man's perfectibility. Christianity has ceased to be hostile to the world; it tends to be reconciled with it in a thoroughly Christian civilisation. Such a staggering change would hardly have been possible had not new and powerful factors been at work in producing it. The medieval world was fluid, with avenues open to the

---

[1] Many modern historians, following Troeltsch, distinguish in the teaching of the Fathers a 'primary' or absolute, from a 'secondary' or relative, natural law, the first corresponding to nature before the Fall, the second to the corruption of man's sinful nature. But these expressions are nowhere to be found in the sources.

future. Nothing had yet taken the place of the old bureaucratic structure of the Empire. The work of building up a Christian community could be started from below rather than from above.

An immense task lay ahead of the medieval man. The present had to be secured, the past reconquered. The lesson of Roman law was that the greatest of all legal systems had been based purely on reason and utility; the lesson of Aristotle, that the State is the highest achievement of man and the necessary instrument of human perfection. How could a Christian community be taught the elementary duties of good life and fellowship? How could Roman law be accepted as the universal law of Christendom? How could the teaching of Aristotle, the pagan philosopher, be adapted to the Christian view of life? If so great a body of wisdom had been discovered without supernatural help, if a basis was to be provided for human relations independently of the higher requirements of Christian perfection, surely there must be a knowledge of ethical values which man can attain with the sole help of his reason. There must be a system of natural ethics. Its cornerstone must be natural law.

This entirely new function for the idea of the law of nature is nowhere more apparent than in the teaching of St Thomas Aquinas. He is the greatest representative of medieval philosophy as well as the most constructive and systematic thinker of the Middle Ages. His great *Summae* contain the most complete statement of that ideal of a thorough Christianisation of life which inspired medieval Catholicism and which found its highest artistic achievement in the *Divine Comedy* of Dante. Although Thomist philosophy was at first bitterly opposed by contemporary schools of thought, it finally won the battle. It has remained ever since the most authoritative expression of what may well be called the Catholic view of life. We can therefore safely choose St Thomas's theory of natural law as the best illustration of the part which that notion was called upon to play in one of the great constructive periods of Western civilisation.

It is, however, impossible to understand that theory correctly without taking a resolute plunge into the vast sea of metaphysics. Before becoming a practical principle which, as we shall presently see, is susceptible of the most various applications, St Thomas's theory of natural law is laid down as an interpretation of man's nature and of his relation to God and to the universe. Natural law is unintelligible unless we realise its close link with the eternal divine order on which the whole creation ultimately rests.

Supposing the world to be governed by divine Providence . . . it is clear that the whole community of the universe is governed by the divine reason. This rational guidance of created things on the part of God . . . we can call the Eternal law.

[Now] since all things which are subject to divine Providence are measured and regulated by the Eternal law . . . it is clear that all things participate to some degree in the Eternal law, in so far as they derive from it certain inclinations to those actions and aims which are proper to them.

But, of all others, rational creatures are subject to divine Providence in a very special way; being themselves made participators in Providence itself, in that they control their own actions and the actions of others. So they have a certain share in the divine reason itself, deriving therefrom a natural inclination to such actions and ends as are fitting. This participation in the Eternal law by rational creatures is called the Natural law. Thus when the Psalmist said (*Psalm* iv, 6): 'Offer up the sacrifice of justice,' he added, as though being asked the question, what is the sacrifice of justice, 'Many say, who sheweth us good things?', and then replied, saying: 'The light of Thy countenance, O Lord, is signed upon us.' As though the light of natural reason, by which we discern good from evil, and which is the Natural law, were nothing else than the impression of the divine light in us. So it is clear that the Natural law is nothing else than the participation of the Eternal law in rational creatures.

(*Summa Theologica*, 1a 2ae, quae. 91, art. 1 and 2)

I have given St Thomas's definition in full. I shall now try to disentangle the different points which seem to me to call for attention in this context. The first is the conception of natural law as the expression of the dignity and power of man.

Alone among created beings, man is called to participate intellectually and actively in the rational order of the universe. He is called to do so because of his rational nature. Reason is the essence of man, the divine spark which makes for his greatness. It is the 'light of natural reason' which enables us to 'discern good from evil'. St Thomas's notion of the light of reason is of capital importance. It probably goes back to Platonic and Augustinian sources, and has remained also in later days closely associated with the notion of the law of nature. It has been suggested that St Thomas rationalised the illumination doctrine which St Augustine had derived from Plato.[1] He certainly used that doctrine in a humanist rather than in a mystical sense. The dignity and power of man lead up to an interpretation of life which has been

[1] I owe this suggestion to Fr. F. C. Coplestone, s.j., in a private letter.

very aptly described as a 'Christian humanism'. Man is conceived to hold the unique position of being at the same time a subject of God and His co-operator, a position which Dante—a good Thomist on this point—compared to the horizon 'which lies in the middle, between two hemispheres' (*Monarchia*, III, xvi). Man participates in two worlds; hence the law of his nature includes the qualities which he has in common with all created beings as well as those which are distinctive of his own rational nature.

In a very interesting passage St Thomas described how the first and general precept of natural law—'do good and avoid evil'—can be specified in a concrete order of precepts. Man has in common with all created things the desire for self-preservation. Hence a first group of natural law precepts comprises all that makes for the preservation of human life. But man also has in common with animated beings a further inclination to more specific ends. Hence it is right to say that 'that which nature has taught all animals' pertains to the natural law—such as sexual relationships, the rearing of offspring and the like. But, finally, 'there is in man a certain inclination to know the truth about God and to live in society. In this respect there come under the Natural law all actions connected with such inclinations' (*Summa Theol.*, 1a 2a, 94, 2). St Thomas was a great systematiser. In his classification the definition of Ulpian has found its proper place. But so have the reservations which medieval writers had felt it necessary to make in regard to it. Natural law, the expression of reason, cannot fail to be an essentially human concern.

The second point which calls for attention is the manner in which natural law is conceived as providing the basis of morality. This is a direct consequence of the dignity and power attributed to human nature. The central idea is here a particular notion of the relationship between the evidence of nature and that of Revelation. In giving a clear formulation to this idea, St Thomas was fulfilling, as it were, what had been the deepest and most intimate aspiration of medieval Christianity. His assertion that 'Grace does not abolish Nature but perfects it' is nothing but the translation into metaphysical terms of the attitude which I have already analysed and described. It is the crown of that 'Christian humanism' which is the essence of his philosophy.

The celebrated formula expresses not only an entirely new interpretation of the relationship between reason and faith, between philosophy and Christianity. It also contains a new and different notion of the capacities of human nature and of the effect of sin upon it. The idea of sin and its consequences could not but remain for St Thomas a fundamental dogma of the Christian faith. But, as he expressly puts it, sin itself has not invalidated 'the essential principles of nature'. Its consequences concern only the possibility of man's fulfilling the dictates of 'natural reason', not his capacity to acquire knowledge of them. In other words, they do not impair the existence of a sphere of purely natural—i.e., rational—values. It is in this sphere that the foundation of social and political institutions must be assessed.

Thus the possibility was opened up of giving a rational explanation and justification of ethical imperatives, as well as of all those institutions which earlier Christian thinkers had conceived as the result of sin and as its divine remedy. It was a momentous discovery, for it made it possible to accept the Aristotelian conception of ethics and politics and to graft it, as it were, on the Christian interpretation of life. This is not the place to examine the historical significance of the Aristotelian revival and its manifold consequences in the field of social and political theory.[1] But it is important to remark that it would not have been possible for St Thomas to accept and revive Aristotle's theory of the State had his notion of natural law not provided the necessary instrument. A positive value could be attributed to the State as the highest expression of natural morality. Man could be conceived as a political animal, finding in the life of the community the harmonious integration of his individual life. The contrast between nature and convention, though never openly rejected, ceased for a time to play any prominent part in political theory.

Yet natural law was not only the foundation of morality and of all social and political institutions. It was also the paramount standard by which these institutions could be judged. This is the third point which must be kept in mind in order to understand the doctrine correctly. In this point also St Thomas brings out clearly and logically what had been in the minds of his contemporaries. The Christian community must be based on justice. And justice, as disclosed to man in the precepts of natural law, must prevail over any other command or authority. 'Whatever has been recognised by usage, or laid down in writing, if it contradicts natural law must be considered null and void.' The words of

[1] For further information I venture to refer the reader to my book on *The Medieval Contribution to Political Thought* and to my Introduction to Aquinas, *Selected Political Writings*, 1948.

the Canonist are faithfully re-echoed by St Thomas—and an adequate explanation is provided.

St Augustine says: 'There is no law unless it be just.' So the validity of law depends upon its justice. But in human affairs a thing is said to be just when it accords aright with the rule of reason: and, as we have already seen, the first rule of reason is the Natural law. Thus all humanly enacted laws are in accord with reason to the extent that they derive from the Natural law. And if a human law is at variance in any particular with the Natural law, it is no longer legal, but rather a corruption of law.   (*Summa Theol.*, 1a 2ae, 95, 2)

This is no academic statement devoid of any practical significance. The words must be taken literally. They mean that allegiance to the State—even though it be the highest embodiment of natural morality—can be only conditional. Unjust laws are not properly laws. 'They do not, in consequence, oblige in conscience.'

Man is bound to obey secular rulers to the extent that the order of justice requires. For this reason if such rulers have no just title to power, but have usurped it, or if they command things to be done which are unjust, their subjects are not obliged to obey them, except perhaps in certain special cases, when it is a matter of avoiding scandal or some particular danger.   (*Summa Theol.*, 2a 2ae, 104, 6)

Thus, in certain cases, disobedience may not only be a possibility, but a duty. A theory of resistance can be built up on such premises. The final decision, however, is a matter of complex casuistry. It does not rest solely with the individual. We must be careful not to misconstrue the medieval theory of resistance into a theory of revolution.

In fact, despite the stress which is laid upon the absolute and immutable character of natural law, the notion of it seems to be curiously flexible and adaptable. Positive laws are not expected to be moulded upon it as upon a rigid pattern. A considerable sphere of freedom is left to the human law-giver in the interpretation and application of its general precepts. St Thomas indeed goes so far as to admit that natural law can change. It can change by 'addition', as when new institutions become necessary in view of the development of human activities. It can change by 'subtraction', when 'something ceases to pertain to the Natural law which was formerly part of it'. It is thus quite clear that natural law can be superseded on grounds of utility. In certain cases it seems to indicate simply a condition of things which would prevail if, in the interest of human life, human reason had not been led to adopt new devices. Thus it is possible to speak of a 'common possession of all things', and of an 'equal liberty of all men'. Neither private property nor slavery were imposed by nature. Natural law was not altered but simply added to by their adoption (*Summa Theol.*, 1a 2ae, 94, 5).

This seems to bring us back to the pragmatism of the Roman lawyers. But it is the attitude to history which calls for attention. We tend to consider the very notion of natural law as a typical form of unhistorical thinking. The assertion of absolute and immutable values seems to imply the denial of evolution and development. A correct appraisal of St Thomas's notion of natural law may lead us to modify these conclusions. However different it may be from our own, a deep feeling for history pervades his legal philosophy. The largest possible allowance is made for historical circumstances, the largest compatible with belief in truth and in justice. History is not the last resort, nor can it provide man with the ultimate standard. 'The Lord has said *I am the Truth*, not *I am Custom or Constitution.*'

Lastly, we must consider the limitations of natural law. They considerably qualify the significance of the whole theory. The law of nature is not the only law which guides man on his way to perfection. Other laws are necessary. Human laws must be established to draw out all the conclusions of natural law, and 'to restrain evil men from wrongdoing by force and by fear'. Divine laws were revealed in order to lead man to his heavenly destination, to remedy the weakness of human judgment, to probe the secrets of man's heart and thus to leave no evil unforbidden and unpunished. All law, eternal and natural, human and divine, is linked together in a complete and coherent system. As Hooker remarked—and Hooker was probably one of the ablest, and certainly one of the most unbiased defenders of Thomist legal philosophy—'as the actions of men are of sundry distinct kinds, so the laws thereof must accordingly be distinguished . . . If we measure not each by his own proper law, whereas the things themselves are so different, there will be in our understanding and judgment of them confusion' (*Ecclesiastical Polity*, II, i, 2).

But in order fully to appreciate the inherent limitations of natural law we must never forget that, in the Thomist conception, the natural order is only the condition and the means for the attainment of a higher order. If 'Grace does not abolish Nature', neither does nature abolish grace. Reason and faith go hand in hand, but reason is the handmaid. In the end it is faith alone which can lead man to his 'end of eternal blessedness'. The gradual progress of the soul towards God is symbolised in Dante's long and perilous voyage. The words which the poet attributes to Virgil can well be applied to St Thomas's notion of natural law:

> . . . So far as reason plead
> Can I instruct thee; beyond that point, wait
> For Beatrice; for faith is here thy need.
> (*Purgatorio*, xviii, 46–48, trans. Binyon)

And in the same way as Virgil hands over his pupil to Beatrice on the summit of the mountain of Purgatory, so does the law of nature constitute for man only a step, although a necessary step, towards perfection.

This is the essential qualification of the Thomist conception of natural law, and we must always keep it in mind lest we entirely misconstrue St Thomas's endeavour to base a natural system of ethics on it. Natural law is the token of the fundamental harmony between human and Christian values, the expression of the perfectibility of man and of the power and dignity of his reason. But the system of ethics which is based on these assumptions cannot properly be called a 'rationalist' system. The proud spirit of modern rationalism is lacking. There is no assertion of man's self-sufficiency and inherent perfection. There is no vindication of abstract 'rights', nor of the autonomy of the individual as the ultimate source of all laws and of all standards.

No doubt a system such as this can be said to contain a recognition, and indeed a defence, of human personality. It can be developed, as has been done by some modern Thomists,[1] into a codified system of human rights based on the Christian view of the supreme value of the individual soul, the goal of Redemption. But on closer inspection it is only too evident that the 'rights of the human person' of the Thomist are something entirely different from the 'rights of man' which will be examined in the following chapter. The assertion of those rights is always based on the existence of an objective standard of justice. The emphasis is on natural law, not on natural rights. What is stressed is the duty of the State rather than the rights of the individual, the restoration of the right order of things rather than the perilous experiment of

[1] J. Maritain, *The Rights of Man and Natural Law*, 1944.

revolution. In fact, it is not from the individual that we are asked to start, but from the Cosmos, from the notion of a world well ordered and graded, of which natural law is the expression.

The modern Thomist will insist that the proper foundation of natural law is a metaphysical foundation. But the metaphysics which he has in mind is the Christian, or rather the Thomist. His starting point is that of St Thomas: 'supposing the world to be governed by divine Providence'. The theorists of natural rights also had their metaphysics. They also had their providence. But it was no longer the Thomist, perhaps it was not even the Christian providence.

Thus once again the real significance of the notion of natural law seems to lie more in its function than in the doctrine itself. The stroke of genius of medieval writers was to have grasped its importance for the foundation of a natural system of ethics, distinct though not separate from Christian or revealed ethics. Natural law was the instrument for solving a problem which, from the Christian standpoint, might otherwise seem insoluble or non-existent. Augustinianism and Thomism are often said to constitute the two correlative though not necessarily contradictory poles, so to speak, of Christian thought. The Thomist interpretation of Christianity is unthinkable without the notion of natural law.

That notion has remained a lasting inheritance of legal and moral philosophy. Its importance, one might say, transcends the setting of circumstance and time which explain it historically. It represents a fundamental attitude of the Christian towards the problem of life and society. It has outlived St Thomas as well as medieval Catholicism. The Protestant Hooker made full use of it against the intransigent Augustinianism of the Puritans. It is more than a paradox that this notion should have provided the basis for a defence of the Church of England and indeed of what would nowadays be called the English way of life. The best appreciation of the medieval notion of natural law can be given in Hooker's own words: 'these School-implements are acknowledged by grave and wise men not unprofitable to have been invented'.

R. W. and A. J. CARLYLE, *A History of Medieval Political Theory in the West*, vols. II–V.

D

O. VON GIERKE, trans. MAITLAND, *Political Theories of the Middle Ages*, 1900/1922.
J. N. FIGGIS, *Political Aspects of St Augustine's 'City of God'*, 1921.
B. JARRETT, *Social Theories of the Middle Ages*, 1926.
C. H. MCILWAIN, *The Growth of Political Thought in the West*, chs. v–vi.
SIR M. POWICKE, *The Christian Life in the Middle Ages*, 1935.
E. GILSON, *The Spirit of Medieval Philosophy*, 1936.
A. P. D'ENTRÈVES, *The Medieval Contribution to Political Thought*, 1939.

French books: O. LOTTIN, *Le droit naturel chez Saint Thomas d'Aquin et ses prédécesseurs*, 1931; H. X. ARQUILLERE, *L'Augustinisme politique*, 1934.

German: O. SCHILLING, *Naturrecht und Staat nach der Lehre der alten Kirche*, 1914, and *Die Staats- und Soziallehre des hl. Thomas von Aquin*, 1923; E. BERNHEIM, *Mittelalterliche Zeitanschauungen in ihrem Einfluss auf Politik und Geschichtsschreibung*, 1918.

The references to the *Decretum Gratiani* are from the Leipzig edition (Friedberg) of 1879; those to St Thomas Aquinas from my edition of *Selected Political Writings*, 1948.

For the attitude of the Canonists to natural law, W. ULLMANN, *Medieval Papalism*, 1948, should now be consulted. I regret that I was unable to make use of it as the present essay was already with the printer at the time of its publication.

4

A THEORY OF NATURAL RIGHTS

The representatives of the French people, constituted in a National Assembly, considering that ignorance, oblivion or contempt of the Rights of Man are the only causes of public misfortunes and of the corruption of governments, have resolved to lay down, in a solemn Declaration, the natural, inalienable and sacred Rights of Man, in order that this Declaration, being always before all the members of the Social Body, should constantly remind them of their Rights and their Duties; that the actions of the Legislative as well as of the Executive Power, being liable at any moment to be referred to the end of all political institutions, should be more respected; that the grievances of the citizen, being henceforward based upon simple and indisputable principles, should always be conducive to the preservation of the Constitution and to the happiness of all.

These solemn words form the preamble of the *Déclaration des Droits de l'Homme et du Citoyen*. Together with the fall of the Bastille, the Declaration adopted by the French National Assembly on 26 August 1789, opened the way to the French Revolution. The proclamation of the 'natural, inalienable and sacred rights of man' marks the end of an era and the beginning of contemporary Europe.[1] How tempting it is to consider it only the final act in two thousand years of uninterrupted development! According to many historians, the theory of the rights of man had 'been implicit in political thought ever since the Stoics and as a result of Rome's transmission of Stoic conceptions of equality' (McIlwain). I have in the preceding chapters raised some doubts as to the continuity

[1] See note at the end of this chapter.

of that development. They will be further confirmed if we submit the modern theory of natural rights to the same critical examination to which the Roman and the medieval notions of natural law have been subjected.

Once again it seems best to begin by considering the outstanding features of the theory. They can be reduced to three. The first is its rationalism. The 'natural rights of man' are conceived to be equivalent to 'simple and indisputable principles'. The second, its individualism. The talk is about the 'natural, inalienable rights of *man*'; and men, it is said, in the first of the seventeen articles contained in the Declaration, 'are born and remain free and equal in rights'. The third outstanding feature of the theory is its radicalism. The exercise of power is 'liable at any moment to be referred to the end of all political institutions'; and the end of all political institutions, we read in Article 3, 'is the preservation of the natural and imprescriptible rights of man'. Even more forcibly, the American *Declaration of Independence* had asserted, thirteen years earlier, that 'whenever any form of government becomes destructive of these ends, it is the Right of the People to alter or abolish it'.

The rationalism of the theory first calls for attention. There had always been a rationalist bent in the notion of the law of nature. It had been closely associated with the working of 'natural reason'. It had been identified with the dignity and power of man. But reason to the Roman lawyer was perhaps only another name for experience. For the medieval philosopher it was the gift of God. In both cases the evidence of reason had to be implemented, and indeed confirmed, by some other evidence—of fact or of faith. But now the evidence of reason is in itself sufficient. 'We hold these truths to be self-evident,' wrote the American Fathers. The French re-echoed the idea of the existence of 'simple and indisputable principles' as the ultimate standard and the basis of political obligation.

Rationalism is an ambiguous word. It would take a long time to define it. It would take still more to trace its subtle ramifications and the infinite varieties of its manifestations. 'The appearance of a new intellectual character is like the appearance of a new architectural style; it emerges almost imperceptibly, under the pressure of a great variety of influences . . . All that can be discerned are the slowly mediated changes, the shuffling and re-shuffling, the flow and ebb of tides of inspiration with issues finally in a shape identifiably new.' This remark by a recent student of 'rationalism in politics'[1] fully applies to the modern theory of natural law. Both in the American and in the French Declaration the rationalist style is easily identifiable, and startling enough. But it is not so easy to trace its origin and to ascertain the moment in which it shows itself unmistakably for the first time. The emphasis laid on the continuity of the natural law tradition has led, in this as in other instances which we have examined, to some misconstructions which must be carefully assessed.

Hugo Grotius, a Dutchman (1583–1645), has long been considered the founder of the modern theory of natural law. This judgment goes back to Pufendorf (1632–94), the first holder of a chair of Natural Law in a German university, and the greatest academic expounder of the theory in the seventeenth century. Pufendorf praised Grotius as the *vir incomparabilis* who dared to go beyond what had been taught in the Schools, and to draw the theory of the law of nature out of the 'darkness' in which it had lain for centuries. That judgment is still repeated in many handbooks. Along with Bacon and Descartes in the field of philosophy, with Galileo and Newton in the field of experimental science, Grotius has a special place reserved in the field of jurisprudence as one of the prophets of our brave new world.

This view has been challenged by some modern historians. They have gleefully set to work revising the accepted version and displacing Grotius from his pedestal. There is nothing new nor original—so the story is now told—in the notion of natural law which Grotius used as the foundation of his treatment of the *Laws of War and Peace* (1625). The tradition of natural law had continued to flourish in Europe all through the sixteenth century, notwithstanding the fact that the unity of Christendom had been torn asunder by the Reformation of which Grotius was a son. That notion had been accepted by Catholic as well as by Protestant writers. Grotius did nothing but borrow it from the late Scholastics, particularly from the Spanish theologians and legal philosophers to whom he acknowledged his indebtedness. His thought, therefore, is 'a direct continuation of the great Natural Law tradition which stretches from St Augustine to Suarez, and which culminated in St Thomas.'[2] His famous dictum that natural law would retain its validity even if God did not exist (*etiamsi daremus*

[1] M. Oakeshott, 'Rationalism in Politics' in *The Cambridge Journal*, vol. I, 1947.
[2] A.-H. Chroust, 'Hugo Grotius and the Scholastic Natural Law Tradition' in *The New Scholasticism*, vol. XVII, 1943.

non esse Deum), can be traced back to earlier writers. It is far less revolutionary than it seems, and it is actually accompanied by very important cautions and qualifications.

Once again the quest for precedents has led historians to forget that a doctrine must not be judged by the letter, but by the spirit. There is no doubt that all the great thinkers who open up our modern age have their roots in the age that preceded them. But the fact that Descartes—as has been conclusively shown—drank deep at the well of Scholastic philosophy is certainly no reason for mistaking him for a Schoolman. Nor is the possibility of tracing a large literature *On the Government of Princes* in the Middle Ages an excuse for overlooking the startling novelty of Machiavelli's *Prince*. If Grotius—like Machiavelli and Descartes, and many other great thinkers—was considered by his contemporaries and his immediate successors to have broken with the thought that preceded him, we must try to understand the reasons which led to that opinion. These reasons are not difficult to ascertain. They throw light upon the emergence of that 'rationalist' notion of natural law which found its complete expression one and a half centuries later.

It is not in its content that Grotius' theory of natural law breaks away from Scholasticism. It is in its method (Cassirer). His definition of natural law has nothing revolutionary. When he maintains that natural law is that body of rules which man is able to discover by the use of his reason, he does nothing but restate the Scholastic notion of a rational foundation of ethics. Indeed, his aim is rather to restore that notion which had been shaken by the extreme Augustinianism of certain Protestant currents of thought. When he declares that those rules are valid in themselves, independently of the fact that God willed them, he repeats an assertion which had already been made by some of the Schoolmen for reasons which will be discussed in the following chapter.[1] He is careful to put forward that view in such a way as to avoid any suggestion of blasphemy.

What we have been saying would have a degree of validity even if we should concede that which cannot be conceded without the utmost wickedness, that there is no God, or that the affairs of men are of no concern to Him.   (*De Iure Belli ac Pacis*, Prolegomena, §11)

This is a purely hypothetical argument. It is quite clear that

[1] See below, Chapter 5, p. 71.

Grotius, still deeply imbued with the spirit of Christianity, would never have conceded that God did not take any part in the affairs of men. The law of nature is implanted in man by God. It has therefore unquestionably a divine origin (ibid. §12). The revealed laws of God confirm and assist men in their knowledge of the law of nature (§13).

But Grotius's aim was to construct a system of laws which would carry conviction in an age in which theological controversy was gradually losing the power to do so. He therefore proceeded on the hypothesis further than anyone had done before him— much further than even the judicious Hooker, whose inclinations and thought bear so close a resemblance to his. He proved that it was possible to build up a theory of laws independent of theological presuppositions. His successors completed the task. The natural law which they elaborated was entirely 'secular'. They sharply divided what the Schoolmen had taken great pains to reconcile.

The doctrine of natural law which is set forth in the great treatises of the seventeenth and eighteenth centuries—from Pufendorf's *De Iure Naturae et Gentium* (1672) to Burlamaqui's *Principes du Droit Naturel* (1747), and Vattel's *Droit des Gens ou Principes de la Loi Naturelle* (1758)—has nothing to do with theology. It is a purely rational construction, though it does not refuse to pay homage to some remote notion of God. But, as C. Becker remarked, God is increasingly withdrawn from immediate contact with men. The laws of nature are to Jefferson the Laws of Nature's God. The French legislators solemnly put themselves 'in the presence and under the auspices of the Supreme Being'. But Nature's God or the Supreme Being are not more akin to the God omnipotent of the Creed than Deism is to Christianity. What Grotius had set forth as a hypothesis has become a thesis. The self-evidence of natural law has made the existence of God perfectly superfluous.

Here we touch on another point in which Grotius's influence was decisive. If natural law consists in a set of rules which are absolutely valid, its treatment must be based upon an internal coherence and necessity. In order to be a science, law must not depend on experience, but on definitions, not on facts, but on logical deductions. Hence, only the principles of the law of nature can properly constitute a science. Such a science must be constructed by leaving aside all that undergoes change and varies from place to place.

I have made it my concern to refer the proofs of things touching the law
of nature to certain fundamental conceptions which are beyond question;
so that no one can deny them without doing violence to himself. For
the principles of that law, if only you pay strict heed to them, are in
themselves manifest and clear, almost as evident as are those things
which we perceive by the external senses.

(*De Iure Belli ac Pacis*, Prolegomena, §39)

The analogy with mathematics is at hand. It provides the best
illustration that natural law cannot be altered even by God.

Measureless as is the power of God, nevertheless it can be said that
there are certain things over which that power does not extend . . . Just
as even God cannot cause that two times two should not make four,
so He cannot cause that that which is intrinsically evil be not evil.

(*De Iure Belli ac Pacis*, I, i, x)

It provides the new methodological assumption which Grotius
prides himself on having introduced into the study of law.

With all truthfulness I aver that, just as the mathematicians treat their
figures as abstracted from bodies, so in treating law I have withdrawn
my mind from every particular fact.   (ibid., Prolegomena, §58)

Grotius claimed for his treatment of legal problems the merit of
clarity, self-evidence and coherence. These qualities were fully
appreciated by his successors.

   Nowhere is the 'rationalist' character of the new conception
more apparent than here. The analogy between mathematics and
justice had precedents which went back to Plato. It was fully
developed by Pufendorf and Leibniz, and survived even in
Montesquieu. It was destined, however, to decline in the eighteenth
century under the impact of empirical and utilitarian thought. But
the idea that the theory of law should be based on clarity, self-
evidence and coherence, remained the dominating mark of legal
philosophy down to the revolutionary era.

   Rationalism indeed is here the very synonym of anti-historicism.
The evidence of history cannot shake the absolute validity of
natural law. Its only interest is to provide an object for further
generalisations, or illustrations of the 'ignorance' and 'darkness'
which has long befallen humanity and which reason must dispel.
Vico, a lonely voice, pleaded in vain for a different conception.
For him, the 'ideal, eternal law' could be fully revealed only in

the long ordeal and suffering of mankind. But for the rationalist thinker the self-evident law of nature was in want of no confirmation. It could make history if necessary. It actually did so in the end.

Rationalism, however, is not the only distinctive character of the modern conception of natural law. Its impact upon thoughts and events would not have been so great if it had only expressed a particular manner of thinking. It was an assertion of values as well. The new value is that of the individual. Individualism is the second outstanding feature of modern natural law. The word is not less ambiguous than rationalism. There had been a Greek individualism as well as a Roman. There is a Christian individualism which has deeply pervaded our religious interpretation of life. The quest after 'origins' would again lead us far back, perhaps to Protagoras' dictum that man is the measure of all things.

But when we read the American or the French Declarations we know that we are confronted with a complete architecture, about the style of which there can be no mistake. It is a political philosophy based upon a particular notion of the individual, of society and of their mutual relationship. What Jefferson called the 'station' to which nations and men are entitled under 'the laws of Nature and of Nature's God' has become the determining factor in political obligation. It is a pattern of ideas for which it is difficult to find precedents in history, and it has left an indelible mark upon our civilisation.

As with the emergence of rationalism, it is impossible to determine with absolute certainty the moment when modern individualism was born. The part played by the Renaissance and the Reformation in shaping the new conception of man has often been analysed and described. We all agree, I surmise, that it is at some time in the beginning of the modern era that we must locate the rise of that individualistic principle which held several generations under its spell, until it finally found the way to a sweeping transformation of the whole social and political structure of the Western hemisphere. There is, however, one moment from which we can date the introduction and the coherent application of the individualistic principle in political philosophy. It is the moment at which political theorists turned to the idea of contract for their interpretation of the relationship between the individual and the community. It is the moment when the doctrine of the social contract first makes its appearance.

I am speaking, of course, of the social contract proper, the

notion of an agreement between individuals as the origin of civil
society. Political theory has known other uses of the contractual
idea, such as the contract of government or the contract of submission. This is a theory which 'has nothing to do with the origin
of society itself, but, presupposing a society already formed,
purports to define the terms on which that society is to be
governed' (Gough). This theory had medieval roots, and it played
an important part in the religious and civil dissensions which mark
the beginning of modern Europe. It lingered on even in later days,
and it is sometimes not easy to distinguish it from the social
contract proper. But the theory of the social contract, apart from
occasional precedents which can be found in ancient writers, is an
entirely modern product. It is the distinctive mark of the political
theory of individualism. It is closely associated with the modern
theory of natural law.

Indeed, the theory of the social contract would hardly have
been possible had not the modern notion of natural law provided
its basis. There was nothing new in the assertion that man is a
rational being, capable of guiding himself and of deriving from
his reason a standard to judge his environment. There was
nothing new in the notion that man is born free and equal to all
other men; in the idea of an original state of nature; in the quest
for an explanation of the change which had come about with the
rise of social and political institutions. It is only a shifting of
accent on these commonplaces of natural law theory which can
explain why all of a sudden we are faced with a doctrine which
purposely sets out to construe civil society as the result of a deliberate act of will on the part of its components.

The shifting of accent is the same which we have analysed in
the transformation of natural law into a purely rational and
secular principle. The accent is now on the individual. The
social contract was the only possible way left for deducing the
existence of social and political institutions once the reason of
man was made the ultimate standard of values. The construction
bears the unmistakable mark of rationalist thinking. It provided
what Mr Oakeshott would call a political 'crib': in his recent
article on *Rationalism in Politics*, Mr Oakeshott has convincingly
shown that one of the main concerns of rationalist thought was to
provide such cribs in all fields of learning.

The social contract was a crib. It was also a blue-print. Its
different interpretations all have one character in common.
Their starting point is the individual. Their basis is the modern,

secular notion of natural law and the 'station' of man which is derived from it. This is true even of the contract which gives rise to the 'great Leviathan', to Hobbes' 'mortal God'. Hobbes' political theory is the extreme outcome of rationalism and individualism—as it were the *reductio ad absurdum* of both. The different interpretations of the contract and of its consequences are merely the result of different interpretations of human nature, that is, of the impact of natural law upon man.

Man may be throughout a reasonable creature, or he may be dominated by lust or fear. Accordingly, the manner of conceiving the 'station' of man will vary, as well as the interpretation of what Cicero had already called the *causa coëundi*, the reason for men joining together in society. But if we take the most widely different authors—say Hobbes and Locke—we cannot fail to be aware of the fact that the essential elements—the form and the substance—of the contract remain unvaried in all. 'Formally', the contract is a manifestation of individual will with the object of establishing a relationship of mutual obligation which would not otherwise exist by the law of nature. 'Substantially', the content of the contract is the 'natural right' of the individual, which is exchanged against a counterpart of equal or greater value—the benefits of society and the security of political organisation. The social contract may effect a complete transformation of the original right, as is the case with Hobbes and Rousseau. Or it may leave that right unaltered, and have no other purpose than to secure it, as Locke was anxious to maintain. But in all cases the contract is the necessary pattern of all legal and political obligations.

How did it come about—Maitland asked—that political theory borrowed from the lawyers the notion of contract, 'that greediest of legal categories', and made it the basis of the State? The answer can only be given in the words of Kant, who reaped the fruit of the age-long development. The idea of contract was the only possible means of setting the natural rights of the individual within the framework of the State.[1] The theory of the social contract may have been to begin with a theory of the origins of political society. It was also and primarily a rational explanation of the State, the only explanation compatible with the pattern of thought laid down in the modern notion of natural law.

But the mention of 'natural rights' brings us back to the *Déclaration* and to the third outstanding feature of modern natural law. Radicalism is a less ambiguous word than indi-

[1] Kant, *Rechtslehre*, §47.

vidualism or rationalism. The modern theory of natural law was a rational construction. It was an assertion of the value of the individual. But it was also and foremost a vindication of rights. As such, it could become a theory of revolution. It had become one by 1776 and 1789. Curiously enough, there was nothing revolutionary in modern natural law in its beginnings. Jefferson's radical assertion, that any form of government which proves destructive of the 'inalienable rights' of man should be altered or abolished, is more reminiscent of the uncompromising statements of medieval lawyers and philosophers than of the abstract speculation of the earlier theorists of modern natural law.

Medieval political theory had elaborated a doctrine of resistance to 'unjust' or 'unlawful' government. That doctrine lived on through the Renaissance, the Reformation and the Counter-Reformation. It was given prominence and actuality in the great social and political upheavals of the sixteenth century. It was fully developed by that group of writers who, for their advocacy of the right of rebellion, came to be named *Monarchomachi* (literally the enemies of kings). That group includes Protestant as well as Catholic authors. It is interesting to note that, as recent historians have pointed out, Protestant writers seem to be inclined to justify the right of resistance on grounds of history or of scripture rather than of natural law. The tendency towards rational and 'natural law' arguments is more prominent among the Catholic *Monarchomachi*.

However that may be, the school of natural law of which Grotius is considered the founder had little to do with either group. On the Continent, that school flourished under the benign rule of the absolute princes, when the problem of resistance was no longer an issue and new interests were focussed on legal and political thought. In England, both the Puritan and the Glorious revolutions had centred on practical issues rather than on abstract speculations. Ever since Burke, the contrast between the assertion of the 'rights of Englishmen' and the vindication of the 'rights of man' has become a commonplace in the interpretation of English history.

The question then is how did it come about that the doctrine of natural law, which Grotius had lifted up to the highest regions of abstraction, and which had from the start assumed the character of a scientific rather than a practical principle, became a revolutionary doctrine which changed the face of the world? This is a large question which would involve the discussion of the several factors which contributed to the unprecedented development of thought during the century and a half that divides the appearance of *The Laws of War and Peace* from the first shot fired at Concord by the 'embattled farmers' whose guns were 'heard round the world'. But there is one point which throws light on the process as it were from within: a point which ought to have been kept in mind from the beginning and which must now be squarely faced and assessed.

The modern theory of natural law was not, properly speaking, a theory of law at all. It was a theory of rights. A momentous change has taken place under cover of the same verbal expressions. The *ius naturale* of the modern political philosopher is no longer the *lex naturalis* of the medieval moralist nor the *ius naturale* of the Roman lawyer. These different conceptions have in common only the name. The Latin word *ius* is the cause of the ambiguity. It has its equivalent in most European languages, except in English.[1] The fact is significant. As Hobbes pointed out with his usual shrewdness:

> though they that speak of this subject use to confound *ius* and *lex*, *rights* and *law*: yet they ought to be distinguished; because RIGHT consisteth in liberty to do, or to forbear: whereas LAW determineth, and bindeth to one of them: so that law and right differ as much, as obligation and liberty. (*Leviathan*, pt. 1, ch. 14)

The different meanings of the word *ius* had of course long been familiar to the lawyers who had been brought up in the study of the Roman law. They had carefully distinguished between 'objective' and 'subjective right', between the *norma agendi* (the rule of action) and the *facultas agendi* (the right to act) which can both be indicated by the same name of *ius*, and which are indicated in English by the different names of law and of right. But they had never overlooked the fact, which Hobbes seems either to ignore or implicitly to deny, that the two meanings of *ius* are not antithetic, but correlative. In the language of the law-schools, *ius* could be used in an 'objective' as well as in a 'subjective' sense: but the latter always presupposes the former. There is a *facultas agendi* in as much as there is a *norma agendi*. There is a 'right' in as much as there is a law.

The distinction is capital if we are to understand the full

---

[1] For a detailed analysis of the different meanings of *law, right* and *ius* see Sir J. Salmond, *Jurisprudence* (8th ed., 1930), app. I.

implications of the modern theory of natural law. The great majority of natural law writers in the seventeenth and eighteenth centuries would not have accepted Hobbes' anarchical conception of 'natural right' as opposed to 'natural law'.[1] To them natural law was the necessary presupposition of natural right. Locke, in his *Second Treatise of Government* (ch. vi, §59 and 63) makes the point very clearly. He says that the natural freedom of man is nothing else than his knowledge of the law of nature, in the same way as the freedom of an Englishman consists in his 'liberty to dispose of his actions and possessions' according to the laws of England. But the emphasis is shifting more and more from the objective to the subjective meaning of natural law. Wolff, towards the middle of the eighteenth century, declares quite flatly that the latter is the only proper meaning of *ius naturae* and that

whenever we speak of natural law (*ius naturae*), we never intend the law of nature, but rather the right which belongs to man on the strength of that law, that is naturally.
(*Ius Naturae Methodo Scientifica Pertractatum*, 1741, tom. I, Prol., §3)

On the eve of the American and French Revolutions the theory of natural law had been turned into a theory of natural rights. The old notion which lawyers, philosophers and political writers had used down the ages had become—to use Professor Willey's expression—a liberating principle, ready to hand for the use of modern man in his challenge to existing institutions. Even then, the two meanings survived. The doctrine of natural rights was closely associated with that of a 'fundamental law', the American version of the Continental idea of the law of nature. The *Declarations of Rights*, of which the Virginia Bill opened the series, clearly expressed the belief that a solemn document was necessary to provide 'the basis and foundation of government'.

But it was the vindication of the rights of man which gave modern natural law its tremendous power and vigour. Rationalism, individualism and radicalism combined to give the old word an entirely new meaning. The notion which had been invoked to construct a universal system of law and to provide a rational foundation for ethics, inspired the formulation of a theory of rights which will not easily be cancelled from the heart of Western man and which bears witness to his generosity and idealism.

[1] The opposite view is taken by L. Strauss, *The Political Philosophy of Hobbes*, 1936, p. 156.

I long hesitated whether to choose as the heading of this chapter the opening words of the American *Declaration of Independence* or the preamble of the French *Declaration of the Rights of Man.* I finally decided for the French declaration, though I am fully aware of the soundness of Sir Ernest Barker's remark that 'we who live in Europe too readily see the year 1789 as the year in which it was said: "Behold, I will make all things new." A wider view will show us that the year of change was the year 1776 . . .'

The connection between the two Declarations, or, as the word now goes, between the two ideologies, the American and the French, is still a matter of controversy. It has produced, and not only in English, a large literature which this is not the place to discuss. Perhaps the best illustration of that connection is provided by two documents existing in the Library of Congress in Washington to which O. Vossler first called attention. They are two original drafts of the *Déclaration des Droits de l'Homme* submitted by Lafayette to Jefferson, American ambassador in Paris till September 1789, for discussion and criticism: one of them bears Jefferson's autograph remarks.

Here, at any rate, are the opening paragraphs of the American *Declaration* of 1776, to which many references will have been found in the text of this chapter:

When in the Course of human events, it becomes necessary for one people to dissolve the political bands, which have connected them with another, and to assume among the powers of the earth, the separate and equal station to which the Laws of Nature and of Nature's God entitle them, a decent respect to the opinions of mankind requires that they should declare the causes which impel them to the separation. We hold these truths to be self-evident, that all men are created equal, that they are endowed by the Creator with certain unalienable Rights, that among these are Life, Liberty and the pursuit of Happiness. That to secure these rights, Governments are instituted among Men, deriving their just powers from the consent of the governed. That whenever any form of Government becomes destructive of these ends, it is the Right of the People to alter or to abolish it, and to institute new Government, laying its foundation on such principles and organising its powers in such form, as to them shall seem most likely to effect their Safety and Happiness.

C. E. VAUGHAN, *Studies in the History of Political Philosophy before and after Rousseau,* 1925.

C. BECKER, *The Declaration of Independence,* 1922; and *The Heavenly City of the Eighteenth Century Philosophers,* 1932.

B. F. WRIGHT, *American Interpretations of Natural Law,* 1930.

C. G. HAINES, *The revival of Natural Law Concepts,* 1930.

H. J. LASKI, *The Rise of European Liberalism*, 1936.
J. W. GOUGH, *The Social Contract*, 1936.
B. WILLEY, *The Eighteenth Century Background*, 1940.
C. J. FRIEDRICH, *Inevitable Peace*, 1948.
SIR E. BARKER, 'Natural Law and the American Revolution', in *Traditions of Civility*, 1948.
D. J. BOORSTIN, *The Lost World of Thomas Jefferson*, 1948.

German books: O. VON GIERKE, *Johannes Althusius und die Entwicklung der naturrechtlichen Staatstheorien*, 1880/1913 (English trans. B. Freyd, *The Development of Political Theory*, 1939); W. DILTHEY, *Weltanschauung und Analyse des Menschen seit Renaissance und Reformation* (*Gesammelte Schriften*, II); G. JELLINEK, *Die Erklärung der Menschen- und Bürgerrechte*, 4th ed., 1927; O. VOSSLER, *Die Amerikanischen Revolutionsideale in ihrem Verhältnis zu den Europäischen*, 1929, and *Studien zur Erklärung der Menschenrechte*, 1930; E. CASSIRER, *Die Philosophie der Aufklärung*, 1932; (English trans. F. C. A. Koelln and J. P. Pettegrove, *The Philosophy of Enlightenment*, 1951).

French and Italian: B. FAY, *L'esprit révolutionnaire en France et aux Etats Unis à la fin du XVIIIᵉ siecle*, 1924; B. GROETHUYSEN, *Origines de l'esprit bourgeois en France*, vol. I, *L'Eglise et la Bourgeoisie*, 1927; P. HAZARD, *La crise de la conscience européenne 1680–1715*, 1932; D. MORNET, *Les origines intellectuelles de la Révolution Française 1715–1787*, 1947; G. DEL VECCHIO, *Su la teoria del contratto sociale*, 1906.

The references to GROTIUS, *De Iure Belli ac Pacis Libri Tres*, are from F. W. Kelsey's translation (*The Classics of International Law*, publication of the Carnegie Endowment for International Peace, no. 3, 1925).

5

THE ESSENCE OF LAW

Another and different approach to our subject can now be suggested. Enough evidence has been provided of the historical function of natural law. The time has come to assess its general value. That value, if any, can consist only in a specific contribution to the knowledge of law and to the understanding of legal phenomena.

The doctrine of natural law was closely associated with historical development. But some of its features are constant. The theorists of natural law were faced with much the same problems as confront the modern legal philosopher. The first of these problems is that of the essence of law. It is a problem of form or of structure. It is a problem of definition. 'Is law an act of the will or of the intellect?' Is the existence of a superior and an inferior the necessary pattern of legal experience? The question may be put in these or in other terms, but it is still controversial. The old discussion about the nature of *ius*—whether *ius quia iustum* or *ius quia iussum*[1]—was more than an etymological quibble.

Natural law provided a definite answer. It stands or falls with a particular notion of law. The very condition of its existence is that the identification of law and command be overcome or abandoned. Its logical outcome is an extension of the concept of law which is much more far-reaching and exacting than is at first realised. This is nowhere more apparent than in the many challenges which natural law had to meet in its age-long develop-

[1] This is a play upon words, *iustum* meaning 'just', and *iussum* 'commanded'.

E

ment. We must begin by examining these challenges. The grouping which is adopted in this chapter should not be taken to imply a chronological succession. It is rather a description of types or modes of thought which have recurred at different epochs. We are here concerned only with what they have in common.

The most direct and obvious challenge comes from the legal field proper. It is the challenge of what in our days is called legal positivism. It is the challenge of a particular experience in which command and obedience appear as the essential attributes of law. But the Austinian definition of law is no present-day novelty. It has more than one precedent in the past. There were legal positivists long before Austin. There is an understandable bias towards positivism in all lawyers. Here is a quotation from Cicero which may serve to remind us how old the isssue is:

ATTICUS: Then you do not think that the science of law is to be derived from the Prætor's edict, as the majority do now, or from the Twelve Tables, as people used to think, but from the deepest mysteries of philosophy?

MARCUS: Quite right; for in our present conversation, Pomponius, we are not trying to learn how to protect ourselves legally, or how to answer clients' questions. Such problems may be important, and in fact they are . . . But in our present investigation we intend to cover the whole range of universal Justice and Law in such a way that our own civil law, as it is called, will be confined to a small and narrow corner.

(*De Legibus*, I, v, 17)

Clearly Cicero's idea is that the essence of law cannot be fully understood unless we go beyond the 'popular view' that law is simply a command or a prohibition (ib., I, vi, 19). Positive law is unable to tell us the last word about the real nature of legal experience. 'The civil law of the Roman people' should be 'confined to a small and narrow corner'.

Actually Roman law became the law of the civilised world. It provided the mainstay of Europe's legal education for centuries to come. And the notion of law which was embodied in the Roman texts was the outcome not so much of philosophical speculations as of a particular historical experience. Law was to the Romans the object of a deliberate act of legislation. Law was the expression of the will of the Roman people, or of the Emperor to whom the original power of the people had been transferred. It was left for later generations endlessly to discuss the nature of that transference, and to derive from the Roman texts conflicting evidence in favour of monarchy or of democracy.

But the real importance of those texts lay in the notion they contained, that all law must go back to an ultimate power which expresses and sanctions it. The holder of that power is the source of the law. He is therefore above the law—*legibus solutus*. The Byzantine prince, as he emerges from the pages of Justinian's law-books, is the living embodiment of the law—*lex animata*, νόμος ᾿έμψυχος. He is such, not in the sense in which Aristotle had conceived the excellent king to be a living law because of his exceptional personal qualities, but in a strictly legal sense, because of his office of law-giver, because of the attribute of sovereignty which is inherent in legislation. Thus, in the Roman tradition, sovereignty and law became correlative notions.

Sovereignty of course is a comparatively modern expression. Bodin, a French sixteenth-century writer, claimed to be its inventor.[1] But, as he himself admitted and his contemporaries were quick to point out, the notion went back to a tradition of thought which had already borne its fruits in the Middle Ages. Long before the theorists of the State, the theorists of the Church had resorted to the notion of a *potestas legibus soluta* to make good the claim of the medieval Papacy to world domination. And in turn the idea of a supreme and ultimate power from which all laws proceed went back to the Roman texts that the Bolognese lawyers had rediscovered in the eleventh century. From them a new and revolutionary notion of law was revealed to medieval Europe.

The importance of the doctrine of sovereignty can hardly be overrated. It was a formidable tool in the hands of lawyers and politicians, and a decisive factor in the making of modern Europe. It was also an object of passionate controversy. It met with enthusiastic support and with unbending resistance from different quarters and in different countries. But it also appeared to undermine the very possibility of natural law thinking. Natural law is not properly law if sovereignty is the essential condition of legal experience. It is not possible to conceive a law of nature if command is the essence of law. How then can it be explained that the notion of natural law survived, and indeed blossomed into new life, even after the doctrine of sovereignty had been finally accepted as the necessary presupposition of the modern State?

The answer to this question provides a further qualification of

[1] Jean Bodin, *De la République*, 1576.

Figgis' famous dictum about the *damnosa hereditas* of Roman law. For Roman law was no doubt the vehicle of the doctrine of sovereignty. But it was also one of the vehicles of natural law, which it fostered with all its glamour and authority. And a correct reading of the Roman texts certainly provided the means for circumscribing the notion of sovereignty within precise and well-defined limits. These limits were those of positive law. The notion of sovereignty was—at least in origin—a strictly legal, not a philosophical notion. Unless we bear this in mind we shall be unable properly to understand the peculiar contribution of Roman ideas to political theory.

Sovereignty was not to the Romans a synonym of lawlessness. On the contrary, in a famous passage of the *Corpus Iuris Civilis*, the Emperor is described as deriving his power from the law and as being subject to its authority (*Codex*, I, 14, 4: Const. 'Digna Vox'). This is no contradiction to the notion of sovereignty. The fact that positive law is laid down in the form of a command and proceeds from the will of the sovereign does not mean that the holder of sovereignty is immune from all legal obligation. The point is set out with a wealth of imagery by medieval theorists of sovereignty. 'The Pope' writes one of them 'is an animal without reins and without bridle, the man who is above the positive law. Yet he must impose on himself reins and bridle, and live according to the established laws and observe them, unless special cases arise and particular causes require him [to alter them].'[1]

Clearly, the notion of sovereignty does not cancel the notion of legal obligation. Positive law does not exhaust the whole range of legal experience. There may be laws other than the commands of the sovereign, laws with a different structure yet nevertheless binding and formally perfect. The laws of the international community can look to no ultimate power for their enforcement. Natural law is devoid of sanctions. Yet both are properly called laws and are binding even on the sovereign. In the words of Albericus Gentilis—the Italian jurist, who taught Roman law at Oxford from 1587 to 1608—the 'absolute' Prince is a prince who is *above* positive law but *under* natural law and the law of nations.[2]

---

[1] Aegidius Romanus, *De Ecclesiastica Potestate*, 1302 (Ed. Scholz, 1929), lib. III, cap. 8.

[2] Albericus Gentilis, *Regales Disputationes Tres*, 1605 (Disp. I, *De Potestate Regia Absoluta*, p. 17). He in turn refers to Baldus, the medieval jurist, as his source for the distinction. A. Gentilis is better known as the author of the *De Iure Belli* (1598) and as one of the founders of modern international law.

This doctrine was a product of the Roman law-schools of the Continent. In England it was unpopular and alien. But it provided the programme of legal and political thinking for the next two centuries. Never did the ideas of natural and of international law flourish so happily and undisturbed as in the age of princely 'absolutism'. This is a clear indication that the challenge of legal positivism could be successfully met if the nature of sovereignty were correctly appraised, and the definition of law as a command were not taken as the final answer to the problem of legal experience.

The trouble is that the 'voluntarist' notion of law was not always limited to the legal sphere proper. A different challenge to natural law could take shape the moment that notion was extended to all moral imperatives. Philosophers and theologians were more formidable foes than the professional lawyer. Mention must now be made of a much more insidious menace to the doctrine of natural law, the Nominalist theory of ethics.

Nominalism meant not only a crisis in Scholastic method, a quarrel about 'universals' and an anticipation of some aspects of the modern theory of knowledge. It also meant a radical change in the approach to morality. The vindication of the primacy of the will over the intellect led to the denial that ethical values can have any other foundation but the will of God that imposes them. The notion of God as an unlimited and arbitrary power implied the reduction of all moral laws to inscrutable manifestations of divine omnipotence. The basis of the 'natural system of ethics' was discarded. Natural law ceases to be the bridge between God and man. It affords no indication of the existence of an eternal and immutable order. It no longer constitutes the measure of man's dignity and of his capacity to participate in that order, a standard of good and evil available to all rational creatures.

This is how a recent historian describes the impact of Nominalism on ethics: 'An action is not good because of its suitableness to the essential nature of man—but because God so wills. God's will could also have willed and decreed the precise opposite, which would then possess the same binding force as that which is now valid—which indeed, has validity only as long as God's absolute will so determines. Law is will, pure will without any foundation in reality, without foundation in the essential nature of things' (Rommen). It is as if the notion of sovereignty were here applied to the divine law-giver himself. The consequences were soon apparent.

Nominalism is, of course, used here only as a general name for a vast movement of thought and opinion. It may be doubted whether all the implications of 'voluntarist ethics' are already traceable in Duns Scotus (1266–1308). But certainly they are fully drawn out by William of Ockham (1300–50). And the notion of the moral law as the expression of the divine will passed over from the Nominalists to the Reformers—to Wycliff, and later on to Luther and Calvin.

The 'sovereignty of God' is the pivot of Calvin's theology and ethics. The similarity between Calvin's notion of God as *legibus solutus* and the modern conception of sovereignty is a fascinating subject for research and reflection. The analogy has been pointed out many times, and attention has been called to Calvin's early training in the law as a possible source of his notion of God's sovereignty. In turn, it has been maintained that his notion could not fail to affect legal and political theory, and that many fundamental concepts of modern political theory are nothing but 'secularised' theological concepts. Both views have some element of truth, though it would certainly be unwise to overrate it.

Protestantism did not necessarily lead to a complete break with the old tradition of natural law. The impact of the Reformation upon the continuity of legal and political thought is still the subject of controversy among scholars. But it seems obvious enough that the Thomist conception of natural law, as a mediatory element between God and man, and as an assertion of the power and dignity of human nature, would have been out of place in the Reformers' theology, and actually they found little or no room for it.

The Reformation marked a return to the rigid alternatives which had been stressed by St Augustine and have been analysed in one of the preceding chapters.[1] It brought about a profound transformation of moral and political standards, which in turn could not fail to leave traces and to exert an influence upon the new conception of natural law which was the product of the Age of Reason. But, as far as the controversial literature of the period is concerned, the evidence, as has already been pointed out[2], is that the continuity of natural law thinking is more apparent among Catholic than among Protestant writers. The voluntarist bent of Protestant ethics may well afford an explanation of the comparative disparagement, among Protestant controversialists

[1] See above, pp. 40–1.
[2] See above, p. 60.

and political writers, of natural law in favour of the divine law of the Bible on one hand, and, on the other, of the positive law of the State conceived as ultimately grounded upon the will of God. That the 'divine right of kings' is a typical product of this age is certainly significant.

One point, at any rate, is certain: that the revival of natural law which takes place towards the turn of the sixteenth and seventeenth centuries is essentially a rejection of the 'Nominalist' or 'voluntarist' theory of law. This is apparent in Hooker. It is equally apparent, and historically far more important, in Grotius. For Hooker was mainly restating the old Thomist arguments against his Puritan opponents. But Grotius was the founder of the modern theory of natural law.

Thus Grotius' famous proposition, that natural law would retain its validity even if God did not exist, once again appears as a turning point in the history of thought. It was the answer to the challenge of voluntarist ethics. It meant the assertion that command is not the essence of law.

This, I think, is what must be kept in mind in order correctly to appraise the 'precedents' of Grotius' much quoted dictum. The daring assertion that natural law is independent of the will of God had already been made by the Schoolmen, though not by Thomas Aquinas himself. The Spanish Jesuit Suarez, in his treatise *On the Laws*,[1] which Grotius quotes with great respect, gives a convenient summary of Catholic authors on the subject. There were indeed many, Suarez pointed out, who had taken the view that natural law, as an indication of what is 'intrinsically good or intrinsically bad', does not depend on the will 'of any superior'.

These authors seem therefore logically to admit that natural law does not proceed from God as a law-giver, for it is not dependent on God's will, nor does God manifest Himself in it as a sovereign (*superior*) commanding or forbidding.

Indeed, some of these authors had gone so far as to say that

even though God did not exist, or did not make use of His reason, or did not judge rightly of things, if there is in man such a dictate of right reason to guide him, it would have had the same nature of law as it now has.

This, very likely, was the source of Grotius' statement about

[1] Franciscus Suarez, *De Legibus ac Deo Legislatore*, 1619, lib. II, cap. vi.

the validity and character of natural law. He was using an old argument, but the challenge which he endeavoured to meet was not an entirely new one either. The Nominalist doctrine that the will of God is the ultimate source of morality had played a prominent part in Protestant theology and ethics. Grotius was a Protestant, but, as a follower of Arminius, he rejected the extreme Calvinist view of the absolute sovereignty of God. But he was also a jurist, and his vindication of natural law was further devised to meet the new and dangerous challenge of the absolute sovereignty of the State. Grotius' capital importance lies in the fact that he succeeded where others had failed. He secured a new lease of life for the doctrine of natural law and for the notion that law is not merely an expression of will.

There was, however, a third possible line of attack on natural law which proved more devastating than the challenge of either legal positivism or voluntarist ethics. It was indeed more than a challenge. It was a complete reversal of positions. The notion of law as the expression of will could be met on purely legal grounds by restricting its validity to positive law and denying its application to other groups or types of legal experience. It could be met on the philosophical or theological plane by proving its inadequacy to explain the nature of God and of moral imperatives. But it is difficult with any of these arguments to meet a theory which as it were turns upside down the very pattern of natural law thinking. It is impossible to reconcile the notion of natural law with the doctrine of the 'ethical state'. This doctrine is usually associated with the name of Hegel.

The association is correct. For it is with Hegel that the final break with natural law occurs in legal as well as in political theory. Already in one of his earlier works—an essay on 'The Scientific Treatment of Natural Law' (1802)—Hegel had called into question the whole tradition of thought which had centred on natural law.[1] Its theorists, he pointed out, had either contented themselves with generalisation from existing institutions which they were anxious to justify, or else been inspired by a purely 'negative' attitude to ethics, thus exasperating a dualism between the ideal and the real which they had been unable to bridge. Hegel pleaded for a 'positive' approach to the problem. The real task of ethics, he maintained, is to understand and assert the

[1] G. W. F. Hegel, *Über die Wissenschaftlichen Behandlungsarten des Naturrechts*, in *Hegels Schriften zur Politik und Rechtsphilosophie, Sämtliche Werke*, vol. VII, Ed. Lasson, 1913.

'totality' of ethical life. 'The absolute ethical totality is nothing but *ein Volk*—a people or nation.'

The momentous implications of this entirely new approach to law and morality were developed by Hegel in his *Philosophy of Right* some twenty years later (1821). The full title of the book is *Natural Law and Political Science in Outline*.[1] But there is no trace in it of natural law in any of its traditional meanings. *Recht* or *ius* Hegel defines in the most extensive sense as the realisation of 'free' or 'ethical' will. It therefore comprises all possible manifestations of moral life. Positive or civil law is but one of its aspects. Of ethical life the national State is the highest embodiment. Its 'right' therefore stands above any other. The State is the ethical whole, the incarnation of God in history. Its basis 'is the power of reason actualising itself as will'. The rational will is the presupposition of all law and morality.

Hegel's theory of the 'rational will' goes indeed far beyond the old quarrel whether reason or will constitutes the essence of legal experience. The doctrine of the ethical State is a complete substitute for the doctrine of natural law which had accompanied Western thought throughout its long history. It entirely reverses the relationship between the ideal and the real, which was the necessary presupposition of natural law thinking. The claims of natural law are to Hegel the outcome of the antagonism 'between what ought to be and what is'. It is an ineradicable bent of the human mind to contrast them. But true philosophy must overcome this antagonism. It must reconcile man to the historical world, which is his own creation. 'The great thing is to apprehend in the show of the temporal and transient the substance which is immanent and the eternal which is present' (*Philosophy of Right*, Preface and addition 1).

It is no easy task to appraise Hegel's teaching correctly. His famous dictum, 'What is rational is actual and what is actual is rational', certainly allows of a twofold interpretation. It does not necessarily imply, as is often assumed, a plea for conservatism, a glorification of existing institutions as such. In one place, indeed, Hegel openly states that 'in considering the Idea of the State, we must not have our eyes on particular States or on particular institutions. We must consider the Idea, this actual God, by itself' (ibid., addition 152).

Ideals can have a greater actuality than facts. Hegel's conception of the interplay of the ideal and the real could easily be

[1] The references are to T. M. Knox's translation, Oxford, 1942.

turned into the most explosive theory of revolution. Marxism was an offspring of Hegelianism. But there can be no doubt that Hegel's conception of history marks the end of natural law thinking altogether. It eliminates for all purposes that notion of an ideal law which, as we shall presently see, is another constant feature of the theory of the law of nature. Ideals cease to be immutable and eternal. They are the outcome of history. It is before the bench of history that ideals must be tried.

History had indeed been the stumbling block of all natural law theories. Lawyers, philosophers and theologians had tried in vain to account for the apparent indifference of historical development to any pattern of right or wrong. Political theorists of the past had found it difficult to square the bitter facts of political life with the requirements of justice. After Machiavelli had brought the crude contradictions between morals and politics into the limelight, the convenient doctrine of *raison d'état* had been invented to explain, if not to justify, the encroachments of political necessity on the field of accepted morality.

But now that history was transfigured into the unfolding of the Absolute, now that the State was conceived as the embodiment of moral life, the exigencies of *raison d'état* could appear in a different perspective. The opposition between morals and politics could be declared to be the result of 'superficial ideas about morality', and the welfare of the State to have claims to recognition 'totally different from those of the welfare of the individual'. Not the abstract precepts of natural law—'the many universal thoughts supposed to be universal commands'—but the 'concrete existence' of the State should dictate its behaviour. It may happen that a higher morality is revealed 'in the form of hussars with shining sabres', and the vain harangues of the moralist will be silenced by the 'solemn cycles of history'. Against the apparent injustice of the State there is no appeal but to history, for 'the history of the World is the World's court of judgment' (*Philosophy of Right*, 337, §§340; addition 188).

I have no intention of dwelling at greater length on the niceties of Hegel's political theory. It would certainly be unfair to attribute to the German philosopher the sole responsibility for later developments of thought which have borne such bitter fruit not only in his own country but also for the whole of Europe. Actually the notion that will can be creative of moral values is not strictly speaking an invention of Hegel's. Hegel himself acknowledged his debt to Rousseau. Rousseau's theory of the 'general will' is the real source of the theory of the ethical state.

It is difficult to say how clearly Rousseau was conscious of breaking with the natural law. 'Rousseau is a Janus-like figure in the history of natural law. He turns to it, and belongs to it: he turns away from it, and belongs elsewhere' (Barker). But Rousseau is responsible for the doctrine that 'whoever refuses to obey the General Will shall be compelled to do so by the whole body'—for 'this means nothing else than that he will be forced to be free'. And we have only to look at Rousseau's way of solving the problems which had been the crux of natural law thinking to realise the complete change which has come over legal and political theory:

On this view, we at once see that it can no longer be asked whose business it is to make laws, since they are acts of the General Will; nor whether a prince is above the law, since he is a member of the State; nor whether the law can be unjust, since no one is unjust to himself; nor how we can be both free and subject to the laws, since they are but registers of our wills.

(*Du Contrat Social*, 1762, bk. II, ch. VI, trans. G. D. H. Cole)

There can be little room left for old-fashioned discussions about the nature of justice and the essence of law when human will is made the supreme arbiter of all human values. Speaking of precedents, we may well note here that Rousseau had a striking and untimely forerunner in a medieval writer. Marsilius of Padua, a fourteenth-century Italian, had stated in so many words a theory of the general will in his *Defensor Pacis* (1324). According to him, not only are laws the expression of the will of the people, but it is because they are the expression of the will of the people that laws are good and just. Natural law had never reigned quite unchallenged, not even in the Middle Ages.

Compared to Hegel, Rousseau or Marsilius, the author of *Leviathan* (1651) seems almost a moderate thinker. For all his insistence on sovereignty, for all his denial that natural law can properly be called a law, for all his assertion that it is positive law that lays down the 'distinction of Right and Wrong', Hobbes is nearer to the positions of voluntarist ethics than to those of the ethical state. His conception of law is the Nominalist conception. His ethical theory rejects the notion of absolute values. His State is an artificial, not an historical product. In the definition of the 'mortal God' it is the adjective that matters. The 'great Leviathan' still lacks the soul with which Rousseau and Hegel endowed it.

Let us bring matters to a head and attempt a conclusion. So far, only the negative side of the question has been examined. But it is the positive side that matters. In order to meet the challenge to natural law its supporters seem to have constantly fallen back upon certain fundamental premises. I submit that these premises are the necessary conditions of natural law thinking. Natural law was a definition of law. It implies an extension of the notion of law which may well perplex the modern student. I know of no better illustration of this point than the one which is given by Hooker. That 'learned and judicious divine' had a real gift for bringing out, in an age of passionate controversy, the gist of an argument. This is what he wrote in the first book of his great treatise on *The Laws of Ecclesiastical Polity* (1594):

They who are thus accustomed to speak apply the name of *Law* unto that only rule of working which superior authority imposeth; whereas we, somewhat more enlarging the sense thereof, term any kind of rule or canon, whereby actions are framed, a law. (*Eccles. Polity*, I, iii, 1)

'Somewhat more enlarging the sense thereof': the words bear the mark of Hooker's well-known caution and balance. But they bring out the essentials. Hooker's title to greatness is that, more than any other writer, he can claim to stand between two ages and to constitute a link, if there is any, between the old and the new schools of natural law. I think that both the medieval and the modern theorists of natural law, however divergent their views might have been on other matters, would have agreed on the necessity of 'enlarging the sense' of law which Hooker stresses.

Hooker's definition of law as 'any kind of rule or canon whereby actions are framed' is almost word for word the definition of Thomas Aquinas. 'Law'—St Thomas maintained—'is a rule or measure of action in virtue of which one is led to perform certain actions and restrained from the performance of others' (*Summa Theol.*, 1a 2ae, 90, 1). Even friendly critics had been reluctant to follow St Thomas so far. 'Such a description,' wrote Suarez, 'seems to be too broad and general' (*De legibus*, I, i, 1). It is curious to find an Anglican more faithful to St Thomas than a Jesuit. But Hooker had perhaps the clearer grasp of the issue.

He was set on breaking the spell of the Nominalist God. He knew that the notion of sovereignty could be harnessed only on certain conditions. He was putting St Thomas' words into good

English vernacular: 'the being of God is a kind of law to His working.'[1] But he was also handing on to later generations the notion of a law-abiding God and of a well-ordered universe. 'Of law there can be no less acknowledged, than that her seat is the bosom of God, her voice the harmony of the world' (*Eccl. Pol.*, I, xvi, 8). This is sound Thomist doctrine. But it has also a strangely eighteenth-century ring:

> The spacious firmanent on high,
> With all the blue æthereal sky,
> And spangled heavens, a shining frame,
> Their great Original proclaim.

The extension of the notion of law is a pronouncement on its nature. Law does not necessarily require the existence of a superior and an inferior. Law does not only command. It does something else besides, which is no less important. Actually natural law *teaches*, according to Locke; according to Grotius it *indicates* a particular quality of actions. This opens up new perspectives to the understanding of legal phenomena. A law which lacks authoritative sanction may yet be law. *Pacta sunt servanda*, the ultimate basis of international law, is such a proposition.

In turn a rule may be laid down as a command and yet not be properly a law. We must learn to distinguish in law the 'compelling' from the 'directing' element. This had led the Schoolmen to a complex casuistry. They had distinguished two aspects of law, the *vis coactiva* and the *vis directiva*. It is the *vis directiva*, the element of justice which is embodied in law, that ultimately matters. And Grotius, going back to the warning of Cicero, had made a similar point:

Those who have consecrated themselves to true justice should undertake to treat the parts of the natural and unchangeable philosophy of law, after having removed all that has its origin in the will of man.
(*De Iure Belli ac Pacis*, Prol., §31)

The emphasis is shifted from *ius quia iussum* to *ius quia iustum*, from the form of the law to its content. And the content of the law is a moral value. The relation between law and morals is the crux of the whole theory.

But even the formal structure of law could not fail to be affected by such premises. If law is not merely a command,

[1] *Ecclesiastical Polity*, I, ii, 2; cf. Aquinas, *Summa Theologica*, 1a 2ae, 93, 4.

if it does not proceed only from the will, law is the outcome of reason. Natural law is a plea for reasonableness in action. But it is also an assertion that only inasmuch as action can be measured in terms of reason does it properly come under the heading of law. It is because law is an act of the intellect that its notion can be extended to 'any kind of rule or canon, whereby actions are framed.' We find this difficult to accept and perhaps even to understand. But let us try to forget for a moment our everyday experience of legal positivism. Let us set aside the ambiguities of the word 'reason' and the widely different meanings with which it was used in turn by the theorists of natural law. What we find is a definite proposition about the essence of law.

Law is a standard, a model, a pattern from which the quality of a particular action, the relevance of certain situations and facts may be inferred. The primary function of law is not to command but to qualify; it is a logical as well as a practical proposition. The notion of law has much wider implications than the professional lawyer would have us believe. Legal valuations are possible where we are no longer accustomed to expect them. Legality is an aspect of moral experience which extends far beyond the legal field proper. I shall try to show in the concluding section of this book that such conceptions can still enrich our minds, and that the old discussions about the essence of law should not be wilfully ignored by the modern legal philosopher.

On the doctrine of sovereignty: LORD BRYCE, 'The Nature of Sovereignty', in *Studies in History and Jurisprudence*, vol. II, 1901; C. N. S. WOOLF, *Bartolus of Sassoferrato*, 1913.

On voluntarist ethics and its impact on Protestantism: G. DE LAGARDE, *Recherches sur l'esprit politique de la Réforme*, 1926.

On the theory of *raison d'état*: F. MEINECKE, *Die Idee der Staatsräson in der neueren Geschichte*, 3rd ed., 1929.

On the theory of the ethical State: B. BOSANQUET, *The Philosophical Theory of the State*, 1925; L. T. HOBHOUSE, *The Metaphysical Theory of the State*, 1918.

For a summary of the discussions on the essence of law: JETHRO BROWN, *The Austinian Theory of Law*, 1912, excursus E.

6

LAW AND MORALS

The relation between law and morals is the crux of all natural law theory. The theory not only requires an extension of the notion of law. It also implies a definite view about its compass. The problem is no longer one of form or of structure. It is a problem of content. The content of law is a moral one. Law is not only a measure of action. It is a pronouncement on its value. Law is an indication of what is good and evil. In turn, good and evil are the conditions of legal obligation.

The problem of the content of law is far from being ignored by present-day legal positivists. They frankly admit that every system of laws corresponds to a particular 'ideology'. They refer to the 'sociological background' as a necessary part of legal experience. They recognise that law is not only a command, but also the embodiment of certain values. The difference lies in the manner of conceiving those values. Natural law theorists would never have admitted that law is merely the expression of the standards of a particular group or society. They believed in absolute values, and they conceived of law as a means to achieve them. 'Law is the furtherance of what is good and equitable.' 'There is no law unless it be just.' 'The end of all political association is the preservation of the natural and imprescriptible rights of man.' I have chosen my quotations at random. We are no longer concerned with what divided their authors. We are concerned with what they had in common.

The close association of morals and law is the distinguishing

mark of natural law theory throughout its long history.[1] The very
enunciation of natural law is a moral proposition. The first
precept of natural law, says Thomas Aquinas, is 'to do good and
to avoid evil.'[2] And Grotius declares that 'the law of nature is a
dictate of right reason which points out (*indicans*) that an act . . .
has in it a quality of moral baseness or moral necessity.'[3] From
this general proposition both the old and the new school of natural
law set out to construct a complete and precise code of rules. The
only difference is the greater caution of the earlier theorists in
drawing out the consequences and applications of their first
'self-evident' principle.

I have already given a sample of the Scholastic manner of
handling the subject. Several groups or categories of precepts
can be deduced from the first and general precept that good
should be done and evil avoided. They correspond to 'the order
of our natural inclinations': self-preservation, the preservation of
the species, life in society. Practically all social and political
institutions—marriage, property, civil authority, etc.—can be
shown to be derived from these original 'values', and thus to
partake of a moral character.

In contrast with this elaborate process of deduction, which
allows for variations according to time and circumstances,
stands the modern and rationalist doctrine of natural law with
its blunt assertion of a constant and necessary pattern of social
and political relations. The natural and imprescriptible rights of
man, according to the *Declaration* of 1789, are 'liberty, property,
security and resistance to oppression'.

Medieval philosophers seem to have been anxious to couch
their ideals in loose and general terms. It is difficult, though not
impossible, to relate these ideals to a particular social background.
The 'bourgeois ideology' is much more clearly defined. It shows
the unmistakable imprint of its age and of the social and political
struggle which it reflected. Yet in both it is a 'table of values' that
provides the foundation of all legal order. In both the assumption
is that the validity of law depends on the measure in which these
values are embodied in it. Only good laws are laws. And for a law
to be good, it must be based, in one way or another, upon natural
law. 'If a human law is at variance with natural law it is no longer

[1] Maitland, it may be remembered, connected the doctrine of natural law
with 'the jural conception of morality' (*Collected Papers*, I, p. 23).
[2] See above, p. 44.
[3] *De Iure Belli ac Pacis*, I, 1, 10.

legal.' 'A society where the respect of rights is not assured has no constitution.'

Shall we then conclude that one, and perhaps the most striking, of the characteristics of natural law theory is to weld together morals and law in such a way that it is no longer possible to distinguish them? This is a capital question which calls for careful elucidation. The confusion between law and morals can have two different aspects which must be separately assessed.

The first and more conspicuous is the moralisation of law, the subordination of law to morals. This is the aspect which is more usually considered, criticised and deplored. It is indeed often alleged as one of the main arguments against natural law and as the reason for its abandonment. Here is a good account of the profound change which has occurred among legal writers in that respect:

If we compare the juristic writing and judicial decision of the end of the eighteenth century with juristic writing and judicial decision of the end of the nineteenth century, the entire change of front with respect to the nature of law, with respect to the source of obligation of legal precepts, and with respect to the relation of law and morals and consequent relation of jurisprudence and ethics, challenges attention. Thus Blackstone speaks of 'ethics or natural law' as synonymous, and of natural law as the ultimate measure of obligation by which all legal precepts must be tried and from which they derive their whole force and authority. Again, Wilson's lectures on law (delivered in 1790–91 by one of the framers of the federal constitution and a justice of the Supreme Court of the United States) begin with a lecture on the moral basis of legal obligation and a lecture on the law of nature or the universal moral principles of which positive laws are but declaratory.

In contrast, the institutional book of widest use in English-speaking lands at the end of the nineteenth century (Holland's *Elements of Jurisprudence*) begins with an elaborate setting off of law from 'all rules which, like the principles of morality . . . are enforced by an indeterminate authority' and conceives that natural law is wholly outside of the author's province. Likewise, Mr Justice Miller, lecturing upon the constitution in 1889–90, finds no occasion to speak of natural law nor of ethics, but puts a political and historical foundation where Mr Justice Wilson had put an ethical and philosophical foundation.

(Pound, *Law and Morals*, pp. 1–2)

This revulsion against what had been one of the deepest rooted traditions of Western thought—that law is subordinate to morals—is in no way restricted to the English-speaking world.

F

I shall try to show in the next chapter that it is among Continental lawyers that the tendency to strip legal theory of all natural law implications was more clearly developed and carried to its logical conclusions. I am here concerned only with the fact that, to modern eyes, the doctrine of natural law appears to involve a contamination of legality with morality, an obsolete and unacceptable moralisation of law. The judgment, if not the blame, is certainly well-founded. The theory of natural law is the outcome of a very old conviction, which goes back to the sources of our civilisation: the conviction that the purpose of law is not only to make men obedient, but to help them to be virtuous.

There is, however, another side to the confusion between law and morals. We no longer feel greatly concerned about its consequences, but there was a time when they were a major issue. The introduction of legal valuations into the field of morality can give rise to serious misgivings. Yet the moment we conceive of moral values as expressed in terms of law, as indeed the very notion of natural law requires us to do, it is difficult to see how these misgivings can be avoided. For this can mean only that, in passing judgment on the moral quality of action, we do nothing more than pronounce upon the conformity of that action to a legal pattern. If morality consists solely in respect for the law, then the Pharisee is a perfect example of moral behaviour. If moral duties can be couched in legal terms, they can be specified with code-like precision. Casuistry will set in and forecast all possible alternatives. Probabilism will help men to solve their doubts about the most appropriate rule to choose for their conduct. Moral experience is reduced to narrow legal categories. The task of the moralist is for all purposes identical with that of the lawyer. He must expound and interpret the law. Eventually he will also indicate how to employ it with discretion and advantage.

I do not intend to suggest that natural law is entirely responsible for these strange perversions. But it is more than a coincidence that the great age of natural law was also the age of legalistic ethics. And it is significant that Pascal, the bitter enemy of casuistry, was no friend of natural law. In that immortal libel, the *Provinciales* (1657), he denounced *la plaisante comparaison des choses du monde à celles de la conscience*, the 'worldliness' which results from the intrusion of legal categories into the field of morality. A truly moral conscience—Pascal pointed out—rebels against the notion that 'the rule may be adapted to its subject'; it is not content with probability, but craves for certainty. In the same way as the moralisation of law was felt to contradict the evidence of legal experience, the legalisation of morals was felt to imperil and to destroy the very essence of morality.

It is hardly credible that our forefathers could have been content for so many centuries with the doctrine of natural law if that doctrine had implied and sanctioned such gross misconceptions. The truth is, I think, very different. No doubt the fundamental assumption of natural law is the close association between law and morals. But that assumption allows for a variety of interpretations. The association of morals and law does not rule out the possibility of a demarcation between them. Actually the history of natural law is a history of painstaking efforts to delimit the two spheres and to get to the core of their difference.

The 'differential characters' of morals and law are much less of a novelty than its modern supporters would have us believe. What is new is the breach between the two, the assertion that law has nothing to do with morals and that natural law lies wholly outside the province of the lawyer. In fact, the problem of the differentiation between law and morals is so closely associated with the development of political thought that one wonders why it is not given more attention by historians. It coincides with the problem of the purpose and limits of State action and with the history of political and religious freedom. It was bound to appear under a different light at different stages. The independence of the State had first to be secured against the all-pervading sway of religion and morality, before the position came to be reversed and the need to secure the freedom of religious and moral experience against the encroachments of State action was revealed.

Thus, in a very broad generalisation, it might be said that medieval writers were concerned to prevent morals from encroaching on law, the writers of the seventeenth and eighteenth centuries to prevent law from encroaching on morals. But the problem remained fundamentally the same, and the results of the efforts to solve it are curiously similar. It is interesting to compare these results with the full-blown theory of the 'differential characters' of law and morals which is usually considered as one of the pillars of modern legal philosophy.

I shall restrict my analysis to the best known and more often quoted of these characters. The first is the 'social' or 'objective' character of law as against the 'individual' or 'subjective' character of morals. This is how the difference is defined by one of the exponents of the neo-Kantian school of legal philosophy:

> The logical function of law exerts its influence where a collision between the acts of two or more agents or an antithesis between two or more wills is possible, and tends to promote objective ordination among them. The moral criterion, on the other hand, supposes an antithesis between two or more possible acts of the same agent and tends to settle internal strife, that is, to establish a subjective ethical order. From this come the diverse elementary characteristics, which delimit the proper sphere of each.   (Del Vecchio, *The Formal Bases of Law*, p. 163)

The main idea behind this elaborate language seems to be that the essential function of law is to make life in society possible. *Ubi societas ibi ius.* Law presupposes society. Morals do not. Moral experience is essentially a matter for the individual. Legal experience is tied to the notion of a community.

If this is the gist of the first of the so-called 'differential characters', I think that in all fairness we should recognise that it was not entirely unknown even to the Schoolmen. Though conceiving of natural law as a moral standard and as the foundation of all laws, they were careful to draw the line between such of its applications which refer to men as men, and those which relate only to men in society. The latter they comprised under the heading of 'human law' or law proper; and the justification, and indeed the very essence of human laws, they found in the fact of social relationship. No doubt natural law, as a moral precept, extends to 'all acts of virtue'. But human laws cover only those aspects of human behaviour which imply a co-ordination with other men. Thus, properly speaking, the laws of men do not primarily aim at promoting virtue, but only at securing a peaceful living together: they do not forbid all that is evil, but only that which imperils society; they do not command all that is good, but only that which pertains to the general welfare.[1] If the social element in law is conceived as a differential character between law and morals, surely that element was clearly perceived already by medieval legal philosophers.

Another much quoted distinguishing mark of law as opposed to morals is the 'coercive' character of legal precepts. The argument is best known to the English reader through Austin's famous enunciation; but it is certainly much older than Austin and has a long history behind it. According to Kant the 'possibility of coercion' is intimately associated with the notion of a legal order.

[1] Aquinas, *Summa Theol.*, 1a 2ae, 72, 4; 96, 2 and 3.

But, as we shall presently see, Kant's deduction of this fundamental aspect of legality goes far beyond the usual acceptance of
coercion as a convenient mark by which to distinguish one group
of precepts from another.

Here, again, one can only say that, if 'sanction' or, to use
Austin's words, the 'enforcement of obedience', is conceived to
be the distinctive attribute of law proper, then even the medieval
theorists of natural law had a grasp of the distinction between
legal and moral imperatives, in so far as they identified the
'discipline of law' with a 'discipline which compels under fear of
penalty'. They actually went so far as to realise that the coercive
character of human or positive law is in its essence contradictory
to that moral element which the law is supposed to embody.

None the less, what they had in view was not the separation
of morals and law, but their unity. All they did was to point out
the different binding force of positive as against moral and divine
precepts, as well as the fact that the introduction of coercion
marks a turning point in the deduction of all laws from the
supreme principles of the law of nature.[1]

By far the most important distinction is that between the
'external' character of law and the 'internal' character of morals.
'Externality' was considered by Kant to constitute the very
essence of legal experience. But the merit of having 'discovered'
and formulated the distinction is commonly attributed to Christian
Thomasius (1655–1728), a representative like Pufendorf of the
German school of natural law, and a champion of freedom of
conscience in an age and in a country in which religious intolerance
was still a matter of accepted policy.

In his *Fundamenta Iuris Naturae et Gentium* (1705) and in a
number of other writings, Thomasius developed the view that
the law of the State, as a coercive order, is debarred by its very
nature from any action and competence in the sphere of morals.
Justice (*iustum*) consists in laying down and respecting the conditions which make human intercourse possible. Its first precept is:
'Do not unto others what you do not want others to do unto you.'
But morals, in the widest acceptation (*decorum* and *honestum*),
exact much more than that. They imply doing to others what
we want others to do to us; they imply a duty to our own conscience. Legal precepts can therefore be only external; they can
have nothing to do with the inwardness and spontaneity of
thought and religion.

[1] Aquinas, *Summa Theol.*, 1a 2ae, 95, 1; 96, 5.

Thomasius was drawing the moral of two centuries of religious strife and persecution. His theory lays the foundations of the modern, secular, tolerant State. Its novelty, however, is practical rather than theoretical. The distinction between external and internal obligation, between the *forum externum* and the *forum internum* is not a discovery of Pufendorf or Thomasius. It goes back, if I am not mistaken, to the Canon law. What is new is the sharp distinction between the two, and the assertion that law, and therefore the State, can and must have no competence in the *forum internum*, viz., in the 'court of conscience'. What is new is the belief that it is possible clearly to delimit the sphere which is beyond the bounds of State action, while, on the other hand, cataloguing the commands of the State under the heading of purely external precepts.

But the notion of the inherent disability of positive legislation in matters of thought or religion, is a notion which has its roots in the oldest tradition of Western thought. For it is indeed the essence of Christian belief to stress the intimacy and freedom of moral and religious experience; nor did the 'external' character of legal obligation escape the notice of earlier writers on ethics and natural law. Thomas Aquinas and Hooker are in close agreement on this point, stressing as they do that the laws of God work differently from the laws of men:

Man, the maker of human law, can pass judgment only upon external action, because 'man seeth those things that appear', as we are told in the book of *Kings*. God alone, the divine Law-giver, is able to judge the inner movements of the will, as the Psalmist says, 'The searcher of hearts and reins is God'.   (Aquinas, *Summa Theol.*, 1a 2ae, 100, 9)

Wherein appeareth also the difference between human and divine laws, the one of which two are content with *opus operatum*, the other require the *opus operantis*, the one but claims the deed, the other especially the mind.   (Hooker, *Eccles. Pol.*, V, lxii, 15)

And long before Aquinas and Hooker, another great Christian writer had given the same thought a solemn expression:

The law of God has taught us what to believe, which the laws of men cannot teach us. They can exact a different conduct from those who fear them. But faith they cannot inspire.
                              (St Ambrose, *Ep.* XXI, 10; Migne, XVI, 1005)

The conclusion of this short summary is simple. There was a

notion of the distinction between law and morals long before the theory of the 'differential characters' was fully developed. Far from being responsible for the confusion of the two spheres, the doctrine of natural law led to a better appraisal of their differences. What divides the old school from the new is not so much the confusion between moral and legal obligation as a different view about the position of the State and of law with regards to morals.

The theory of the differential characters is thus at bottom nothing but a political theory, a theory about the nature and limits of State action which was the outcome of a particular historical situation or the expression of a particular ideal that claimed recognition. That this ideal was the outcome of a better understanding of Christian values is, I think, undeniable. But we must be careful not to mistake the effect for the cause, and not to reverse the historical process which led to the formulation of the 'differential characters'. As Croce ironically remarked, it is not because these characters were suddenly discovered that 'the Catholics ceased to bring the Protestants to the stake, and the Protestants to repay them with the same kindness'. The differential characters between law and morals were the transformation into a political programme of an ideal which was inherent from the outset in Western civilisation. We ought not to forget the blood and the toil which it cost to secure what could henceforward appear as a 'neat philosophical theorem'.

However, another and deeper criticism of the 'differential characters' has been suggested. It must be briefly mentioned because it affords some further arguments for the rehabilitation of the natural law theorists and of their long-forgotten labours. It has been pointed out that these characters, based as they are upon a particular historical experience, can be only approximate and shifting. They cannot survive, on closer inspection, as absolutely valid criteria for distinguishing legal from moral precepts.

Take the social character of law as contrasted with the individual character of morals. It is, of course, true that modern man has come to associate law almost exclusively with the State, and morals almost exclusively with the individual. But are there not moral values which presuppose and foster society as much, if not more, than can the legal order? Are there not laws outside the range of the State, regularly observed and sometimes felt as more binding by the individual? A purely individual morality is unthinkable; while law, if we consider it in its broadest sense as 'a rule or measure of action', is ever present in practical experience, even to Robinson Crusoe, who made himself a rule to read the Bible 'a while every morning and every night' and to make his way of living as 'regular' as possible—thus saving himself from despair and preserving his very humanity.[1]

Nor is the coercive character of certain laws or groups of laws a distinguishing mark of law proper. For one thing, as Lord Bryce pointed out,[2] compulsion is no final explanation of the observance of law, nor is physical force the only type of compulsion. On the other hand, there are a number of laws, that not even the legal positivist would deny to be laws, which lack proper sanctions. Such are, apart from international law, the fundamental laws of a given constitution. The very notion of sanction, it has been pointed out many times, is not quite so simple as Austin would have us believe; and, at any rate, in the working of law, sanctions have only a complementary function. When a law is infringed, sanctions may operate; but they cannot succeed in restoring the situation once it has been altered: *factum quod infectum fieri nequit.*

Finally, as far as the external character of law is concerned, nowhere is the approximate character of the distinction more apparent. The valuation of an action as external or internal can never be a matter of general agreement. In our days, the State exacts military service from its citizens, and actually requires them to be good soldiers. In Queen Elizabeth's days, the government enforced Church attendance, but denied the charge of 'commanding opinions'. Which of the two cases is nearer the notion of law as a purely external command? How can we prove that law is never concerned with the internal side of action? What do we make of such legal concepts as *bona fides* or *dolus* which involve a subtle valuation of motives? What of that 'mental element' which plays so decisive and elusive a part in criminal liability?

Clearly such criticism as this can lead only to the conclusion that the distinction between law and morals should not be based merely on a generalisation from our present experience, but on a deeper analysis of the inmost nature of legal and moral obligation. It also leads to the recognition that there must be closer links between the two spheres than is realised prima facie. But this brings us back to the position of the theorists of natural

[1] Defoe, *Robinson Crusoe*, sect. X.
[2] 'Obedience', in *Studies in History and Jurisprudence*, vol. II, 1901.

law and to a more charitable view of their merits. It is indeed strange enough to discover that much of the criticism which I have summarised can easily be put into traditional natural law language. But it is even more significant to find that the theorists of natural law, because of their very assumption of an indissoluble link between law and morals, have left us some precious evidence for the correct appraisal of their mutual relationship. They may have unduly stressed the moral aspect of law or the legal aspect of morals. But, as has already been shown, they were well aware of the differences between them and showed a surprisingly clear insight into their real nature.

Thus, for example, with regard to the social character of law and the individual character of morals, they would probably have denied that the distinction is as simple as that. Life in society, they would have pointed out, is a moral duty. There is no aspect of life which can be said to be morally indifferent. Moral values tend of necessity to be realised in social, that is, in legal terms. These notions they would have expressed in different ways according to their different inspiration. Aquinas stressed the political nature of man. Grotius was content with an *appetitus societatis*. But the common aim of both the old school of natural law and the new was to emphasise the moral foundation of law as well as the part which law plays in moral experience. The proper scope of justice is 'to promote an objective order among men'. Justice is therefore essentially *ad alterum*. Yet metaphorically we can speak of justice as present even 'in him that leads a solitary life': for law is nothing but the rule of right reason.[1]

Or take the coercive character of law as opposed to the freedom and spontaneity of morals. We may have good reasons for fearing any doctrine which is based on the assumption that it is the purpose of law to make men 'virtuous'. But are we so sure that we can, even at the present day, draw a clear line between the precepts which can and cannot, or which should and should not, be enforced by positive legislation? Are there not many examples of moral duties still forcibly sanctioned by law? The problem is a different one, and the theorists of natural law saw it clearly. Coercion they fully realised to be contradictory to the moral quality of action. But equally well they realised its inadequacy of obedience. The discrimination between morals and law they sought not in the precepts themselves but in their working. Good

[1] Aquinas, *Summa Theol.*, 2a 2ae, 58, 2.

laws must be obeyed 'for conscience sake'. It is, therefore, only to evil men that law can appear merely as compulsion.

In this sense virtuous and just men are not subject to the law, but only the wicked. For whatever pertains to constraint and to violence is against the will. But the will of the good is at one with the law, whereas in the bad the will is opposed to the law. So, in this sense, the good are not under the law, but only the bad.

(Aquinas, *Summa Theol.*, 1a 2ae, 96, 5)

Here is indeed a very old idea, which goes back to the very sources of Christian teaching. 'If ye be led of the Spirit, ye are not under the law' (*Gal.* V, 18). This is not the place to discuss whether its extension from the field of religious to that of moral experience is justified. But the striking analogy certainly throws light upon the real difference between legal and moral obligation. It accounts better than many 'sociological' arguments for the basic fact of obedience. Surely not even at the present day does the 'good' citizen think of law merely in the shape of the police-man or the law-court. Nor, on the other hand, does he long hesitate to break laws which he deems morally indefensible, at least when he is sure that he can do so with a fair chance of impunity. Is not this the best possible proof that 'good' laws are binding *in foro conscientiae*?

Last, but not least, comes the 'external' character of law as opposed to the 'internal' character of morals. Once again we find natural law theorists deeply aware of the issue. But when they say, as Hooker says, that laws 'but claim the deed'; or when they emphasise, as Thomas Aquinas emphasises, that the object of justice is 'external operation', they are not taking 'externality' in the same way as we do to be a mark by which to fence and delimit the proper field of State action. We can hardly expect them to share our modern views about the comparative claims of religion and politics, nor our notion of the sacred rights of the individual conscience.

I cannot help thinking, however, that both Aquinas and Hooker would probably have been surprised to hear us speak of the modern State as strictly confined to 'externals'. They would have had little difficulty in pointing out that even in our days opinions are far from being politically irrelevant, and that 'purges' are only a more cilivised version of the stake. The plain fact is that the demarcation between 'externals' and 'internals' is as shifting and approximate today as it was in the hey-day of natural law theorising. It is difficult to see on what theoretical grounds certain duties which are imposed by the modern State, such as military service, can be described as purely external duties.

Clearly, the distinction cannot lie in the duties as such, but in the manner in which they are imposed and finally fulfilled. And this the old theorists of natural law knew very well, better perhaps than we do. What they had in mind, when they stressed the difference between legal and moral obligation, was that the purpose of law cannot go beyond external conformity. It can enforce virtuous actions, but it cannot secure that these actions should be carried out as they would be by the virtuous man, *eo modo quo virtuosus operatur*.[1] To our efforts to justify conscription in contrast to compulsory Church attendance, they would have objected, I surmise, that whether the law-giver chooses to enjoin the one or the other he will never quite succeed in making a good soldier and even less in making a truly religious man.

All this brings us to a conclusion. We should be more careful not to speak of natural law as a confusion between law and morals. It is undoubtedly true that the very notion of natural law implies their close association. But so does the modern definition of law as an 'ethical minimum', which Jellinek made so popular among the jurists.[2] Natural law is a vindication of that minimum. But it is not a denial that a distinction between the two spheres of ethics exists and should always be kept in mind for a correct understanding of legal and moral phenomena. In fact, if the theorists of natural law foreshadowed that distinction, they did so not in the empirical terms of a generalisation from a given historical situation, but in a truly philosophical sense, as an analysis of the nature of legal and moral obligation. It is possible to find in their now forgotten and discredited speculations a surprisingly clear grasp of the difference between legal conformity and the moral value of action, which one would almost be tempted to relate to Kant's incomparable analysis of the categories of legality and morality.

With Kant the 'differential characters' are finally freed from all empirical implications. Kant's deduction of the 'external' and 'coercive' essence of law represents the conclusion and crown of the long effort to reach a distinction between law and morals.

[1] Aquinas, *Summa Theol.*, 1a 2ae, 96, 3, ad 2um.
[2] G. Jellinek, *Die sozialethische Bedeutung von Recht, Unrecht and Strafe*, 1878.

But it also provides the conditions for an entirely new and critical approach to the problems of legal philosophy.

B. CROCE, *Philosophy of the Practical, Economic and Ethic*, 1913.

G. DEL VECCHIO, *The Formal Bases of Law*, 1921.

R. POUND, *Law and Morals*, McNair lectures in the University of N. Carolina, 1924.

C. K. ALLEN, *Legal Duties and other Essays in Jurisprudence*, 1931 (Legal Morality and the *Jus Abutendi*—Legal Duties).

Droit, Morale, Moeurs, IIᵉ Annuaire de l'Institut International de Philosophie du Droit et de Sociologie Juridique, 1936.

7

THE IDEAL LAW

It has been the purpose of this enquiry to show that the theory of natural law provided answers to many problems which still face the modern legal philosopher. No assessment of that theory would, however, be complete without taking into account what may well be said to constitute its most constant feature all through the ages: the assertion of the possibility of testing the validity of all laws by referring them to an ultimate measure, to an ideal law which can be known and appraised with an even greater measure of certainty than all existing legislation. Natural law is the outcome of man's quest for an absolute standard of justice. It is based upon a particular conception of the relationship between the ideal and the real. It is a dualist theory which presupposes a rift, though not necessarily a contrast, between what is and what ought to be.

This must not be taken to mean that the doctrine of natural law is at heart a revolutionary doctrine. Nothing indeed would be more remote from the truth. If natural law played a revolutionary part at certain epochs of Western history, it is equally true that, during most of its age-long development, the doctrine was limited to a mildly progressive, and at times to a frankly conservative function. The recognition of the existence of an ideal law did not necessarily imply that positive law should be overruled by it in cases of conflict. Natural law could serve as well to support revolutionary claims as to justify an existing legal order. It could even lead to the glorification of a particular system of law, as when Roman law, after its reception on the Continent as the 'common' law of Europe, came to be considered as the *ratio scripta,* or as when Sir Edward Coke described the English Common law as 'nothing else but reason'.[1] Justice Holmes humorously described this particular outcome of natural law by remarking:

It is not enough for the knight of romance that you agree that his lady is a very nice girl—if you do not admit that she is the best that God ever made or will make, you must fight. There is in all men a demand for the speculative, so much so that the poor devil who has no other way of reaching it obtains it by getting drunk. It seems to me that this demand is at the bottom of the philosopher's effort to prove that truth is absolute and of the jurist's search for criteria of universal validity which he collects under the head of natural law.

(Holmes,'Natural Law' in *Harvard Law Review,* 1918)

This is not a very charitable judgment: but there is no doubt that natural law was the *belle dame sans merci* who inspired the crusading spirit of old-time jurisprudence. That spirit has gone. It has given way to a realistic approach which is in keeping with an age of prosaic undertakings. The study of the ideal law is no longer conceived as being of any relevance to the lawyer. 'The juridical science of the nineteenth and twentieth century expressly declares itself incapable of drawing the problem of justice into the scope of its enquiries' (Kelsen). It actually prides itself on being able to master and to construct into a system any given legal material without resorting to the delusion of natural law. The abandonment of natural law marks the rise of modern jurisprudence. This is the fundamental fact which we must keep in mind in order to understand, if only from a negative angle, what natural law ultimately stood for. It may well be that after we have examined the achievements and limitations of modern jurisprudence, the case for natural law may once again be assessed in a positive manner.

The rise of modern jurisprudence is marked by the abandonment of natural law and by a new or 'positive' approach to legal experience. But the notion of natural law as the embodiment of justice and as the ultimate ground of the validity of all laws had been criticised long before the advent of positive jurisprudence. Nor can the new approach be described as the outcome of any particular doctrinal standpoint. The word 'positivism', if one cares to use it in this connection, can indicate only an attitude rather than a definite philosophical creed. Indeed, the oldest argument

[1] *The Institutes of the Laws of England,* pt. I (1628).

against natural justice is the sceptical argument. It goes back to
the very beginnings of speculative thought. It has a long history
which stretches down from the Sophists to the present day. I need
only refer the reader, for a classical treatment of the subject, to
Hume's *Treatise of Human Nature*, book II, part ii, or to the
section in Cicero's *Republic* (III, vi–xx), where Carneades' argument is set forth with sufficient vigour and clearness to remind us
how little there is that can be called entirely new in legal and
political philosophy.

Modern or positive jurisprudence is not necessarily based upon
scepticism, nor does it imply a denial that the problem of justice
exists. Modern jurists may be willing to leave the discussion of
the ultimate reason why law should be regarded as binding to the
legal philosopher, without taking a definite stand about the
existence of natural law. Nor do they accept as a matter of course
the 'monist' view of the coincidence of the ideal and the real
which, as we have seen in a preceding chapter, consecrated the
law of the State as the embodiment of moral values. All they do
is to put the problem of the ideal or natural law, as it were, within
brackets. However influenced they may have been or still are by
one or other philosophical current, their implicit or explicit
philosophy is not the determining factor. They are indeed anxious
to convince us that theirs is not a philosophical, but a 'scientific'
concern.

This, I understand, is apparent among English jurists. To the
foreign observer English jurisprudence—with some notable
exceptions—may still seem to have a flavour of utilitarianism as a
distinctive national characteristic. And indeed, if we think of
Austin, we may well believe that the cradle of modern English
jurisprudence was utilitarian philosophy. But Austin himself, if I
am not mistaken, was careful not to tie his notion of jurisprudence
to any particular philosophical assumption. He actually avoided
any final pronouncement on the possibility of evaluating legal
experience from a standpoint other than that of the 'analytical'
jurist. Of general jurisprudence he wrote:

It is concerned directly with principles and distinctions which are
common to various systems of particular or positive law; and which
each of these various systems inevitably involves, let it be worthy of
praise or blame, or let it accord or not with an assumed measure or test.
(Austin, *Lectures*, Campbell's ed., I, 33)

He seems clearly to admit that 'the goodness or badness of

laws' might be tried 'by the test of utility (or by any of the various tests which divide the opinions of mankind)'. He contented himself with declaring that with this kind of undertaking general jurisprudence 'has no immediate concern'. The problem of the ideal law is neither denied nor declared insoluble. It is simply put within brackets as irrelevant to the task of the jurist.

Very similar remarks can be made about Continental jurisprudence. This was, as is well known, the outcome of the 'Historical school', and it is significant that the standard-bearer of that school—F. C. von Savigny (1779–1861)—was also the founder, or at any rate the most authoritative exponent, of the systematic treatment of law which still obtains general recognition and application in the law-schools of the Continent. Now the Historical school—the programme of which was laid down in Savigny's famous book, published in 1814, *Of the Vocation of Our Age for Legislation and Jurisprudence*—meant, if not a new philosophical theory of law, at least the expression in the field of law of a great philosophical revolution. It was an aspect as well as a result of the great tide of Romanticism which, foreshadowed in the eighteenth century, swept Europe as a counterblow to the French revolution.

As its name clearly indicates, the Historical school was essentially a vindication of growth and development against the abstract rationalism which had become the distinguishing mark of natural law theory in its last stage of development. It stressed that the origin and the explanation of legal phenomena must not be sought in the individual, but in collective life; that law is the product of the particular genius of each nation (*Volksgeist*); that legal experience should not be arrested and as it were crystallised in statutes and codes, but allowed to grow and bear fruit in its full vigour and vitality.

How then can it be explained that the untiring advocate of the historical study of law should also have been the exponent of a systematic treatment which seems to be mainly inspired by the rationalist quest for order, coherence and unity? Savigny's *System of Present-day Roman Law* (1840–49) brought to perfection a method which had long been applied, in Germany and elsewhere, in the study of the common (Roman) law of Continental Europe. It added little or nothing to the pattern that the great *Pandektisten* had elaborated, which had come to be considered as the necessary introductory or 'general' part (*Allgemeiner Teil*) of jurisprudence. Under that heading the notions of law, objective and subjective right, juridical relationship, personality, facts, things and so forth, had been abstractly assessed and defined. These notions have remained down to the present day the elements of legal study and training on the Continent.

Now it might well be questioned whether the acceptance by Savigny of any of these abstract categories was not in contradiction to the notion of law which he championed. These categories were derived from the essentially individualistic conception of law which had inspired the Continental law-schools for centuries. Surely they needed recasting if they were to be fitted to a new conception of law as the expression of the organic life of society. It must also be remembered that the final outcome of the Historical school, as Sir Ernest Barker has pointed out,[1] was a vindication of 'national' law (in the particular case of Germany, of German law) as against Roman law, the impact of which was bound to be more and more resented as alien. The 'Germanist' doctrine of group-personality, the 'organic theory of the State', the struggle against individualism in the field of public and even of private law, all trace their beginnings to the Historical school.

But the point which must here receive our attention is the paradox of the parallel birth of the historical interpretation of law and of modern, positive jurisprudence. The Historical school had begun by stressing the growth and development of law, it ended by fostering its scientific study. It had begun with an apology for history. It ended with an apology for jurisprudence. The paradox is worth considering more closely, for it is one of the crucial episodes in the rise of modern juristic thought, and it throws light upon its fundamental nature.

The explanation of the riddle can be found only in the correct interpretation of Savigny's intentions, as well as of the real aims and purposes of the historical doctrine. Already in the *Vocation* Savigny had pointed out that the life of law is, as it were, twofold. Law has a 'political' life inasmuch as it expresses the realities of a given social structure. But law has also a 'technical' life, which begins the very moment it undergoes its 'scientific' elaboration at the hands of the jurist.[2] Law is no doubt the product of the *Volkgeist* and the outcome of history. But it can be assessed and appraised only through the labours of the professional lawyer.

The complete change of front from the old natural law approach

[1] Introduction to Gierke, *Natural Law and the Theory of Society*, pp. liv–lv.
[2] F. C. von Savigny, *Of the Vocation of Our Age for Legislation and Jurisprudence*, trans. Hayward, 1831, pp. 22–29, 62.

G

is here apparent. The rationalist school had led to an exaltation of the law-giver as the agent for the realisation of justice. The Historical school led to an exaltation of the jurist as the interpreter of historical growth and development. But this does not mean that the followers of the Historical school intended to substitute historical growth and development for the notion of absolute justice. Its greatest representatives, such as Savigny, Puchta and Stahl, remained unshaken in their Christian belief in an order of justice based upon the existence of a transcendent God. They must not be mistaken for Hegelians. Theirs was at bottom a 'dualist' theory: they never accepted the fundamental assumption of Hegel's legal philosophy, that the ideal finds its revelation in history. The cult of history they had in common with all the Romantics. But historicism was a method to them, rather than a philosophy. They, too, were putting the ideal law within brackets. Jurisprudence was called in to fill the vacuum.

It filled it so well and so thoroughly that, for a time, the old quest for the ideal law seemed to have been written off from the tasks of the jurist and the lawyer. The achievement of nineteenth century jurisprudence is a great and positive one. The age of science produced a science of law worthy of its ambitions. Anyone who is acquainted with the immense amount of ingenuity which generation after generation of jurists spent in constructing the majestic edifice of modern jurisprudence, cannot easily believe that such labours could have been in vain.

To bring order, coherence and unity into the system of law, to provide the law-giver with a clear map of his province, the lawyer and the judge with a body of concepts which should enable them to perform their duties with the greatest amount of precision and ease: this was, for nearly a century, the distinguishing mark of legal theory on the Continent. And it is indeed on the Continent rather than in English-speaking countries that Austin's programme of a 'general jurisprudence' has been carried out to the full. 'As principles abstracted from positive systems are the subject of general jurisprudence, so is the exposition of such principles its exclusive or appropriate object.' German *Rechtwissenschaft*, with its relentless pursuit of an ever-increasing degree of systematic perfection and of formal abstraction, can and must be taken as the best illustration of the fate of legal theory after the spell of natural law had been broken.

This is not the place to discuss the character and value of legal science, or, if we may indeed identify the two terms, of modern jurisprudence: its claim, that is, to possess the character of a science, as well as the possibility of its universal application. These are not two different problems, but one: for indeed, if we admit the claim of jurisprudence to be 'the formal science of positive law'—as Holland defined it—I can see no reason why we should not admit that jurisprudence may be 'particular' or 'general' according to the greater or lesser degree of induction and generalisation which has been performed in the collection and elaboration of legal material. If jurisprudence is an empirical science, then clearly it is so from beginning to end, nor is there any substantial change, either in its methods or in its results, whether it restricts itself to the *Dogmatik* or scientific elaboration of a particular legal order, or whether it progresses to a 'general theory of law' (*Allgemeine Rechtslehre*) which 'takes up . . . several systems of law and seeks for legal institutions which have appeared in history on more than one occasion' (Stammler).

What I am concerned with here is a different question. It is the claim of modern jurisprudence to have entirely eliminated the problems which had for centuries been considered and discussed under the heading of the natural or ideal law, the claim to self-sufficiency, if I may so call it, of modern jurisprudence, viz., to provide the student of the law with the sufficient and necessary criteria for the understanding and interpretation of legal pheno-mena. In order to assess to what extent that claim is justified we must now examine the answer which modern jurisprudence has given to the problem of the validity of the laws which are the object of its study.

The existence of that problem was certainly never denied by the 'positive' jurist. On the contrary, it is because it purported to restrict itself only to the study of laws 'actually valid' that modern jurisprudence was led to lay all the emphasis on the adjective 'positive'. That term can have a meaning only as a term of contrast. 'There is no law but positive law', wrote Stahl;[1] natural law precepts 'possess neither the requisite definiteness nor the binding force of law'. But Bergbohm, the 'diligent tracker of natural law', was perfectly right to point out that, from the point of view of legal positivism, the very use of the adjective 'positive' with regard to law is nothing but a pleonasm.[2]

The real question was to determine which laws are sufficiently 'definite', or 'binding', or 'positive' to deserve the name of laws.

[1] F. J. Stahl, quot. by H. Rommen, *The Natural Law*, p. 117.
[2] K. Bergbohm, *Jurisprudenz und Rechtsphilosophie*, I, 1892, p. 49, 51 ff.

It is on this point that the difficulties began, and that the peculiarities of legal empiricism soon became apparent. It gradually dawned upon lawyers and jurists that the validity or 'positiveness' of law cannot consist, or at least cannot consist solely, in the mere fact of its enforcement. The use of force, or the possibility of its use, is only the outward or material aspect of positive law. From a strictly juridical or 'formal' point of view the validity of a particular law cannot depend upon its varying degree of effectiveness. It consists in the fact that that particular law belongs to a system which is singled out and recognised as the only positive and valid system.

That this system, to nineteenth-century jurists, was the system or legal order of the State, has only a relative importance. The formal or logical side of their argument is the side which calls for attention. To say that the positiveness of law derives from its belonging to a positive system is in fact only a different way of saying that the recognition of its validity as a law depends on the possibility of referring it back, directly or indirectly, to a common source from which all legal precepts ultimately proceed. This is what the jurists, borrowing an old term with which we are already acquainted, indicated under the name of sovereignty. Sovereignty became the sacred dogma of positive jurisprudence, because it was the condition of the positiveness of law. Sovereignty may be, and indeed is, a fact. But from the juridical angle it was also, and essentially, a formal criterion: the criterion which made it possible to recognise a rule or a body of rules as part of a positive order, and therefore to pronounce on their validity as laws.

Thus the restriction of all law to positive law and the quest for a systematic construction of the legal order went hand in hand. They are indeed the two fundamental aspects of modern jurisprudence. Its tendency to become more and more 'formal' was only a consequence of its purpose to be a 'positive' science, that is, to steer clear of any criterion of validity of law—such as natural law—extraneous to the system.

We have of late grown accustomed to consider this 'formal' character of jurisprudence as self-evident. I have no doubt that we are greatly indebted to the 'pure theory of law', developed by Kelsen and his school, for a sounder appreciation of the logical issues of the juristic method. But the process which led modern jurisprudence to an increasing degree of abstraction had long been at work. It is interesting to look back upon it and to see how the concepts which had at first provided the basis of positive jurisprudence were gradually transformed, as it were by an internal logic. The process is curiously reminiscent of the old discussions about the essence of law which have been examined in a preceding chapter.

Positive jurisprudence had started from the identification of law and command. It ended with the elimination of will from the field of law altogether. This is apparent not only in the sphere of 'public law', in the untiring efforts of 'classical' German jurisprudence (Jellinek, Laband, etc.) to construe the State as a *Rechtsstaat*. It is equally apparent in the sphere of 'private law', as anyone can easily gather who is acquainted with the great debate on the *Willenstheorie* which divided nineteenth-century jurists.

The tendency was to eliminate any intrinsic, original power of the will, whether of the State or of the individual. To admit such a power, it was argued, is nothing but a natural law proposition: for where can will derive its juridical value from except from law itself? Surely, if we admit, as Savigny admitted, a 'natural capacity' of the human person to set in motion legal consequences; or if we ascribe, as Windscheid ascribed, a 'creative force' to the individual will in laying down legal precepts, we deprive State sovereignty of its essential function as the ultimate source of all rules which have positive validity.

In turn, even sovereignty is a misnomer. It seems to indicate that the will of a man or of a body of men is endowed with some original legal value—a natural law proposition! From a purely juridical, that is, from a strictly 'formal' and 'positive' standpoint, it is clear that the will of this or that man or body of men is creative of law only because there is a superior law (the law of the constitution) which attributes to that will a juridical relevance.

The tendency among up-to-date writers is in fact to substitute some other expression for the word 'sovereignty', wherever it would have been used in the past. Thus we hear it now said that the legal order can be conceived only as 'complete' and 'exclusive'. Exclusive, because the recognition of a particular legal order as positive implies that the rules which compose it are, for the jurist, the only valid ones: all other rules are not properly laws but mere facts.[1] Complete, because the admission that there may be 'gaps' in the law is nothing but a delusion, which springs from the belief that there may be situations or facts 'intrinsically' juridical—a residue of natural law thinking. From a really 'positive' standpoint,

[1] This principle has been applied with remarkable success in the theory of Conflict of Laws, or Private International Law, as it is called on the Continent.

unless these situations or facts are given relevance by a law, they are, as far as the legal order is concerned, simply non-existent.

We seem to be forced to the conclusion that command is not the essential attribute of law. The function of law is to qualify, to provide, as it were, a term of reference for certain situations and facts by ascribing a particular meaning to them, or inserting them in a relation of condition and sequence. The widespread adoption of the word 'norm' in modern juristic terminology is, from this point of view, particularly significant. For that word does, it is true, involve the notion of an 'ought', but also and primarily that of a standard or model or pattern; and the 'injunctive' character is at any rate in no way essential to an 'ought' proposition. Thus, modern legal thought has been led to emphasise more and more the logical character of law, and to conceive of juridical categories as mere symbols or names for indicating the relevance of certain situations and facts from a given 'normative' angle. The parallel between law and language is ready to hand, as well as the comparison of jurisprudence and grammar.[1]

This description of the characteristics of modern legal thought may sound strange to English ears. The tendencies which I have described may perhaps be suspected as fundamentally alien. Jurisprudence on this side of the Channel has preserved a solid core of commonsense which has guarded it from the perils of overabstraction. It may also be doubted whether all the conclusions of Continental juristic thinking are applicable to a type of legal experience such as that of the Common law, entirely different from the tradition of Roman law on the Continent.[2]

There is, however, one point which of late has attracted attention in England also. I would like to refer to it as one of the best illustrations of the final outcome of present-day legal theory, as well as one of the most carefully thought-out attempts to provide an answer to the problem of the validity of law which, as I have pointed out, was from the outset one of the inspiring motifs of positive jurisprudence. It is the notion of the 'basic norm', which Kelsen and his followers have stressed as the necessary presupposition for a systematic construction of the legal order. The notion is well known, and readily understood in the light of what has already been said about the logical issues of the juristic method.

[1] See below, pp. 114.
[2] For the 'typically English approach' to the problems of legal theory I need only refer the reader to Professor Goodhart's stimulating lecture, *English Contributions to the Philosophy of Law*, New York, 1949.

The 'basic norm' is, according to Kelsen, the condition of completeness and self-sufficiency in a given legal order—in other words, of its 'positiveness'. 'The basic norm of a legal order is the postulated ultimate rule according to which the norms of this order are established and annulled, receive and lose their validity.' 'The quest for the reason of validity of a norm is not—like the quest for the cause of an effect—a *regressus ad infinitum*; it is terminated by a highest norm which is the last ground of validity within the normative system.' In other words, the basic norm is the necessary hypothesis on which the jurist sets to work: his first and primary task is indeed that of discovering the common ground of validity in each and every norm or group of norms which constitute the system.

This, Kelsen maintains, is possible for any given legal material: for the determination of the basic norm 'implies no categorical statement as to the value of the method of law-making or of the person functioning as the positive legal authority; this value is a hypothetical assumption'. Thus the basic norm of national law in the modern sovereign State is that the commands of the sovereign (a man or a body of men) are to be obeyed; the basic norm of the international legal order is that *pacta sunt servanda*, and so forth. Each and every order will appear as a hierarchical system, every part of which derives from the basic norm its ultimate ground of validity.

I can see no serious objection to Kelsen's theory of the 'basic norm' as the condition of correct legal thinking. On the contrary, I think that the theory throws considerable light upon the real nature of jurisprudence. In grounding his whole construction upon a hypothetical premise, the jurist may well claim that he is doing nothing but what is done in all other empirical sciences. But what should always be borne in mind is that scientific constructions are based upon 'working' hypotheses. The fundamental task is therefore for the scientist to choose his hypothesis correctly. The moment it ceases to work, the question of rejecting it arises, and of superseding it with another and better one.

I find it difficult to see how the jurist who accepts the postulates of the 'pure theory of law' for what they are worth—as an admirable system of formal logic applied to the law[1]—can avoid asking himself some similar question. The basic norm of a national system of law—that the commands of the sovereign are to be obeyed—can have a meaning for the jurist (who will then be able to declare that the system is a positive system) only inasmuch as

[1] H. J. Laski, *Grammar of Politics*, 4th ed., p. vi.

the commands of the sovereign are in fact obeyed. Similarly, the basic norm of international law, *pacta sunt servanda*, can provide the foundation of the international order only inasmuch as there is such an order in which *pacta sunt servata*: which is, I suppose, what international lawyers, from Grotius onwards, have, correctly or incorrectly, assumed.

In other words there is, and must be, a point at which the basic norm—the hypothesis—is converted into a fact—a thesis— unless its validity be derived from some other or further hypothesis, from a norm which will no longer be positive but can only be a proposition of 'natural law', a pronouncement on justice.

Thus, in its latest and most up-to-date developments, modern jurisprudence has really done nothing more than shift to a higher plane the old problem which used to be discussed under the heading of the ideal or natural law. The following quotation from Kelsen seems to me particularly significant:

That a norm of the kind just mentioned is the basic norm of the national legal order does not imply that it is impossible to go beyond that norm. Certainly one may ask why one has to respect the first constitution as a binding norm. The answer might be that the fathers of the first constitution were empowered by God. The characteristic of so-called legal positivism is, however, that it dispenses with any such religious justification of the legal order. The basic norm is only the necessary presupposition of any positivistic interpretation of legal material.   (Kelsen, *General Theory of Law and State*, p. 116)

How this passage reveals the Achilles' heel of modern legal positivism! For the recognition that the ultimate test of the validity of law lies *beyond* law itself is nothing but a natural law proposition. In peaceful days, when the actual observance of law (be it of the commands of the State or of treaties solemnly entered upon) was unchallenged, 'positivism' could find in 'facts' its ground and perhaps its justification. But the moment 'facts' are called into question, the moment a 'choice' must be made between two or more possible alternatives,[1] I can see no reason why the old argument of natural law, which purported to value the facts and to direct the choice, should not be reconsidered.

[1] Kelsen gives an example of such an alternative in the case of the relationship between national and international law. The choice between the two hypotheses of the 'primacy' of the one or the other he declares to be merely a matter of 'political ideology'.

The typically German dilemma of either blind force or blind faith with which Kelsen leaves us stranded can never be entirely satisfactory. Positivism may indeed dispense with the quest for the ultimate foundation of the legal order. But this makes it entirely powerless when a vital issue is involved, such as the defence or the destruction of that order. It is tragically significant that the country where formal jurisprudence was developed to its utmost perfection was also the country where legality offered least resistance to the challenge of new and disruptive forces. Events seem to have brought us back once again to long-forgotten responsibilities.

I would like to conclude this long argument with the mention of some recent examples of the inadequacy of legal positivism to solve the problem of the ultimate validity of law. Examples of this kind are, in our troubled days, only too frequent. I remember a time, not very remote, when there was in my country not one but four different legal orders, all of which could have claimed some degrees of 'positiveness'. I prefer to use a simpler example which was given by Professor Goodhart in an interesting article.[1]

A statute is promulgated during the war by the Netherlands Government in London, purporting to bind Dutch subjects in Holland. Professor Goodhart asks 'is this law?'—by which he means, I presume, 'is it positive law?', law the validity of which can be ascertained by the criteria of positive jurisprudence. Now, as Professor Goodhart points out, the statute was certainly a law from the point of view of the Netherlands Government, who regarded themselves as having the right to issue it, independently of the fact whether it could ever be made efficacious. Yet, on the other hand, the German authorities would never have regarded it as a law, not even if every citizen in Holland had obeyed it. From the standpoint of a third party, such as the British courts, the question might have been dubious. 'The real difficult question arises, however, when we consider the position of the inhabitant of Holland.'

Professor Goodhart suggests that, at the end of the war, the Netherlands courts would have considered his particular views as immaterial. They would have confined themselves to assessing the actual observance or violation of the statute. And, indeed, so they should according to 'positive' jurisprudence. But, as Professor Goodhart frankly admits, 'this does not mean that the view of the

[1] 'An Apology for Jurisprudence', in *Interpretations of Modern Legal Philosophies*, 1947.

individual is unimportant. On the contrary, a large part of political history has been concerned with disputes between individuals and governments regarding the authority of the latter to declare law.'

I submit that what Professor Goodhart seems to consider a political issue is what our benighted ancestors would have called a clear issue of natural law. I submit that this issue can be solved only on the traditional lines of calling the validity of positive law into question, and that it is impossible for the individual to do so unless he decides on the justice of the law which he is asked to obey. But I further submit that it is possible to find in quite recent developments of legal theory and practice a clear indication of a return to the obsolete notions which positivism had criticised and declared to be unacceptable.

That the whole question of the trial of war criminals at the end of the war would raise a 'natural law' issue was an authoritative opinion which events have fully confirmed.[1] No doubt the provisions for the Nürnberg Tribunal were based, or purported to be based, on existing or 'positive' international law. Apart from the preliminary and controversial question of individual responsibility under international law, the violation of international treaties, of the laws and customs of war, and above all of Article I of the Preamble to the Fourth Hague Convention of 1907 (the 'Martens clause' which formally included the 'laws of humanity' and the 'dictates of the public conscience' within the boundaries of international law) certainly provided a 'positive' basis for the prosecution.

But I strongly suspect that the boundaries of legal positivism were overstepped, and had to be overstepped, the moment it was stated that the trials were a 'question of justice'. The principle *nullum crimen sine poena*, on which the sentences were grounded, was a flat contradiction of one of the most generally accepted principles of positive jurisprudence, the principle *nulla poena sine lege*. Whether or not the assertion of that principle constitutes a dangerous precedent is not for me to judge. All I suggest is that the words used by the Court ('So far from it being unjust to punish him, it would be unjust if his wrong were allowed to go unpunished')[2] are clearly reminiscent of old natural law argumentations. The rejection of the defence of superior orders makes that

[1] Lord Wright, 'Natural Law and International Law' in *Interpretations of Modern Legal Philosophies*, 1947; 'War Crimes under International Law' in *Law Quarterly Review*, 1946.
[2] *The Times*, October 1946.

reminiscence even more poignant: for it is nothing less than the old doctrine that the validity of laws does not depend on their 'positiveness', and that it is the duty of the individual to pass judgment on laws before he obeys them.

Thus, after a century of effort to eliminate the dualism between what is and what ought to be from the field of legal and political experience, natural law seems to have taken its revenge upon the very champions of the pernicious doctrine that there is no law but positive law, or that might equals right, since for all practical purposes the two propositions are perfectly equivalent.

R. POUND, *Outline of Lectures on Jurisprudence*, 5th ed., 1943 (a complete bibliographical guide).
SIR P. VINOGRADOFF, *Common-sense in Law*, 10th imp., 1933.
C. K. ALLEN, 'Jurisprudence—What and Why?' in *Legal Duties*, 1931.
Modern Theories of Law, Ed. by J. JENNINGS, 1933.
J. W. JONES, *Historical Introduction to the Theory of Law*, 1940.
W. FRIEDMANN, *Legal Theory*, 1944.
W. W. BUCKLAND, *Some Reflections on Jurisprudence*, 1945.
G. W. PATON, *A Text-Book of Jurisprudence*, 1946.
J. STONE, *The Province and Function of Law*, 1946.
H. KELSEN, *General Theory of Law and State*, 1946, with an Appendix on *Natural Law Doctrine and Legal Positivism*.
Interpretations of Modern Legal Philosophies, Essays in honour of Roscoe Pound, 1947.

A useful selection from authors can be found in J. HALL's *Readings in Jurisprudence*.

For the interpretation of Savigny, which is outlined in this chapter, I wish to acknowledge my indebtedness to an excellent Italian book by G. SOLARI, *Storicismo e diritto privato*, 1940.

For a further analysis of 'formal' jurisprudence and for a survey of the immense literature on the subject, I must refer to my book, *Il Negozio Giuridico*, 1934.

Mention should be made here of the remarkable efforts made by French jurisprudence to disentangle itself from the impact of positivism. Under the influence especially of Gény (*Science et technique en droit privé positif*, 1914–1924), a renaissance of natural law thinking has taken place among French legal writers which could well be the object of a separate study

8

CONCLUSION

The time has now come to bring this long argument to a tentative conclusion. The validity of that conclusion can be tested only by the light which it throws upon the problem at issue. A great jurist of the last century who devoted his life to the historical study of law, once wrote that the undying spirit of natural law can never be extinguished. 'If it is denied entry into the body of positive law, it flutters around the room like a ghost and threatens to turn into a vampire which sucks the blood from the body of law.'[1] The present essay is an attempt to account for the ghost and perhaps to exorcise it.

I suggested at the beginning of this enquiry that we should try to assess the meaning of natural law from two different angles, the historical and the philosophical. But on closer inspection these two lines of approach cannot but appear as fundamentally contradictory. The very notion of an 'historical function' is hardly compatible with that of a 'permanent value'. History may well tell us the part which the doctrine of natural law has played in the building up of our cultural heritage. It may convince us of the importance of spiritual factors in the shaping of events and of positive institutions. But it will also make us painfully aware of the 'relativism' of all natural law theories. It will provide the unfriendly critic with further grounds for dismissing such theories as typical 'ideological superstructures' in the interplay and clash of historical forces.

Political ideology is the term which modern historians tend to

[1] O. von Gierke, *Natural Law and the Theory of Society*, I, p. 226.

substitute whenever natural law would formerly have been mentioned. From a strictly historical standpoint the two expressions may well seem equivalent. As the former Master of Balliol once pointed out, even the doctrine which, at the present day, most emphatically claims to be based on a 'scientific' interpretation of history, can easily be construed into a theory of natural right.[1] Yet, on the other hand, the champions of historical relativism (of which Marxism, if I interpret it correctly, is certainly an aspect) will have little difficulty in showing that the most solemn assertions of 'natural rights'—such as, to take one of the more recent examples, the *Universal Declaration of Human Rights*, adopted on 10 December 1948, by the General Assembly of United Nations in Paris—are nothing but ideological programmes, or indeed war machines, to be used and tested in the battlefield of history.[2]

The question then is, whether the historical explanation of the notion of natural law can be accepted as the final explanation. In that case the proper place for its assessment is the history of political thought rather than the study of legal philosophy. My contention is, that legal philosophy also has something to say on the subject, and that a notion which has proved to be constructive and valuable to man has a claim to be assessed not only *sub specie historiae* but *sub specie aeterni*.

This obviously presupposes a particular view of the function of legal philosophy, and may seem to bring us on to highly controversial ground—for on what indeed do legal philosophers agree except on the most conventional platitudes?[3] I shall assume that they agree at least on the existence of a fundamental problem: the problem *quid ius?*—'what is law?' which, as Kant pointed out, puts the jurist in the same embarrassment in which the logician is put by the question 'what is truth?'[4] I believe that the doctrine of natural law is nothing less than an attempt to answer that question, and that this attempt provides the explanation of the constant

[1] A. D. Lindsay, *K. Marx's Capital*, An Introductory Essay, 1925.
[2] The volume *Human Rights*, A Symposium, published by UNESCO (1949), provides the best running commentary on the fundamental 'conflict of ideologies' which underlies the compromise finally agreed upon in the UN Declaration.
[3] For a description of the 'function' of legal philosophy see Pound, *An Introduction to the Philosophy of Law*, 4th imp., 1930, ch. I, where the close connection between natural law thinking and philosophical speculation about law is aptly illustrated.
[4] Kant, *Einleitung in die Rechtslehre*, sect. B.

return of natural law, as well as the only constant feature of natural law thinking.

As an answer to the problem *quid ius*? natural law is, first and foremost, a rejection of all empirical solutions, such as purport to derive the notion of law from a process of induction ever more generalised and extended. Kant compared a 'purely empirical theory of law' to 'the wooden head in Phædrus' fable, which may be beautiful, but alas! has no brain'.

Kant was indeed the most forceful exponent of natural law theory in modern days, when he maintained that the jurist should turn 'to pure reason for the source of his judgments in order to provide a foundation for all possible legislation'. But he is also the most coherent and persuasive critic of legal empiricism when he points out that knowledge of what the laws actually 'say or have said' will never enable the jurist to know what law *is*, but only what *pertains to* the law (*quid iuris*) in a given place and at a given time. I think that the survey which has been made in the preceding chapter of the aims and methods of modern legal science provides a striking confirmation of such criticism.

Yet, on the other hand, the notion of natural law has nothing in common with the theories which some modern legal philosophers, claiming the authority of Kant, have put forward as an answer to the question *quid ius*: viz., that the notion of law is a purely logical category, which may enable us to recognise the existence of law but not to pronounce on its goodness or badness. I gravely doubt whether any of the greatest natural law theorists—from Cicero to Kant—would have accepted the neo-Kantian distinction between the 'concept' and the 'ideal' of law. To them, the concept and the ideal coincided. Theirs would never have been merely a theory of *richtiges Recht*. It was the *gerechtes Recht* they were after.[1] Natural law was indeed to them the supreme 'legal category'. It enabled them to 'distinguish' or identify law within the indistinct mass of practical human experience. But it 'valued' as well as it 'distinguished'. To the question *quid ius*? the theorists of natural law unanimously answered *ius quia iustum*.

Thus the doctrine of natural law is in fact nothing but an assertion that law is a part of ethics. I do not think that the judgment can be seriously challenged from the historical side,

---

[1] The distinction between *richtig* (correct) and *gerecht* (just) as applied to law (*Recht*) was a favourite theme of the neo-Kantians. It was intended to correspond to the two different angles—the logical and the moral—from which the problem of law can be viewed.

though I am willing to admit that the 'ethical' character of law may have been stressed to a greater or lesser extent by different writers. I suggest that we look a little more deeply into the full implications of the assertion.

In order to provide a satisfactory answer to the question *quid ius*, the proposition *ius quia iustum* certainly requires some further qualification. It obviously can not be merely a question of definition, nor of carving out, as it were, a particular slice of experience which we agree to indicate by the name of law according to definition. It is further necessary to account for that very experience, to explain not only *what* laws are, but *why* they exist, the reasons which make legal phenomena an inevitable aspect of human life and behaviour. I have no doubt that for Kant the question 'what is law?' really meant 'how is law possible at all?' (*wie ist Recht überhaupt möglich?*). I am not here concerned with Kant's 'transcendental' deduction of ethics. I am rather concerned with the possibility of testing the old doctrine of natural law from this modern and critical standpoint.

I submit that the doctrine can stand the test successfully. For if we admit that the very assertion of natural law is an assertion that law is a part of ethics, its essential function can appear only as that of mediating between the moral sphere and the sphere of law proper. The notion of natural law partakes at the same time of a legal and of a moral character. Perhaps the best description of natural law is that it provides a name for the point of intersection between law and morals. Whether such a point of intersection exists is therefore the ultimate test of the validity of all natural law thinking.

Now the existence of such a point can to my mind hardly be denied when we look at the question from the purely legal angle. I need not remind the reader of the conclusions reached in the preceding chapter. That a strictly empirical treatment of law, such as that which modern jurisprudence purports to achieve, ultimately leads to a problem which the positive jurist is unable to solve, is all that need be admitted. It may be objected that this problem is not necessarily a 'moral' problem, and that the linking up of a given legal system either to the factual existence of sovereignty, or to the recognition of a particular political ideology, is the best guarantee of the final elimination of the 'moral' element, of the 'metaphysical' notion of natural law from the theory of positive law.

But let us not be deceived by such sham substitutions. The

'factual' existence of sovereignty can provide a convenient peg for the jurist only inasmuch as he accepts the equation of might and right as a final proposition. And as for 'political ideologies', they are only too clearly an assertion of values; nor does the relativism in which they are cloaked, and the 'emotional aura' they foster, alter their fundamentally moral (or immoral) character. Natural law they resemble as Satan resembles God. These blood-thirsty idols are proving to be far more exacting than the old gods of truth and of justice. Such doctrines at any rate purport to provide us with judgments on the goodness or badness of laws. And the goodness or badness of laws is obviously a matter which pertains to the moral sphere proper.

Now let us look at the same problem from the other, the moral, angle. Natural law was an endeavour to formulate in legal or 'normative' terms certain fundamental values which were believed to be absolutely valid. With this claim to absolute validity I am not here concerned. It is the task of the moralist to assess it. But I would like to call the reader's attention to the notion that values must be given a 'normative' expression in order to have a meaning. We are told by modern analysts that the sentence 'this is good' has a 'meaning' only as expressing an attitude or as an incitement to action.[1] Natural-law theorists would probably have agreed, though on very different grounds and for totally different purposes. They stressed the necessity of translating the notion of 'good' into the precept 'do good and avoid evil', and this, they maintained, is the first generative proposition of natural law, and hence of all legal precepts.

This really amounts to a recognition of the 'inevitability' of legal or normative propositions in the field of practical experience. Taken in this, the broadest sense possible, laws are nothing but the outcome of the quest for clear and definite standards of valuation whenever action is involved. This is perhaps the place to recall Vico's profound remark about the *verum* and the *certum* in law. The 'truth' of the laws—according to the Italian philosopher—is the moral value which they embody, 'the light and splendour of natural reason'. But the moral element in law must not blind us to its other and necessary aspect, the crude appearance which values assume when they are embodied in positive legislation, when they are 'particularised' or cashed, as it were, in a system of authoritative precepts.

[1] Ogden and Richards, *The Meaning of Meaning*, 4th ed., 1936, p. 125.

The certainty of laws involves an obscuring of reason, in so far as in them reason is supported merely by authority. And this makes us experience the laws as hard to obey, and yet we are constrained to obey them because of their being certain.

(Vico, *Scienza Nuova Seconda*, 1744, cxi, cxiii)

If these considerations be granted, perhaps we may have an argument to persuade both the jurist and the moralist that the old speculations about natural law were not entirely purposeless.

The jurist is the man of the *certum*. It is right that he should be so, that he should stress the *dura lex sed lex*, the advantage of even imperfect laws over the absence of any law whatsoever. But his 'certainty' can be only a comparative one. New values may emerge, challenging the existing order and clamouring for recognition. Other legal orders exist, based upon different assumptions and yet securing the allegiance of men. Or it may be that the 'certainty' of the legal order is inadequate, that even the most 'complete' and 'exclusive' system of laws cannot foresee all possible emergencies.[1] In all such cases the student of law is made painfully aware of the limits of his 'certainty'. This is the reason why the claims of natural law are to him so disturbing. He is made to realise the unceasing interplay of 'values' and 'norms', of *verum* and *certum*. He is forced to admit that the ultimate ground of the validity of law can lie only in the values which it embodies.

I am, of course, fully aware that the notion of natural law can be acceptable to the jurist only inasmuch as it offers an instrument for the better understanding of legal phenomena, a means of sharpening the tools which he employs. But, as I have already remarked, certain recent developments of legal theory are in this respect particularly instructive. We have seen the jurist recognise that 'law' does not necessarily coincide with the law of the State. We have found him aware that his 'choice' is a purely arbitrary one, a matter of ideology—and indeed how could he deny the close links which make modern legal positivism a typical outcome of nineteenth century State worship? Yet, on the other hand, we have found the jurist conceding that there is no logical impossibility in the 'scientific' construction of any given legal material, be it the law of the State or the law of the Church, the laws of

---

[1] This is particularly interesting in the case of continental code-law, where express reservations are made for the possibility that neither positive law nor custom may provide a sufficient basis for decision, and the necessity of recourse to the 'general principles of law' or other criteria is clearly indicated (e.g., *Swiss Civil Code*, art 1; *Italian Civil Code*, art. 3 *Disp. Prel.*, etc.).

H

primitive societies or those of the international community—not to speak of the innumerable other laws which in the variety of their intercourse men have come to consider as binding, and indeed 'rigorously obey'. In all such cases the student of law is led back to the basic questions which inspired former discussions about the nature of law.

The abandonment of the 'voluntarist' conception of law in modern jurisprudence, the very change in juridical terminolgy of which the substitution of 'norm' for 'precept' or 'command' is a clear indication,[1] both seem to point towards a better appraisal of certain notions with which natural law theorists have made us familiar. Such are the notions that the primary function of law is not to command but to qualify, and that legal valuations partake of a logical as well as of a practical character. These notions had been fully displayed by the theorists of the law of nature when they stressed that law is an act of the intellect besides and before being an act of the will. It is fascinating to see these old notions re-emerge, in modern legal theory, in the form of the analogy, to which I have already called attention, between law and language.

If law be considered primarily as a 'sign' or an indication of a quality, language and law cannot fail to appear closely similar. The parallel is further confirmed by the similarity between the work of the jurist and that of the grammarian and linguist. Both purport to formulate the general rules applying to the use of certain symbols or signs which men use for qualifying certain given situations. Both lead to an increasing degree of abstraction and 'formalism', and are thus liable to the same fallacy of forgetting that the rules which they lay down have a meaning only in so far as they refer to a living reality. Grammars and dictionaries, phonology and morphology do not make a language. Jurisprudence is unable to say the final word about law.[2]

[1] See above, p. 102.

[2] The analogy of law and language can be traced back to the Historical school, which developed it in accordance with the Romantic interest in folk-lore and *Sittengeschichte*. The similarity between the work of the grammarian and that of the jurist was to my knowledge first pointed out by B. Croce in an essay on legal philosophy in 1907; but references to grammar and grammatical rules have always been frequent among students of law at all times.

The relationship between law and language has recently been approached from an entirely new angle in this country and in the USA. It is mentioned in C. L. Stevenson's book, *Ethics and Language*, 1946, and discussed in greater detail by G. L. Williams in *Law Quarterly Review*, 1945-6. An excellent contribution to the analysis of legal language has been made by Professor Hart (*The Ascription of Responsibility and Rights*, Aristotelian Society, 1949).

The lesson of natural law, if it were to be recalled in this connection, would, I suppose, be simply to remind the jurist of his own limitations. No philological effort will ever be able to explain a work of art. Nor can jurisprudence reach the ultimate core of law and account for its existence. The lesson of natural law is that the logical character of law does not necessarily imply a denial that law is a part of ethics. What language is to thought, norms are to values. Ultimately, it is on the basis of these that man makes his choice and determines his action. The transformation of a norm into a command is essentially a matter of subjective appreciation. Surely there is no command where there is no obedience.

Here, indeed, is where the moralist will have his word to say, and will decide whether the old speculations on the nature of law are entirely superseded. If he be the man of the *verum* he will not ignore that the certainty for which conscience craves is not that of transient laws, but that of absolute values. He will provide such grounds for obedience as are capable of carrying conviction. But he will also take into account the unrelenting quest of man to rise above the 'letter of the law' to the realm of the spirit. He will draw the dividing line between mere conformity to the law and the real value of action, between the Pharisee and the truly moral man.

I have endeavoured in this book to show how deeply concerned the theorists of natural law were with these issues. We ought not to forget the great debt we owe them. They were the first to explore the ambiguous borderland between law and morals. They were the first to secure the comparative independence of the law-giver as well as the inviolable rights of the individual conscience. They were the first to analyse the complex interplay of legal and moral obligation, the mysterious process by which the truly honest man abides by the law and yet is free from its bondage. We must be careful before we reject their eloquent plea that law is a part of ethics. We must ask ourselves whether there is not a permanent element of truth in their contention that law and morals are closely intertwined and yet fundamentally different; that it is from the idea of the good that all 'normative' judgments proceed, and yet that the essence of moral experience is freedom.

I know of no better description of this process than that given by Kant in a famous passage which I would like to quote as the conclusion of this essay. Kant's ethics may appear, and probably are, not entirely immune from a 'legalistic' bias. But nobody had

a clearer grasp than Kant had of the incommensurable difference
between legality and morality.

A perfectly good will . . . [cannot] . . . be conceived as *necessitated* to
act in conformity with law, since of itself, in accordance with its subjective constitution, it can be determined only by the concept of the
good. Hence for the *divine* will, and in general for a *holy* will, there are
no imperatives: '*I ought*' is here out of place, because '*I will*' is already
of itself necessarily in harmony with the law. Imperatives are in
consequence only formulæ for expressing the relation of objective laws
of willing to the subjective imperfection of the will of this or that
rational being—for example, of the human will.   (Kant, *The Moral
Law: Groundwork of the Metaphysic of Morals*, trans. H. J. Paton, p. 81)

This point where values and norms coincide, which is the
ultimate origin of law and at the same time the beginning of moral
life proper, is, I believe, what men for over two thousand years
have indicated by the name of natural law.

Additional Essays

A

THE CASE FOR NATURAL LAW RE-EXAMINED

The lectures printed in this chapter were delivered at the University of Notre Dame on 9 and 10 October 1954, at the invitation of the President and the Dean of the Law School. Their purpose was to initiate a discussion about the use and scope of a journal of natural law studies. That they should appear in the first issue of this journal is a generous reward and a great honour for the lecturer. I have made no substantial alteration of the text: I wish my talks to read as they were given. The introductory lecture is omitted at my request. A very few words will suffice to explain my line of approach and my intentions.

The case for natural law is not an easy one to put clearly and convincingly. It must needs appear in a different light according to the angle in time or in place from which it is looked at. In England, for a number of reasons, that case has never been a popular one.[1] At the time when I was preparing these lectures I happened to ask an eminent scholar for his views on the debate about natural law that was taking place in the *Canadian Bar Review*. Professor Goodhart is no declared enemy of 'old-fashioned' jurisprudence. As will appear from these lectures, I believe that we see eye to eye on many important issues. But his comment was not very encouraging. 'I have a suspicion,' he wrote, 'that the various

[1] 'It is surprising to find how small a contribution to English jurisprudence in these years has been made by writers in the natural law tradition': Hart, 'Philosophy of Law and Jurisprudence in Britain (1945–1952)', 2 AM. J. COMP. L. 355, 362 (1953). For the famous phrase, *in Anglia minus curatur de iure naturali quam in aliqua regione de mundo,* see my *Medieval Contribution to Political Thought* (1939), chs. v and vi.

disputants are arguing about different things. Once you are in agreement concerning your basic premise, then it is probable that logical reasoning will lead you to the same conclusion; but the real difficulty lies in finding a common basic premise. A person who believes in a Divine Being and a future world will have one premise, while a person who is an agnostic will have another. As reasonable men, they will probably differ concerning the conclusions which they will eventually reach, having started from different premises.'

These lectures are an attempt to resolve the difficulty indicated by Professor Goodhart. They take their start from the opposite end to his; they leave 'premises' as much as possible out of discussion. Dean O'Meara's letter of invitation contained one suggestion which I found particularly to my taste and particularly helpful: that we should turn to natural law for an 'illumination of problems' rather than for a 'blueprint of detailed solutions'. It so happened that in an essay published some years ago[1] I had tried to show that natural law can shed light on a number of problems. The nature of law, the relationship between legal and moral obligation, the necessity of referring positive law to some ideal standard: on each of these problems I believed, and still believe, that natural law has a word to say, that, indeed, natural law is perhaps nothing other than a name for the right answer. I concluded that the best way for reassessing the case for natural law was to reassess the value of that answer.

If I borrowed my division from an old book, I have done my best not to borrow anything else besides it. This time my concern was with the present rather than with the past; I hope that I may have poured some new wine into my old bottles. It is one of my happiest recollections of Notre Dame that I actually met there many of the authors whose views I was about to discuss in these lectures; the others I had only just left behind, my daily companions at Oxford. My intention was to start a friendly discussion among friends. I must acknowledge an equal debt to those with whom I agree and to those with whom I differ.

(I) THE PROBLEM OF THE NATURE OF LAW: THE CONTRIBUTION OF NATURAL LAW THINKING

The first problem is that of the nature, or the essence, or, if you prefer to put it even more simply, of the definition of law—and of

[1] See above, pp. 13–116.

what natural law has to contribute to the age-long controversy centring around it.

Surely the old problem is not as dead as it looks. Even in quite recent days and in very respectable quarters it is still chosen as a subject for academic discussion at the highest level. It seems to me, in fact, highly significant that only last year the new Oxford professor of jurisprudence—Professor Herbert Hart—should have chosen it as the subject of his inaugural lecture.[1] This lecture is a clear indication that there is no objection for the modern jurist to start, as of old, from the beginning, viz., from the old problem of the nature of law and of its definition.

On the first page of Professor Hart's lecture we read the following: 'The perplexities I propose to discuss are voiced in those questions of analytical jurisprudence which are usually characterised as requests for definitions: What is law? What is a state? What is a right? What is possession? I choose this topic because it seems to me that the common mode of definition is ill-adapted to the law and has complicated its exposition.' In the next two paragraphs Professor Hart adds: '. . . compared with most ordinary words these legal words are in different ways anomalous'. They '. . . do not have the straightforward connection with counterparts in the world of fact which most ordinary words have and to which we appeal in our definition of ordinary words.'

I have taken the liberty of quoting from Professor Hart's inaugural lecture in order to prove my point that discussion of the definition or essence of law is not so out of fashion as is usually believed. I am of course well aware that there are some remarkable novelties in the manner in which the discussion is approached. The philosophy prevalent in many Anglo-Saxon universities— and of which Oxford has become the stronghold in recent years— is one that is mainly occupied with the analysis of language. Strange and alien and in some ways parochial as this particular brand of philosophy appears to me, I have no doubt that its methods, and indeed even its temper, can in many ways prove peculiarly relevant to legal studies and to jurisprudence; and I shall presently return to some of Professor Hart's most striking and interesting suggestions. For the time being I trust that I am not misreading his words if I take them as evidence that *de legum natura* still animates the mind of the legal philosopher. Nor do I think that the legal philosopher should be at all annoyed if I

[1] Hart, *Definition and Theory in Jurisprudence* (1953), an inaugural lecture delivered before the University of Oxford on 30 May 1953.

remind him that this is a question with a very long and very respectable history behind it. Any acquaintance with the history of jurisprudence reveals that all through the ages the problem of defining what law is has almost constantly been in the mind of the jurist. If authority is needed on this point, Professor Rommen's admirable book provides ample evidence that the problem of the nature of law was in fact part and parcel of past discussions about the law of nature.[1]

Surely the old discussion *utrum lex sit actus intellectus seu voluntatis* was more than a Scholastic quibble. But surely natural law implied a particular answer. Natural law thinking implies a certain attitude towards the problem of the definition of law. Wherever that attitude can be traced, we may be almost sure that natural law has had its say; we may even be justified in using 'natural law' as a provisional heading. In the discussion whether law is an *actus intellectus* or an *actus voluntatis*, natural law theorists have always and invariably sided with the first part of the alternative.

I think that this conclusion applies not only to the medieval Schoolmen, but also to the modern 'secularised' theory of the law of nature. Both Grotius and Locke certainly accepted the view that the essence of law is not will but reason. So did, unless I am mistaken, the Fathers of the American Constitution. There are, of course, some notorious exceptions. Hobbes, the best known among them, with all his talk about the law of nature, is really outside that tradition of natural law still so much alive in the Declaration of Independence. Hobbes is in fact the forerunner and founder of that theory of law which has ignored natural law altogether. That theory has come to be known by a name which is usually taken to express the 'modern' attitude towards the problem of law: the theory of 'legal positivism'. It is an ambiguous name: I shall use it here for that line of thought which rejects any quest after the reason or justification of the law, and which no doubt, in the old discussion whether the essence of law is reason or will, would have sided in favour of the second part of the alternative. As the basic, almost scriptural text for that theory, I would choose the following passage from Hobbes: 'And first it is manifest that Law in general is not Counsel but Command, nor a Command of any man to any man, but only of him whose command is addressed to one formerly obliged to obey him.'[2]

[1] Rommen, *The Natural Law* (1947).
[2] *Leviathan*, ch. 26.

From Hobbes to Austin and from Austin to the present-day 'positivist': the line seems as continuous and unbroken as it is from Cicero to the Founding Fathers. Yet the continuity of certain lines of thought should not blind us to the differences which may and do separate one age from another. I am not sure that modern legal theory, with all its insistence on 'positivism', would still stand, without many qualifications, by Hobbes' definition of law as the command of the sovereign. I have an impression, in other words, that contemporary legal thought, though still terming itself 'positivist', has, on the whole, abandoned the will-theory of law and is groping for some new and more satisfactory definition. Actually every treatise on jurisprudence nowadays seems to contain a preliminary section devoted primarily to showing that the identification of law with command is not an adequate explanation of legal phenomena.

I should not be surprised if that doctrine had long been abandoned in England. It has always seemed to me a strange paradox that both Austin and Hobbes should have maintained their full right of citizenship across the Channel. But it is not for me to say whether Hobbes' and Austin's theory of law can be reconciled with the common law tradition. What seems to me even more significant is that the will-theory of law should be losing ground on the continent of Europe, where it does seem after all infinitely better adapted than in England to the actual facts of legal experience. Here indeed the old tradition of Roman law has played a large part in fostering the notion that law is the expression of a sovereign will, whether of the prince or of the people. And that tradition has also undoubtedly concurred in fostering the growth of highly centralised States, in which one single authority gradually absorbed all the functions of lawmaking, and stripped society of what Montesquieu called 'les corps intermédiaires': a process which Tocqueville has admirably described in his book *L'Ancien Régime et la Révolution*, where he shows it at work long before the French Revolution proclaimed the dogma of the one and indivisible sovereignty of the people.

The reasons for this abandonment have become commonplaces of modern jurisprudence. The will-theory of law, it is pointed out, does not provide an adequate explanation of certain important aspects of legal experience. It does not, for example, explain the nature of constitutional law. The laws of a constitution, whether written or unwritten, are not commanded; they are accepted. They have no 'sanction' in the normal sense of the word; nor can such sanctions be said to exist even in those constitutions providing a mechanism for the control of the constitution itself, for *quis custodiet custodes*? Nor can insurrection as the 'last resort'—as the right of the people to rebel against arbitrary rule—be properly called the sanction of the constitution. Surely no modern constitution embodies any recognition of such a right. In short, the will- and sanction-theory of law simply will not work with constitutional law, and, as Professor Goodhart puts it very well, 'an interpretation of law which leaves out constitutional law seems . . . clearly inadequate'. I think all modern students of jurisprudence would agree on this point.

I need hardly mention the other classic example of the inadequacy of the will-theory of law, viz., the case of international law. It is clearly impossible to consider international law as law in the terms of the Hobbesian or Austinian definition. There is no sovereign power to command; 'sanctions' there may be, but no proper system of coercion, unless we construe war itself as the sanction of international law. This has been done, but it does seem a curious way of conceiving the sanction of law as consisting in its own destruction. It may of course be objected that the whole question is merely a matter of definition:[1] the point, however, is that if we want to understand international law *as* law we must give a definition of law in which the current notion of command and of sanction are left out altogether.

Finally—as I have already pointed out—I must leave it to you to decide to what extent the will-theory of law is a stumbling block in the Anglo-Saxon approach to the legal problem. Here I can only refer to a recent article which has made a deep impression on me, as an indication of American awareness of the same problems worrying us on the continent of Europe.[2] Professor Lon Fuller's criticism of the 'predictive' theory of law—the theory enunciated in Holmes' famous dictum about 'the prophecies of what the courts will do in fact'—only confirms me in my conviction that, if the will-theory of law has been found inadequate even by Continental lawyers brought up in the tradition of centralised sovereignty, it could hardly fail to be found so 'in the jurisdictions of the common law'. Professor Fuller's vindication of 'the antinomy of reason and fiat that runs throughout the law' is

[1] See Professor Glanville Williams' article, 'International Law and the Controversy Concerning the Word Law', *British Year Book of International Law*, (1945), p. 146.
[2] Fuller, 'Reason and Fiat in Case Law', *Harvard Law Review* (1946), **59**, 376.

certainly one of the most interesting and most recent instances of the dissatisfaction of the jurist with the attempt at 'stating law purely in terms of power relations without reference to its ethical bases'.

At this point I must make it perfectly clear that, in my view, the defeat or abandonment of the will-theory of law is not necessarily an indication of a return to natural law thinking. I can think of new and more subtle forms of legal positivism in which the emphasis on will, power, sanction or command which characterised Hobbes' or Austin's approach is no longer essential. In fact, it is characteristic of the modern approach to the problem of law to discard the notion of will from that of law altogether.

The first and foremost instance I would like to quote in this connection is that of Kelsen's 'pure theory of law'. I am well aware that Kelsen's theory can be interpreted in many different ways; and I am quite willing to concede that, as a 'sanction theory' of law, it can, in some way, be linked to the traditional 'positivist' approach to law—to the notion that law is the command of the sovereign. But if we look at the case a little more closely we can easily see that things are not quite so simple and that in Kelsen himself, and more clearly in that Kelsenian school flourishing on the Continent in recent decades, there is ample indication that the pure theory of law tends to be an entirely formal construction of the legal order in which the element of will—in fact every consideration of the 'content' of the law—can and must be entirely eliminated. The moment in fact that we conceive of the legal order as a construction in degrees—a *Stufenbau*, as Kelsen puts it—in which every legal proposition derives its validity from the step that precedes it; the moment, in other words, we conceive the whole legal system as merely a system of reciprocal coherence and implication—that moment indeed we shall have no need or use for a 'will' to set as it were the whole system in motion. We are in fact bound to recognise that the very notion of a 'will' or a 'sovereign' is nothing other than a 'personification' and an illusion.

Actually, to the Kelsenian, 'sovereignty' is no more than the primary assumption necessary and sufficient for the understanding and the coherent interpretation of a given legal order. The choice of that assumption is a mere matter of convention; though, once the choice is made, the validity of every and each legal proposition will derive from it. There is no intrinsic legal value which a rule can claim apart from the system; in fact, there is no law except 'positive' law. Natural law holds no brief with Kelsen and his followers.

I turn now to another, quite different approach to the problem of the nature of law which provides a good illustration of what I have called the 'positivist' attitude in modern legal thinking. Here again the emphasis is no longer on will or command. Yet there is no indication that the abandonment of the will-theory of law should point towards a revival of natural law thinking. The kind of approach of which I am speaking strikes me as particularly fashionable among present-day English legal and political theorists. It is based on an analogy which seems to have a special appeal to the English—the analogy between law and the 'rules of a game'. Actually—though I am not aware that any of my Oxford friends who make use of the analogy ever refer to their direct antecedent— the analogy can clearly be traced back to the father of legal positivism himself. In his *Questions concerning Liberty, Necessity and Chance*, Hobbes says at one point: 'In the same manner as men in playing turn up trump, and as in playing their game their morality consisteth in not renouncing, so in our civil conversation our morality is all contained in not disobeying of the laws.' This analogy must have pleased Hobbes a lot, for he makes use of it also in the *Leviathan*. Most clearly, and in his own unforgettable way, he repeats it in *A Dialogue of the Common Law*: 'For such authority (of defining final punishments) is to trump in card playing, save that in matter of government when nothing else is turned up, clubs are trumps.'[1] Hobbes was indeed a great writer; he knew how to coin a phrase, and to hit a nail on the head.

Let us turn now to some English writers talking about law and the rules of the game. Professor Hart—I quote again from his recent inaugural lecture—remarks: 'The language involved in the enunciation and application of rules constitutes a special segment of human discourse with special features which lead to confusion if neglected. Of this type of discourse the law is one very complex example, and sometimes to see its features we need to look away from the law to simpler cases which in spite of many differences share these features. The economist or the scientist often uses a simple model with which to understand the complex, and this can be done for the law. So in what follows I shall use as a simple analogy the rules of a game which at many vital points have the same puzzling logical structure as rules of law.'

Since Professor Hart is an Englishman, we should not be

[1] Hobbes, 5 *Works*, p. 194 (Molesworth ed., 1841); 6 *id.* p. 122.

surprised if the game to which he refers is a typical English game, one whose rules are little known beyond English shores—I mean cricket. Personally, I have always considered that there are three things difficult for a foreigner to understand about England. The first is the working of the British Constitution: that can be learned with patient application and sound work. The second is the peculiar essence of the Church of England: that too can be understood with the exercise of some charity and good will. But the real stumbling block for a foreigner is the rules of cricket: they, to be sure, must be learned from early childhood on an English village green! So I cannot help feeling that it is not quite fair on the part of our English friends to force an analogy upon us which we foreigners can hardly be expected to follow in all its delicate and intricate detail. Nevertheless, even without such knowledge of detail, I think it is not altogether impossible to assess what the analogy really amounts to. Let me cite one further quotation from another recent Oxford book.

I am taking this second quotation from a small but provocative book which provides a good insight into what is going on within the walls of my old university. Its author, Mr T. D. Weldon, shows himself well acquainted with those new philosophical methods to which I referred at the beginning of this lecture. The full title of the book is *The Vocabulary of Politics. An Enquiry into the Use and Abuse of Language in the Making of Political Theories*.[1] Mr Weldon is a political philosopher who has a particular gift for bringing out with the utmost clarity (and perhaps with a tinge of boyish perversity) the full implications of a certain line of thought. Here on p. 57, is, what he has to say on the point at issue:

'Let us . . . ask what it means to say that someone has a right to do something. . . . The simple answer which is also the correct one is "Because there is a law in this country to that effect." But this, though correct, is liable to be misleading as will appear shortly. To answer the question fully, one would have to set out fully the whole complicated process by which laws are made and enforced in Great Britain and the way in which legislators themselves are elected. This would be tedious and not many people are competent to do it. Such elaborate elucidations are always boring and usually quite unnecessary. Suppose however the objector goes on to say "Even if it is the law, I don't see why I should obey it." The

---

[1] Penguin Books. First published in 1953.

only further comment possible is "Well, this is Great Britain, isn't it?"

'The position indeed is exactly parallel to that of the cricketer who asks "Why should I obey the umpire? What right has he to give me out?" One can answer only by expounding the rules of cricket, the position of the M.C.C., and so on. Beyond that there is nothing to be done except to say "This is a game of cricket, isn't it?"

'I believe that this is the answer and the complete answer to "What does it mean to say that A has a right to do X?"'

Mr Weldon's manner is certainly challenging. Yet I do not think that I am very far off the mark in saying that the analogy of the game, which is so much in vogue among British legal and political philosophers, does ultimately imply the conclusions which Mr Weldon in the present passage lays down so cogently and neatly. And the question is how to deal with this new and subtle presentation of the positivist case, where law itself, though no longer conceived in the old terms of power relations, is irretrievably and finally severed from any kind of ethical basis.

It should not prove too difficult to point out what is wrong with the analogy between law and the rules of a game. For one thing, I am not sure that we can take that analogy at its face value. As Professor Fuller has pointed out in *The Law in Quest of Itself*,[1] this doctrine which purports to be positive, unemotional, matter-of-fact, is in fact itself steeped in a romantic, emotional aura. On closer inspection, the 'game theory' of law can well appear as 'a quite legitimate attempt to rally to the support of positivism the sporting instinct which takes pride in knowing and observing the rules of the game'. How true is this remark, and how easily one could sustain it from the personal experience of professed sceptics who are clearly intensely loyal and 'moral' men! And we have after all Hobbes' own authority for speaking of a 'morality' of the game itself.

But there are, I believe, stronger and more decisive objections to the purely positivistic approach to law as the rules of a game. For indeed this approach seems to forget that the main difference between law and the rules of a game is that the rules of a game are freely chosen and submitted to. We are free to play cricket; we are indeed—those of us who have not been born and bred in England—free to ignore its rules; and nobody can ever oblige us to learn them. But we are not free to ignore or to disregard the laws

[1] p. 105 (1940).

of the land to which we belong or in which we have made our abode. Hobbes' words, once again, are our great reminders: 'save that in matter of government when nothing else is turned up, clubs are trumps'. If we want at all costs to stick to the analogy between law and the rules of a game, let us admit that it is a peculiar game which we are asked to play, and one which has little to do with the placid setting of a sunny English afternoon.

Finally—and this really leads me to the next subject which I would like to broach—it is not only a question that 'clubs are trumps' in matter of government and that therefore we cannot honestly conceive the legal order as equivalent to the rules of an ordinary game. It is not only a question of choosing the game; it is a question of deciding on its merits. Surely a man who plays cricket or plays a game of cards may have his own views about the rules he is observing. He may find them enjoyable or boring, fit for their purpose or needlessly complicated. Nevertheless he need not depart, while he is playing the game, from a detached and noncommittal attitude about the 'goodness' or 'badness' of the rules as they are. He may keep himself emotionally quite unmoved by that problem, bent, as he probably is, merely on passing time or building up his health or showing his prowess. But I defy anyone to assume and maintain the same noncommittal and phlegmatic attitude concerning the body of laws which condition his entire life and possibility of acting. I firmly believe that it is very difficult, if not quite impossible, to conceive our compliance with law as merely compliance with certain conventional rules whose ultimate justification lies in the mere fact of their existence. I do not think, in other words, that the answer: 'This is Great Britain, isn't it?' is quite akin to the answer: 'This is cricket, isn't it?'

Let me try to make my point somewhat more convincing with the aid of another quotation. You will see that the passage is not quite irrelevant to the analogy between law and the rules of a game. In his famous novel, *La Chartreuse de Parme*, the French writer Stendhal tells us the story of the education of a young Italian, Fabrizio del Dongo, in an utterly corrupt society. Fabrizio, the scion of a noble and influential North-Italian family, had dreamt of adventure and glory in the wake of Napoleon. In the gloomy, oppressive atmosphere of Restoration Italy no career is left open to an ambitious young man except one in the Church. This is what Fabrizio's powerful friends and protectors, Count Mosca and the Duchess Sanseverina, have planned for him; and here are the

I

words of advice of the Duchess to Fabrizio, who is about to enter
a seminary.

> Le comte, quit connaît bien l'Italie actuelle, m'a chargé d'une idée
> pour toi. Crois ou ne crois pas a ce qu'on t'enseignera, *mais ne fais
> jamais aucune objection.* Figure-toi qu'on t'enseigne les règles du jeu
> de whist: est-ce que tu ferais des objections aux règles du whist?

> The Count, who knows the conditions of present-day Italy well, has
> given me a suggestion for you. Believe or disbelieve all the things you
> will be taught: *but never raise any objections against them.* Imagine
> that they teach you the rules of whist. Would you make any objections
> to the rules of whist?

To learn the rules of ecclesiastical life as if they were the rules
of whist! It needed Stendhal's cynical turn of mind to conceive
such an analogy. Yet I do not think there is a lesser degree of
cynicism in the analogy between law and the rules of a game.
Surely such rules as involve grave and vital issues about the
whole pattern and purpose of our life cannot be indifferently 'believed' or 'disbelieved'. Not only do we know very well when and
how to 'raise objections' about them, but it may well be that if
we shrug our shoulders and treat them as mere matters of convention we may prove to be bad citizens—just as Stendhal leaves
us in no doubt that his hero turned out a bad priest. No less than
the choice of an ecclesiastical career for the young Fabrizio, our
compliance with the law involves the acceptance of certain 'values'
as obligatory and final. Actually, I am not sure that an assertion
of this kind of value is not contained in that very answer 'This is
Great Britain, isn't it', which only by a great distortion can be
considered akin to the answer 'This is cricket' or 'This is whist'.
For my part, I cannot bring myself to believe that being a good
citizen of the United Kingdom entails the same obligations as
being a good cricketer; and the trouble with the 'game theory',
as well as with the 'pure theory of law', is that neither seems to
provide an answer to that problem of obligation which used to be
the very core of old-fashioned jurisprudence—if you like, of age-
old natural law.

Now this old-fashioned and outmoded jurisprudence had
developed several devices which did help to approach the problem
of the essence of law in a different way altogether. It taught us,
to begin with, to distinguish in every legal proposition two aspects:
the 'form' and the 'content'. Hence it proceeded to distinguish
and classify laws according to these two aspects, and taught that

there may be laws that are 'formally' perfect and yet 'substantially' inadequate, and others that are 'substantially' laws and yet 'formally' imperfect. Incidentally, I would like to point out that some of these distinctions have survived in our Continental lawbooks, where they have nothing more to do with the problem of 'obligation' which was the main concern of natural law theorists.

It is precisely this distinction between the form and the content of the law—whatever its merits—that both the 'game theory' and the 'pure theory of law' seem to overlook. I would venture to say that, as 'formal' interpretations of the law, both are, in their own way, unexceptionable. Actually we owe them both one great and important result: the elimination of the element of will which played such an important part in the early formulation of legal positivism. Their basic assumption is not the imposition of a will on other wills, the command of a sovereign, the power to coerce; it is merely the 'formal' coherence of the system—if you like, the 'fair play' which is the condition for the game being a proper game. They have indeed opened up new avenues for the understanding of the true nature of legal rules: 'reason', not 'will', is the essence of law; but 'reason' means here simply noncontradiction and possibility of logical deduction and construction.

Nevertheless, with regard to the 'content' of the law, these theories clearly indicate the drawbacks of their 'positivism', or—it might be better to say—their 'agnosticism'. Just as Kelsen assures us that there is no system of law not to be understood and construed according to the principles of the *Stufenbau* and the 'basic norm', and just as the choice of the 'basic norm' is merely a matter of hypothesis, so does the 'game theory' leave us entirely indifferent to the kind of game that is played. Nor does it tell us why on earth we should choose to play it. In other words both theories totally disregard the 'content' of the rules and the law, for it is obviously only by looking at that content that a judgment can be passed on their 'goodness' or 'badness'.

If I am not mistaken, one of the essential characteristics of old-time natural law was the stress laid on the *vis directiva* of law as distinguished from its *vis coactiva*. It was the *vis directiva*—the moral content of the law—that ultimately decided about the 'obligatoriness' of the legal precept. There is no denying that to the modern man a doctrine such as this smacks of 'medievalism'. Yet whether we like it or not, the problem of legal obligation does not seem to be properly solved by the positivist approach; and I cannot help being struck by the fact that it seems to have

cropped up again, almost with a vengeance, in modern jurisprudence. I am thinking here especially of one striking piece of
evidence of which I shall make great use in my next lecture. But
I might as well indicate at this point why, in my mind, Professor
Goodhart's recent lectures—*English Law and the Moral Law*—
are also important with regard to the problem we have so far been
discussing.[1]

Professor Goodhart's starting point is very much the same as I
have taken in this lecture. His argument is the normal argument
followed in every treatment of the basic problems of jurisprudence,
the usual survey and criticism of the many and different definitions
of law that have come down to us through the ages. Better and
more forcibly than I may hope to have done myself in my short
introductory remarks, Professor Goodhart points out the inadequacy of the 'force theory' of law; the importance of his
argument appears most strikingly in his conclusion. We cannot
hope to understand anything about the law unless we first try and
divest ourselves of the view of the law with which the 'force theory'
has made us too long familiar. 'Coercion' and 'obligation' are
widely different terms; their interrelation is a very different one
from what is ordinarily assumed: 'it is because a rule is regarded
as obligatory that a measure of coercion may be attached to it:
it is not obligatory because there is coercion'. Hence the key to
the science of jurisprudence is not, as Austin believed, in the word
command, but in the word *obligation*. Indeed, an entirely new
definition of law can be proposed: 'I should define law as any rule
of human conduct which is recognised as being obligatory.'

Here then is a definition of law which I gladly set down at the
end of this lecture, since it affords unexpected and authoritative
support to the main idea that inspired it. I hope that I have
made it sufficiently clear that my purpose in this lecture was not
merely to confute the 'force theory' of law: this has been done
many times, and I would only have repeated commonplace arguments. My purpose was to show the inadequacy of the 'formal'
approach to the problem of law, an approach forgetting that the
predominant feature of law is neither enforcement, nor regularity,
nor fair play, but obligation. But the problem of obligation is not
and cannot be a merely legal problem: by this I mean that it is
not a problem that can be answered by pointing at the mere
existence of law as a fact—a rule that can be enforced by sanctions

[1] Goodhart, *English Law and the Moral Law* (1953), (Hamlyn Lectures, 4th
series, 1952).

or that must be obeyed for the sake of the game. It is, in fact, a 'moral' problem: a problem that refers us to judgments about 'good' and 'bad', to decisions on basic issues that involve our whole life. And this is where Professor Goodhart's approach indicates the correct line which we ought to follow: indeed he himself does pay homage—though a halfhearted one—to the case for natural law. Once again I would like to quote from him—and this will be my final quotation.

I hope to show in [these] lectures (writes Professor Goodhart) [that] our moral conclusions are of basic importance in the formation of our law. In a static period when both law and morals are accepted as more or less fixed it will not be so necessary to analyse our moral concepts, but when our State law is changing it is then necessary for us to seek for a true interpretation of the moral law with which it is so closely associated. I believe that the so-called revival of 'natural law' thinking at the present time is merely an expression of this point of view. It is because we recognise that law cannot be explained in terms of force that we seek to find the moral law which tends to give it its strength.

Professor Goodhart believes that 'as the classic phrase "law of nature" is so highly charged with emotion and has meant so many different things at various times in history . . . it is preferable to speak of moral law instead'. I shall not take issue with him on this point and at this stage. For the importance of what he cóncedes seems far greater than that of what he denies. There are good reasons for re-examining the case of a doctrine which, but for the name, has constantly advocated the very notion which Professor Goodhart extols: viz., that the problem of law is not a mere problem of definition; that the *vis directiva* is as important an element of law as its *vis coactiva*; that the ultimate question with the law is a question of obligation; that, in one word, there is a close and indissoluble interrelation between law and morals.

(II) THE RELATIONSHIP BETWEEN LAW AND MORALS: THE GIST OF THE NATURAL LAW APPROACH

I devoted my first lecture to the problem of the nature of law, and to a brief survey of some aspects of modern legal theory which seems to indicate a rehabilitation of, if not actually a return to, notions and trends of thought familiar to natural law jurisprudence. In my opinion, two points are particularly striking and significant in that connection: the first is the almost general abandonment of the will-theory of law; the second is the notion that 'obligatoriness' is the distinguishing feature of law over and against other rules of conduct.

I would like to take my start in this lecture from Professor Goodhart's contention that, if 'it is the sense of obligation which gives the rule its legal character . . . the relationship between law and morals is of the utmost importance'. I suggest that Professor Goodhart's recent re-examination of the relationship between law and morals may provide us with a most welcome opportunity for assessing the value of the natural law approach to this very old problem.

Professor Goodhart's main argument in his discussion of the relationship between English law and the moral law can be summed up as follows. Morality has played a particularly important part in the development of the common law. Actually, English law and the moral law are not only closely intertwined; they are rarely in conflict. The type of moral law which has had most influence in English law is one 'based on reason, divorced from other authority'—'a pragmatic natural law and not one based on general principles expressed in authoritative sources'.

It seems to me that three separate questions can be raised with regard to Professor Goodhart's argument. The first question is: is his conception of the moral (natural) law acceptable? The second: is his statement about the harmony between English law and the moral law accurate? The third: is his theory of the relationship between a given system of law and the moral law valid only for English law, or for all legal systems?

I shall leave the first question unanswered for the time being. It will be the subject of my next two lectures. I do not think it is at all useful to discuss what 'type' of natural or moral law can provide the ground of obligatoriness of positive law before ascertaining what is the precise relationship between the one and the other. But I may as well say forthwith that a 'pragmatic' natural law—whatever its merits with regard to the ultimate foundation of English law may prove to be—seems a contradiction in terms. Surely if natural or moral law must provide the ground for the obligation of positive law, we must assume that its validity is an absolute one and not one to be estimated (I am taking this definition from the *Oxford Dictionary*, *sub* 'pragmatism') 'solely by its practical bearing upon human interests'.

The second question is one which I am rather hesitant to discuss at all, for it seems a question for the English rather than for ourselves to ask and to answer. I can only say that Professor Goodhart's claim that English law is substantially in harmony with moral law and the law of nature, carries a very great authority. And I would like to add, for the sake of fairness, that there is little or no smugness in the manner in which Professor Goodhart puts forward that claim, and that he himself points out, very straightforwardly, cases in which the harmony is far from complete.

It would be out of place to list such cases here: some actually add a little touch of humour to the treatment of so grave a subject. For instance, Professor Goodhart remarks—on p. 114—that 'our present death duties are against the law of nature'. But there is one point where—as Lord Justice Denning noted in an excellent broadcast review of Professor Goodhart's lectures[1]—his treatment of the problem cannot fail to appear strangely incomplete, as if he himself had shrunk from facing the full implications of the standpoint he takes with regard to the relationship between law and morals. It is the ultimate issue of constitutional law, where Professor Goodhart's 'philosophy' leads to conclusions which—as Lord Justice Denning points out—are basically at variance with the English doctrine that 'parliament can do anything it pleases except make man a woman'. It is not enough to list the 'basic principles which parliament recognises as binding upon it and conversely which the people regard as binding upon parliament'. Neither is it enough to say that it is 'unthinkable' that parliament should disregard these principles—granting arbitrary powers to one man, extending its life indefinitely, abolishing freedom of speech or the independence of the judiciary. 'It may be inconceivable, but what'—Lord Justice Denning asks—'would happen if parliament did it? . . . The answer of Dr Goodhart would be, I fancy, that such questions can never arise, but I do not think that is a satisfactory answer. The only proper answer, consistent with his philosophy, would be that any such action by parliament would be unconstitutional and invalid. This may be the right view, but it is a view which has not been heard in England for more than three hundred years. . . .' Three hundred years is a fair computation. I take it that to Lord Justice Denning Professor Goodhart's 'philosophy', if argued out to its ultimate consequences, would bring us straight back to the heyday of natural

[1] Lord Justice Denning, 'English Law and the Moral Law', *The Listener*, 25 February 1954, pp. 332–33.

law. I cannot think of a greater tribute to the vitality of that old doctrine.

But the third question which I have ventured to raise with regard to Professor Goodhart's treatment of law and morals calls for most serious attention. Professor Goodhart believes—and I am sure every believer in natural law would agree with him on this point—that the moral foundation of law is what provides law itself with its 'obligatoriness'. But he is careful to make this assertion merely with regard to English law, and indeed he goes so far as to say that this recognition that 'there is a vast difference between obedience to force and obedience to law' is 'the greatest contribution which [England] has made to the civilisation of the world'. He believes 'that in no other country in the world is this obligation [of the rule of law against arbitrary command] recognised more clearly than in England, and that the strength of the law is in large part based on this'. This is indeed very pleasing and encouraging, and no doubt it is also historically accurate and true. It would be grossly unfair to read in Professor Goodhart's words an example of British self-righteousness: I need hardly remind you that he is not an Englishman but an American. But the question is: does this notion of the moral obligation of law hold good only for England, or does it apply to other countries as well? In other words, does the relationship between law and morals appear in a different light if we look at it from England or from the Continent? Personally, I would be inclined to answer this question in the affirmative, and I shall presently give my reasons for doing so. Professor Goodhart himself seems to indicate that this is the case, and once again I shall take the liberty of quoting from his book—this time from a lengthy footnote on page 21.

Professor Goodhart refers to the views of a well-known German legal philosopher, Rudolf Stammler, and to the Neo-Kantian theory of law as an external regulation of human conduct—from which it follows that the inclinations, motives or personal opinions of the person that conforms to the law, as internal processes, are entirely immaterial. Here is Professor Goodhart's comment on this theory: 'It is remarkable to find a legal philosopher accepting the view that it is immaterial whether a person submits out of respect for the law or out of fear. All those who live under the common law may reflect with some pride that Anglo-American history is in large part meaningless unless the distinction between the two is realised.' This time I am inclined to wonder whether Professor Goodhart is not a little bit too complacent about the Anglo-American heritage. This, however, is a question for the historian to answer, and indeed for every one of you to assess in the light of an experience which I have not the privilege to share. My point is a different one: it is that the doctrine which Professor Goodhart rejects seems to have—and not from the historical angle only—some good grounds which cannot and must not be overlooked.

The distinction between 'externality' and 'internality', and the recognition in the former character of the distinguishing mark of legal experience proper, was notoriously developed into a complete theory by the Neo-Kantian school. But its direct antecedent is Kant's distinction between legality and morality, his definition of legality as the possibility of external coercion, from which it follows that law as such can entail only external obligation, while moral behaviour involves motive, and thus the relevance of those internal processes which are irrelevant to the coerciveness of law.

I have always wondered whether Kant's distinction is not, in some ways, a restatement, in strict philosophical terms, of an experience which is deeply rooted in the tradition of Western man. I have always been reminded, in this connection, of a passage from St Paul familiar to all Christians, which enjoins us to respect authority not only for fear but for conscience' sake: *Subditi estote non solum propter iram sed etiam propter conscientiam* (Rom. xiii, 5). Surely this passage seems to endorse that very notion which Professor Goodhart finds strange and startling: does it not state clearly that there are two possible ways of being subject to authority, and of conforming to the law, and that obedience for conscience' sake—that is, out of a feeling of the obligatoriness of the law itself—is a religious or moral duty, and not strictly speaking a legal one? Actually I believe the recognition that law as such does not entail the same kind of obligation as a moral imperative runs through the whole of our European history. Still it is significant that it should have been resorted to and developed into new and unheard-of consequences only at a certain moment in that history—in fact at the very time of Continental absolutism, when men became aware that even though the law of the State has the highest compulsory power, it must and cannot fail to stop short before the inviolable shrine of man's conscience, which no coercion can bind. It is indeed very important to notice that the demand for a clear and sharp demarcation between law and morals arises in the seventeenth century, at the end of a long period of religious strife and social insecurity, when the modern Leviathan comes forward, saying as it were: 'I am going to give you the peace and security for which you crave, provided you obey my laws. But I am asking nothing more from you except the mere fact of obedience. Your religion, your Churches proclaim *da mihi animas cetera tolle.* I shall take the *cetera* and leave *animas* free, for I am not concerned with anything else than outward conformity.' It is on an assumption of this kind, if I am not mistaken, that the modern, secular State came into being in Europe. Looking at it historically, we must admit that the doctrine of the 'externality' of law has some justification.

But we can, if we like, also look in other directions. The problem of the distinction between legal and moral obligation was far from being unknown to medieval jurists and philosophers. I find, for instance, that two points are made by St Thomas Aquinas in his discussion of the law, which have a close bearing on the problem under discussion. One is the existence of purely 'penal' laws, viz., of laws which do not oblige in conscience to what the law commands, but only to the payment of the penalty in case of violation: 'external' laws, laws which we obey *propter iram*, to which we submit for fear of the sanction; laws which have no moral obligatoriness. This problem has caused much ink to flow: note the excellent treatment of it in Fr Davitt's book, *The Nature of Law*, published in 1951.

But there is another aspect of the same problem discussed by the School-men—and well worth mentioning were it only to show that the old natural law theory has had something to say about problems which seem to us so modern and burning. It is the question discussed by St Thomas as he examines how far the law actually can go in turning men to the path of virtue. This is, as it were, the reverse of the problem of the purely penal law. If we accept—as no doubt any natural law theorist is bound to do in the end—Professor Goodhart's contention that law obliges not merely because of fear but because of its intrinsic obligatoriness—if, in other words, we maintain that law has a moral content, a *vis directiva* besides its *vis coactiva*—are we not really asking the law to make men virtuous? But can we really maintain that law can do so? Can morality be enacted? Now St Thomas appears to be extremely sensitive to this problem, and in the *Summa Theologica*[1] he points out—in fact he admits—that though law

[1] 1a 2 ae, 96, 3, ad 2um.

can enforce virtuous actions, it cannot secure the execution of these actions *eo modo quo virtuosus operatur*. Bad men will conform to the law without, by their action, becoming virtuous.

The gist of my argument is this. Professor Goodhart is certainly right in saying that it is not immaterial whether laws are obeyed out of respect or out of fear. He may well be right in maintaining that in no country in the world is the moral obligation of law recognised more clearly than in England; and if this be the case we may well congratulate the English on that score. But the coincidence in Anglo-Saxon countries of moral and legal obligation does not prove that this is always the case. There may be other types of societies where the moral obligatoriness of the law is not recognised, or not felt with the same degree of intensity. Yet such societies are held together by laws—purely 'penal' laws if you like—but sufficient and adequate to ensure peace and order. Out of this recognition that legal and moral obligation do not always coincide the necessity has sprung of drawing the line between respect and fear, between submission to the law *propter iram* and *propter conscientiam*, in fact of distinguishing between legality and morality. It is a very long way from St Thomas to Kant: still there is a link between them in their effort to understand the essence of legal experience. There is no doubt a very great difference in the way in which they conceive the relationship between law and morals; but they are substantially in agreement in conceiving morals and law as two different spheres, and in recognising the limits of law as an essentially external regulation.

This recognition of the limits of law and of the possibility that law may be obeyed merely out of fear, which makes the 'motives' immaterial, is what, if I am not mistaken, your great jurist Holmes called 'the bad man theory of law'. But, to be sure, the 'bad man' theory of law is very often nothing but the consequence of bad government. And I would suggest that if Continental nations have developed that theory which shocks Professor Goodhart so deeply, the reason is that they have not always been very happy in their political experience. Bad governments breed fear, not respect for the law; this has unfortunately been the case all too often on the continent of Europe. I would not like this judgment to be taken too literally. We have had, after all, some good governments. We have some now. But I think that the 'bad man' notion of law is, on the whole, the attitude prevailing on the Continent; and with my long experience of life in Great Britain, and my much shorter experience of life here in the United States,

I have noticed many times that when it comes to the point of discussing the problem of the obligation of law there is a fundamental difference in attitude between you and us. It lies in this: that you will never really persuade a Continental that there is some deep, inherent moral duty to obey the law; obey it he will, but if he can find a loop-hole, he will use it.

I do not want to over-idealise the English. I am quite sure that they too do not always find moral relish in obeying their laws, and I doubt that finding a loophole they may not be tempted to use it. But, on the whole, the Anglo-Saxons are undoubtedly a law-abiding people. On the whole, they obey *propter conscientiam* and not only *propter iram*: while to the average Continental, law is never much more than a necessary nuisance, an external regulation which must be observed to avoid the worst, but certainly not for the sake of a joyful conscience. This attitude is not necessarily an attitude of lawlessness or anarchy. I have heard this point made only too often on the other side of the Channel: let me assure you that not all Latins are black-marketers or racketeers. But there is no escaping the fact that our attitude to law is on the whole a different attitude from yours; it is an attitude which has probably been bred by a long practice of self-defence against the encroachments of the State, and also perhaps by a different experience of social and corporate life, by an age-long difference and contrast of political and religious bonds, by the very fact of belonging, as it were by birthright, to a society different from the 'State', a society like the Church which claims the supreme control of 'conscience', and openly proclaims against the State *da mihi animas cetera tolle*.

I am not sure that this long digression succeeds in justifying the view which Professor Goodhart considers untenable, viz., in showing that there is some element of truth, and that there certainly are some good historical grounds, in stressing 'externality' as the distinguishing mark of legal experience. I need not add that, when it comes to the point of defining the relationship between law as an external regulation of conduct and morals as a consideration of motives and internal processes I am—and cannot fail to be—entirely on Professor Goodhart's side. In fact, I do not think that any believer in natural law could disagree with him on that score. Law may or may not be obeyed for the sake of its obligatoriness. But there is only one ground for the obligation of the law, and this is a moral ground. In discussing the relationship between English law and the moral law Professor

Goodhart has collected his evidence and built up his case from a particularly happy experience: the experience of a nation where, in fact, positive and moral law broadly coincide, and the obligatoriness of the law is admitted and recognised clearly and without discussion. It is what I would call the case of the 'good society': for it is only in a good society that there is no divorce between morals and law and that men obey not out of fear but out of conviction. Let us then say that the 'good society' is the goal which law-givers and politicians should set themselves, the condition of things in which, as Aristotle put it, the 'good man' is also a 'good citizen'. The problem is, can the good society be attained, and if so, by what means? This is, of course, no longer a legal but a political programme; but I have an impression that a political assumption underlies Professor Goodhart's presentation of England as the good society. Is it not ultimately because of the adoption of the democratic principle that, in Anglo-Saxon countries, the harmony of positive and moral law has had the best chance to survive? Democracy seems indeed the modern answer to the problem of ensuring that laws be obeyed not only out of fear but out of conviction, insofar as it implies the consent of the governed to government itself. This, at any rate, seems to me the strongest argument that has ever been put forward in favour of democracy, and it is the argument that was first developed in Rousseau's *Social Contract*.

The mention of Rousseau's name may well seem strange in a discussion of natural law theory. And yet that name is a landmark not only in modern political theory, but in legal theory as well. For it is Rousseau who outlined the case for democracy as the 'good society' precisely on the ground that only by means of the democratic principle can legal and moral obligation be brought to coincide. Once again I would like to go back to a few fundamental texts, and to take the argument, so to speak, straight from the horse's mouth. My first text is from the *Social Contract*, bk. I, ch. 6, where Rousseau states that the fundamental problem of politics is to find 'a form of association . . . in which each, while uniting himself with all, may still obey himself alone, and remain as free as before'. The second passage, from bk. I, ch. 8, reads as follows: 'We might, over and above all this, add to what man acquires in the civil state, moral liberty, which alone makes him truly master of himself; for the mere impulse of appetite is slavery, while obedience to a law which we prescribe to ourselves is liberty.'

Surely these two striking passages are familiar to anyone who
has done some reading in political theory. They are striking and
familiar not only because Rousseau, like Hobbes, is a very great
writer; indeed, the whole eighth chapter of the first book of the
Contrat Social is one that is not easy to forget, for in it Rousseau
describes, in an almost religious language, what happens when
man, having entered the social contract, becomes a citizen, thus
acquiring the full dignity of mankind. It is like a rebirth, a radical
transformation; and I think, for my part, that those writers are
perfectly justified who, pointing out that Rousseau was a son of
Calvinist Geneva, have remarked that there is something almost
Calvinistic in this idea of a rebirth, of the new man, the new
Adam, being made by entering civil society. Truly, what Rousseau
does here is to endow democracy with a moral and religious halo,
because for Rousseau the good society is only that one which can
ensure that man, in obeying the law, obeys himself according to
the democratic principle. Hence only in democracy can moral and
legal obligation coincide, and obedience to the law fulfill a moral
duty. Whether we like it or not, Rousseau remains the supreme
prophet and theorist of modern democracy.

Of course, when we think of Rousseau, we cannot help thinking,
and rightly, of all that comes with him and after him. As Dr
Berlin reminded us in his brilliant lectures over the BBC,[1] this
prophet of freedom turned out to be 'the most sinister and most
formidable enemy of liberty in the whole history of modern
thought'. With Rousseau comes the idea that freedom lies in
obedience, in fact that men can be forced to be free. After
Rousseau we soon drift away from true democracy; in fact we
drift, via the Hegelian State, straight towards the doctrine of
totalitarianism.

But let us cherish no delusion about totalitarian States. I
have myself lived in one for twenty years, and I think I got to
know their techniques long before reading George Orwell's *1984*.
Totalitarian States claim to be the 'good society'. They claim to be
the good society because they maintain that, by belonging to them,
the individual leads *the* good life, that, in other words, by finding
in the State his 'real self', his true moral nature, man will cease to
obey out of fear, but obey out of conscience and full conviction.
It is here, I believe, that we must find the root of that equivocation
of the word 'democracy' that rends the modern world.

Rousseau's definition of democracy as the good society thus

[1] *Freedom and its betrayal*, six lectures, BBC Third Programme, 1952.

appears a landmark as well as a warning. It provides the strongest argument in favour of democracy, indicating that, by means of the democratic principle, the cleavage between legal and moral obligation can be overcome, inasmuch as that principle will ensure that the laws express a prevailing moral conviction. But it also indicates the dangers that lie at hand, and perhaps even the reason why democracy can run amok and turn into the worst kind of tyranny. Rousseau's 'general will', which is always right, is the prototype of the modern tyrant.

I do not think that we in the West can have much use for that sort of democracy. We ought to remember that the Western idea of democracy has sprung from a different seed and grown under different auspices. Indeed, it is precisely at this point that we are made aware of the impact on us of the old natural law thinking. Natural law, with its necessary counterpart of natural rights, has left a lasting mark on our way of conceiving the bond of political obligation. For one thing, it has taught us to conceive politics as a method rather than an end, and to conceive democracy itself as the best method so far devised to realise certain ends, from which alone the 'good life' will follow. But it has also taught us not to assume without reservations that the 'general will' is always right, and that the prevailing moral convictions of a given society are not yet a proof of their absolute value. Natural law is indeed an answer to the problem stated by Rousseau, the problem of reconciling moral and legal obligation, obedience out of fear and for conscience' sake. But it is a very different answer from that given by Rousseau, for it states that only through the recognition of certain supreme values can the law of the State be something other than a mere coercive imposition. Only when the rights of man are secured can democracy be a true democracy.

Surely it is neither smugness nor pride to say that this has been the case with Western democracies. Great indeed is the debt of the modern world to such countries as Britain and the United States, where, through the happy medium of democracy, and not without bitter strife and relentless struggle, the harmony has been secured between the general will and the rights of man, between the rule of law and the respect for the highest values of freedom and morality. But let their present success not blind us, nor make us forget the blood and tears it has cost to achieve it, nor the danger which is always at hand of its being disrupted and destroyed. Suppose it did happen. Suppose one of the instances outlined by Lord Justice Denning actually took place. Have they not taken place in other countries, and within our memory? What then? Surely it would be in keeping with the democratic principle—the supremacy of the general will—to accept even the abolition of democracy, and to do like the Roman Senators whom Tacitus describes as running into servitude. But there can also be another answer, inspired by a view which, as Lord Justice Denning pointed out, has not been heard for a long time—at least in England. And yet we ourselves have seen in our generation brave men and women taking that view: men and women who, rather than submit to injustice and tyranny, took the bitter road into exile, or actually staked their lives for the sake of the cause of humanity. Shall we say that good old natural law took its revenge? I would prefer to frame my conclusions more cautiously.

Any analysis of the relationship between law and morals must lead to the recognition that there is a difference between legal and moral obligation, a difference that does not necessarily entail separation. There must be a name for the relationship between the two, for the principle that spans the chasm that divides them, thus bringing law and morals into harmony. I have suggested elsewhere[1] that this is one of the meanings, one of the essential meanings, in which the term 'natural law' has been used through the ages. It is a convenient name for indicating the ground of obligation of law, which alone can ensure that the law itself is obeyed not only *propter iram* but *propter conscientiam*. And it is a no less convenient name for indicating the limits of the obligatoriness of the law, the crucial point: on it depends whether the injunction of the law is more than mere coercion.

Let me then turn back for a moment and survey our progress so far. If we have not yet found a definition of natural law, we have at any rate come across a number of things which seem to be implied in natural law thinking. We have found that law is no mere command, no arbitrary choice, for it involves a problem of obligation; we have found that it is impossible to understand this problem of obligation without examining the relationship between law and morals; and I have just suggested that, to express the 'point of intersection' between law and morals, our benighted forbears had a name, natural law. And yet I doubt that natural law thinkers, old and new, would rest content with a definition of natural law as nothing but a name for the moral foundation of law, as nothing but the attempt to explain law in terms not of force or convention, but of obligation. They would, I surmise,

[1] **In** the conclusion of *Natural Law* above, pp. 108–116.

consider such a definition as inadequate, and I think they would be right. For the most important feature of natural law is to stress not only the existence of a problem, but actually to provide an answer to it. Natural law theorists would point out that not all solutions of the problem of law and morals are equally valid, and that, if it were a matter merely of explaining the obligatoriness of the law, Rousseau's general will can do that very well. They would emphatically assert that the only valid ground of legal obligation is given by a Law—an unwritten law, an ideal law—to which we can and must refer as the model or standard on which all laws depend and from which they derive their obligation.

We are thus brought to the third, and perhaps the most important, of the three characteristics of natural law thinking, the one to which I propose to devote my last two lectures. Needless to say, I shall endeavour to approach this last and most awkward side of my subject with the same caution I have practised so far. I hope you will bear me no grudge for doing so. There are, after all, many mansions in the House of the Father; and if all natural law theorists agree on the existence of the ideal law, they have differed, and are bound to differ, in the manner of conceiving and defining it. We must therefore examine these differences with an open mind: this, at any rate, is my own personal conviction, and it is based not only on my own misgivings, but on the belief, which I have stressed from the start, that our purpose here is to find a common ground of understanding, and not to hoist a banner or to put forward a 'blueprint' of ready-made solutions.

In brief, then, what I propose to do is to examine how, in different times and in different ways, the ideal law has been conceived and defined. In my mind, these conceptions and definitions seem to fall, roughly, under three main types or headings. These are and must be purely provisional headings. I think in fact that the moment we start classifying 'types' or 'patterns of thought' we run the risk of killing the very thing we are studying. But in very rough outline it seems that the notion of natural law has been, and can be, worked out in three different directions. The first is that of the ideal or natural law as a kind of 'technology'; the second I would call the notion of natural law as an 'ontology'; and the third might perhaps best be described as a 'deontology'.

I am well aware that both classification and headings are open to criticism. I can only say that I am ready to accept any criticism on that score. I shall do my best, not to justify them, but to

K

explain what I actually mean by them. I shall try to approach each of these different versions of the age-old problem of natural law with fairness and sympathy, though I shall not conceal my preference for that version which, in the predicament of our times, seems to me likely to assure the greatest possibility of understanding and agreement.

(III) THE KNOWLEDGE OF AN IDEAL LAW: THE CHALLENGE OF NATURAL LAW THEORIES

My task in the last two lectures is the examination of the various types or headings under which the attempts to define natural law— as the ideal or standard by which all laws can be valued and on which their obligation depends—may be classified. Before beginning this examination, and before even trying to explain if not to justify my headings, one point, which is a common mark of all and each of such attempts, calls for attention.

There is no denying that the very assertion of the existence and possibility of knowledge of an ideal law is the most serious challenge which natural law theory offers modern thought. Natural law is a stumbling block, indeed perhaps a scandal to the modern: and the reason, so we are told, is that the distinction between 'fact' and 'value', the opposition, in other words, between what *is* and what *ought to be*, has become, after Kant, the cornerstone of modern ethics. Kant's doctrine of the 'autonomy of the will' is usually taken to mark the end of the natural law tradition.

I do not propose to discuss this view at this stage, a view which— to my mind at any rate—is subject to many reservations. But I would like to point out that if we want to go back to the real source of the distinction between 'fact' and 'value', if we want to have before our eyes—as we have on some other occasions—a clear and downright statement of the case, we can do no better than turn to a passage from Hume:

I cannot forbear adding to these reasonings an observation, which may, perhaps, be found of some importance. In every system of morality which I have hitherto met with, I have always remarked, that the author proceeds for some time in the ordinary way of reasoning, and establishes the being of a God, or makes observations concerning human affairs: when of a sudden I am surprised to find, that instead of the usual copulations of propositions, *is,* and *is not*, I meet with no proposition that is not connected with an *ought*, or an *ought not*. This change is imperceptible; but it is, however, of the last consequence. For as this *ought,* or *ought not*, expresses some new relation or affirmation, it is necessary that it should be observed and explained; and at the same time that a reason should be given, for what seems altogether inconceivable, how this new relation can be a deduction from others, which are entirely different from it.[1]

I doubt that the main objection to natural law thinking could be put forward with more clarity and cogency than in this classic statement. It is the objection to what in the language of the modern semanticists is called the passage from the indicative to the imperative mood, an objection, one must admit, based on a perfectly accurate description of what natural law theorists are ultimately after. Rather than countering the objection forthwith, I am inclined to accept the description, and indeed enlarge it so far as to venture a new definition of natural law as the attempt to bridge the chasm between *is* and *ought*, between 'fact' and 'value'. The classification I have proposed is in fact nothing other than the story of these different attempts: it remains to see to what extent they have been and can hope to be successful.

One first attempt is that of conceiving natural law as a 'technology'. This is an ugly word, which has gained undue popularity. This is what makes me specially reluctant to use it. But I have my reasons for doing so. Technology, according to the *Oxford Dictionary*, means 'science of the industrial arts'. But I do not think that I am forcing that meaning unduly by suggesting that it is a convenient name for indicating the knowledge of the rules of a particular art or craft (τέχνη)—the 'know-how', as the phrase now goes. And I believe that to many jurists, old and new, natural law was just this: the knowledge of the right rule, of the correct solution to a given problem in law, the answer that lies 'in the nature of things', and which it is only a matter of finding and applying in order to have good laws.

Such at any rate—unless I am grossly mistaken—seems to have been in its broadest sense the Roman conception of natural law, on the importance of which I need hardly linger. Right at the beginning of the *Digest* we find the jurist Celsus defining law— *Jus*—as *ars boni et aequi*. Surely, an 'art' has its rules. Surely, therefore, there must be some means, some instrument for finding out the *bonum et aequum*. *Jus naturale* was that instrument. I am well aware of the ambiguities of the texts that have been handed down to us by Justinian. They are, and always will be, a

[1] *Treatise of Human Nature*, bk. III ('Of Morals'), pt. I, §1.

matter of controversy. Of late, the most authoritative interpreters have warned us against the mistake of conceiving the Roman notion of *jus naturale* as a philosophical construction. They draw a sharp line between the sweeping generalisations of such writers as Cicero and Seneca, and the 'professional constructions' of the lawyers who are included in Justinian's book. *Jus naturale* was to these lawyers not a complete and ready-made system of rules, but essentially a means of interpretation, almost, as it were, the 'trick of the trade' which they resorted to and used in a masterly fashion. In shaping a body of laws which would apply to the whole civilised world they had no abstract theories in mind, but aimed at the workable and practical.

If we consider and compare the several definitions of natural law which are contained in the first section of the *Digest* we undoubtedly find many contradictions.[1] But these contradictions, however puzzling, are comparatively much less important than the fundamental agreement on one point, viz., on the view that there is no problem in law that cannot be solved, provided the *constans et perpetua voluntas* is there, *jus suum cuique tribuendi*. 'What natural reason dictates to all men,' 'what nature has taught all animals'—this is what the jurist and the lawgiver must keep in mind if they are to do their job well and construct a system that may prove *semper bonum et aequum*.

Clearly, this is not a philosophical proposition. It looks much rather like the 'science of an art' according to the definition in the *Oxford Dictionary*. I cannot help being reminded, in connection with this Roman notion of natural law, of what seems to me a modern version of the same conception. I am thinking of Professor Fuller's assertion of the existence of a 'natural order' underlying group life, which it is the task of the judge—and the law-giver—to discover.[2] I would almost be tempted to apply to the Roman notion of natural law his remark, that there is 'nothing mystical' about it, that our attitude in approaching this kind of natural law is not 'that of one doing obeisance before an altar, but more like that of a cook trying to find the secret of a flaky pie crust, or of an engineer trying to devise a means of bridging a ravine'. I rather like to think of the Roman lawyers as cooks and engineers. The pie they cooked and the bridge they built were certainly remarkably good if they proved so successful all through the ages.

---

[1] I have discussed these contradictions at length in ch. 2 of my *Natural Law*.
[2] Fuller, See note 2 above, p. 124.

Their 'technology' was excellent. They did find the best working law for long centuries.

I would hardly dare to press my parallel much further. Yet, in another place, Professor Fuller provides me with some additional proof of what I have called the 'technological' approach to our problem.[1] 'Because of the confusions invited by the term "natural law" ' he has recently recommended a new name for the field of study which natural law used to cover; and he suggests the term 'eunomics' for 'the science, theory or study of good order and workable arrangements'. 'Eunomics,' Professor Fuller assures us, 'involves no commitment to "ultimate ends".' Its primary concern 'is with the means aspect of the means-end relation'. I surmise that one of the tasks of 'eunomics' would be to discover the 'natural laws of social order' as the best working laws in view of the particular ends of a given society.

Now Professor Fuller's theory provides me with the best definition of what I have called the technological notion of natural law. But it also provides me with the main objection which I would move against that notion. In plain, everyday language, the objection is that the 'best working' law is not necessarily the 'best' law. But that objection can also be put in more philosophical idiom by recalling the capital distinction between 'technical' and 'categorical' imperatives, a distinction which, to my mind, could hardly be more pertinent than in this case. The distinction is the one which Kant makes in the *Foundations of the Metaphysics of Morals*, sect. 2: 'All imperatives command either hypothetically or categorically. The former present the practical necessity of a possible action as a means to achieving something else which one desires (or which one may possibly desire). The categorical imperative would be one which presented an action as of itself objectively necessary, without regard to any other end.' Subsequently, Kant distinguishes hypothetical imperatives as 'technical' (belonging to art), and 'pragmatic' (belonging to welfare).

If anything, both the *jus naturale* of the Roman lawyers and Professor Fuller's 'natural law of the social order' are hypothetical or technical imperatives in the Kantian sense. They are hypothetical inasmuch as they are means to an end, and technical insofar as they pertain to an 'art'—though if one chose to call them 'pragmatic' according to Kant's definition this would not alter their 'hypothetical' character. If there were any doubts

[1] 'American Legal Philosophy at Mid-Century', *Journal of Legal Education* (1954), **6**, 457.

about it, here is an illustration given by Professor Fuller which clearly indicates the 'technical' character of the law which, to him as to the Romans, lies in the *natura rei*. Suppose a man wants to assemble an engine: he can obviously do so only if he knows the proper rules of his job. There is no doubt that one such rule (and probably one only) exists. My comment would be that the finding out of this rule has nothing to do with the decision to do the job: our man could very well give up his attempts to assemble the engine and turn to some more congenial occupation. To determine the means for an end is a quite different matter from ascertaining the 'objective necessity' of the end itself: in other words, there is no warrant for turning a technical (hypothetical) imperative into a categorical one.

To conceive natural law as a 'technology' is not to help us solve our problem of obligation. There is no intention to belittle its value and use; indeed these may be great within proper limits. By the help of *jus naturale* the Roman jurists worked out a system of laws which fitted men's needs for many centuries. And the modern lawgiver must keep the 'nature of things' in mind, if he wants his laws to be fitting and efficient. I guess this is what is meant by saying—in the current jargon—that laws must conform to the existing 'sociological requirements'. The penalty for disregarding such requirements may be a heavy one:

Lawgivers are normally fairly sensible and therefore avoid imposing laws . . . which can be obeyed only by a wide departure from normal or probable behaviour. . . . Sometimes they go wrong on this (as the legislators of the United States did with the 18th Amendment)—and then there is trouble. Rationing and restrictions always breed black markets. But . . . lawgivers do not have to act sensibly nor do they have to consider exclusively the interests of their own social group. There is a statistical probability that they will do so, but to suppose that there is any necessity in all this is simply to become confused about the logical grammar of 'law'.

Once again I have quoted from Mr Weldon's little book.[1] I think his rather caustic remarks bring out very neatly the point I have been trying to make. There is no proper link between 'statistical probability' and moral obligation. The penalty for disregarding the 'nature of things' or the 'sociological requirements' does not provide any ground for asserting the absolute validity of the rules or laws deduced from them. Actually such laws are nothing more than statements of facts, even though

[1] *The Vocabulary of Politics* (1953), p. 67.

cloaked in an 'ought' proposition—as when we say: 'if you want to accelerate you ought to press the pedal'. It is a delusion to think that they can provide that bridge between the *is* and the *ought*, between 'facts' and 'values' which we are seeking.

With all its great credentials—which it would be blindness to deny—natural law as a technology does not provide the answer to our problem. Or, if it does so, it is only by assuming an end as the only right end to pursue, by surreptitiously introducing a 'value' behind the 'fact', and discarding the 'hypothetical' for a 'categorical' imperative. Personally, I am not sure that the Roman lawyers did not after all do something of the sort, and I am quite willing to admit that, if this were proved to be so, my strictures on the *jus naturale* would no longer be valid. But in that case we would probably have to subsume the Roman theory of natural law into that second category of natural law thinking to which I am now turning.

I shall devote the remainder of this lecture to examining this second type—if I may call it so—of natural law theory. I must say at once that this second type seems by far the most solidly grounded. The reservations which I shall have to make about it are not so much reservations on its philosophical basis, which is a very strong one; they are inspired by the very difficulty it presents for the common man, as well as by some serious misgivings about its supposed implications.

The second type has a name, a name which it deliberately gives itself. So this time I need not spend many words to justify my terminology. It is the ontological conception of natural law—the doctrine of natural law as an 'ontology' (ὄν, ὄντος—what is). With regard to the problem of bridging the chasm between *is* and *ought*, between 'fact' and 'values', this doctrine would appear to seize the bull by its horns, and to reply to Hume's challenge: there is no chasm; your distinction is a wrong one. The ontological approach welds together being and oughtness, and maintains that the very notion of natural law stands and falls on that identification. This point is so important that I would like to clarify and emphasise it with the help of two quotations.

My first quotation comes from Professor Rommen:

The natural law . . . depends on the science of being, on metaphysics. Hence every attempt to establish the natural law must start from the fundamental relation of being and oughtness, of the real and the good.

From Professor Wild I am selecting the following sentence:

All genuine natural law philosophy . . . must be unreservedly ontological in character. It must be concerned with the nature of existence
in general, for it is only in the light of such basic analysis that the moral
structure of human life can be more clearly understood.[1]

The fact that two thinkers approaching the problem from
different angles agree so completely on this point seems to me
particularly eloquent. Professor Rommen has a further and
important remark:

The idea of natural law obtains general acceptance only in the periods
where metaphysics, queen of the sciences, is dominant. It recedes or
suffers an eclipse, on the other hand, when being . . . and oughtness,
morality and law, are separated, when the essence of things and their
ontological order are viewed as unknowable.[2]

This last contention seems indeed to have very wide implications. It might be taken to mean that the very notion of natural
law is an indication of 'metaphysical' thinking. Thus it would
open up some very interesting lines of research on the 'metaphysics' underlying some 'modern' conceptions of natural law—
such as the conceptions of natural law which were so prominent
and indeed so effective in the seventeenth and the eighteenth
century. But this is clearly not what Professor Rommen has in
mind, for to him there is one system, and one system only, which
bases natural law on the 'ontological order of things'—and this
is the system of Thomist philosophy. There is no denying that
St Thomas Aquinas' doctrine of natural law still represents
the most carefully thought out presentation of the ontological view,
the most complete and thoroughgoing development both of its
assumptions and of its implications.

I do not think that I need spend many words on the merits of
St Thomas' doctrine of natural law. Personally, I would like to
stress that in the eyes of the historian that doctrine is the embodiment of a great tradition, the tradition that proceeds from Greek
and Roman thought and is welded to Christianity. In my view a
further merit of the Thomist conception of natural law is that it
does not reject that technical notion of natural law which the
Roman lawyers had emphasised. On the contrary, it makes the

[1] *Plato's Modern Enemies and the Theory of Natural Law*, (1953), p. 172.
[2] Both quotations from Rommen in this paragraph are from *The Natural Law*
(1947), p. 161.

largest possible use of it; it is just because St Thomas was well trained in the law that his natural law has an eminently practical and realistic cast.

It is, beyond that, an almost unique example of closely knit philosophical argumentation. Its basis—in Professor Rommen's words—is a 'conception of an order of reality' established in its essence by God's wisdom, and proceeding in its existence from God's will. It therefore provides an answer to each and every problem touched upon in this discussion: the relationship between reason and will in law, as well as the relationship between moral and legal obligation. In fact, if natural law is to be defined as the bridge between *is* and *ought*, between 'facts' and 'values', St Thomas' definition of it stands out for its cogency and conciseness: *lex naturalis nihil aliud est quam participatio legis aeternae in rationali creatura*. In the general 'order of reality' man participates because he is a rational being, and hence has the possibility of attaining a knowledge of it. That knowledge thus becomes the condition and the source of all laws pertaining to men: 'being themselves made participators in Providence itself, in that they control their own actions and the actions of others.'[1]

So brief a summary can hardly do justice to St Thomas' theory of natural law. For my part I have tried to do it justice on another occasion,[2] and my purpose here is merely to recall it as a perfect illustration of the 'ontological' approach to our problem. Henceforward I shall willfully assume the role of the *advocatus diaboli*, trying to lay bare the reasons which make for its unpopularity outside a restricted circle of orthodox Thomists. I am still arguing on the assumption that we are here to find a common ground for our case. I still have Professor Goodhart's remark in mind, that 'the real difficulty lies in finding a common basic premise'.

Now it seems to me that in our divided world the first and most serious stumbling block to the Thomist conception of natural law lies precisely in its premise, in that metaphysical premise which both Professor Rommen and Professor Wild tell us is essential to the proper construction of natural law. It is the premise of a divine order of the world which St Thomas recalls at the very beginning of his theory of law, and from which he infers, with unimpeachable logic, the most detailed and specified consequences: *supposito quod mundus divina providentia regatur, ut in Primo habitum est.*[3]

---

[1] *S. Theol.*, 1a 2ae, 91, 2, concl.
[2] *Natural Law* (1951), ch. 3.
[3] *S. Theol.*, 1a 2ae, 91, 1, concl.

Once that premise is granted, the whole majestic edifice of laws can be established on it: eternal law, the natural law, human and divine laws, all are ultimately based on and justified through the existence of a supreme, benevolent Being. In the words of a great English writer, who was also a good Thomist: 'Of Law there can be no less acknowledged, than that her seat is the bosom of God, her voice the harmony of the world.'

I have described this premise of the belief in God and in God's action in the world as a stumbling block. I need hardly add that I would not like to see my words misinterpreted. To be sure, such a belief, far from being a stumbling block to the Christian, is in fact the very essence of his faith. Yet even on this point, as we all well know, Christians have been, and perhaps still are divided. I had my good reasons for taking my last quotation from a Protestant writer, Richard Hooker. Protestant theology has not always been friendly towards the idea of natural law. Thomist natural law is only too often considered to be the exclusive preserve of Roman Catholics. There are, however, encouraging signs that such prejudices are gradually being overcome and the way paved for better understanding among Christians.

In a recent book on the *Law and the Laws*[1] Dr Nathaniel Micklem, Principal of Mansfield College, the Congregational Hall of Oxford, frankly recognises that there was a break in the natural law tradition at the time of the Reformation. He points out that natural law plays very little part in Protestant theology, at least in the theology of the early reformers. But he remarks, 'if the reformers were more pessimistic than the medieval Church they doubted neither that there is a law of nature nor that we may have cognizance of it, *nec tamen extincta est penitus notitia naturalis de Deo* (Melanchton).' Actually, Dr Micklem concludes, the view that natural law commands—that there is an intimate connection between nature, reason and law—'is no fanciful or esoteric theological speculation but a reminder of the *philosophia perennis* significant alike to jurisprudence and theology'.

The last remark undoubtedly shows how very far a modern Protestant theologian can go towards paying homage to the Thomist conception of the law of nature. But the world is not peopled only by Catholics and Protestants. The modern student of law need not necessarily be a Christian. In fact, lawyers have never had a very good reputation on that score: *Juristen böse*

[1] Micklem, *Law and the Laws, being the Marginal Comments of a Theologian* (1952).

Christen! For the agnostic jurist of the present day, and perhaps indeed for the modern man who lives in a 'de-christianised world', it will be very difficult to accept the notion of natural law, if that acceptance is made conditional on the acceptance of the metaphysical premise: *supposito quod mundus divina providentia regatur.* This, to my mind, is the first difficulty for the 'ontological' theory of natural law—a difficulty which may not be a difficulty at all if we simply take the line: 'Well, this is natural law. Take it or leave it.' But we are here to find, if possible, a way of making the argument for natural law acceptable also to people who do not share our own premises.

The second objection is a more practical one. I have spoken of *Juristen* as *böse Christen.* Since I can well expect that such a description might not only cause offence but sound grossly exaggerated, let me try to define their attitude in more general terms as the attitude of men who, having to do with the everyday life and practice of the law, have little time for metaphysical cogitations. It might therefore happen that they accept the 'ontological' notion of natural law because of their religious beliefs, as an essential part of Christian ethics, yet without probing into the problem more deeply; or else that they may have some slight feeling of impatience or embarrassment at being constantly reminded of the necessity of a philosophical and metaphysical training. I am not inventing this objection just for the sake of the argument. A discussion has lately taken place in Italy among Catholic lawyers on the subject of natural law.[1] In reading the reports of that frank and very interesting discussion I think that the feelings I have described can be clearly detected. I would like to quote from the important contribution of Father Joseph Delos, O.P., to the discussion.

Father Delos takes his start from the general idea that inspired the discussion, the idea that there must be 'a principle which provides the condition *sine qua non* of positive law':

Certainly, [he says], this is our common thought. I am taking this agreement into account in order to ask one further question. How are we lawyers to find and to clarify that principle?

Let me explain my question: the theologian studies and works out that principle, he knows its origin and assesses its value; but we are not theologians. The philosopher does the same: but we are not philosophers. We are lawyers, and this means that we are addicted to a

[1] The outcome of that discussion was published in a volume entitled *Diritto Naturale Vigente* (*Quaderni di 'Justitia'*, I, 1951).

particular science which has an object of its own: the rule of positive law. Is there no way, no method which we can call our own? I believe there is; and thus that 'principle which provides the condition *sine qua non* of positive law' may in turn be explored by the theologian, by the philosopher—be he a moralist or a metaphysician—and by the jurist as well, each of them doing his job with the method that is proper to his own discipline; and this third manner—that of the jurist—of presenting a truth that is essentially one, will not fail to be an enrichment of human knowledge. Let me add that for many lawyers this will be the main way—for some indeed the only way—of satisfying their intellectual needs.[1]

I have cited this passage at length because it seems to me in many ways of great significance. If a theologian and a philosopher of Father Delos' calibre declares *nous ne sommes pas des théologiens, nous ne sommes pas des philosophes*, this can surely not be taken merely as a profession of modesty. It rather means that, *qua* jurist, he feels that he must as it were divest himself of his quality, of his capacity as a theologian or a philosopher, and that he must do so in order to make his position equal to that of the jurist, and understandable to him. There is, there must be *un chemin, une méthode* proper to the jurist—and different from that of the metaphysician and the theologian. For my part, I cannot help reading Father Delos' words as a healthy reminder that it is better not to drive too many metaphysical nails into the jurist's head in our presentation of the case for natural law. Surely that case can be made without running the risk that, in refusing the 'metaphysical premise', he may refuse natural law as well, thus throwing away the baby with the bath water.

[1] Je prends acte de cet accord pour poser la question: Comment, nous juristes, allons nous faire pour trouver et élucider ce principe?

Je précise le sens de la question: le théologien recherche et trouve ce principe, il en connaît l'origine et il en expose la valeur; mais nous ne sommes pas des théologiens. Le philosophe agit de même: mais nous ne sommes pas des philosophes. Nous sommes juristes, c'est à dire que nous sommes adonnés à une science particulière qui a son objet: la règle de droit positive. N'y a-t-il point un chemin, une méthode, qui nous soient propres? Je le pense; et ainsi, 'le principe qui est la condition *sine qua non* de la validité du droit positif' pourra être présenté tour à tour par le théologien, par le philosophe moraliste et métaphysicien, par le juriste enfin—chacun travaillant selon la méthode propre à la discipline qui est sienne; et cette troisième présentation—celle du juriste—d'une vérité essentiellement une, sera un enrichissement pour la connaissance humaine. J'ajoute que pour beaucoup de juristes, ce sera même la principale—pour certains même, la manière unique—de satisfaire à leurs exigences intellectuelles.

The points I have raised so far are less objections than subjects of meditation. Now I must limit myself to a very brief mention of one or two further points which I think can be raised—and are often raised with regard to the ontological approach to natural law. One of them is the mistake of stressing its deductive possibilities too much, and thus turning it into the 'blueprint of detailed solutions' against which Dean O'Meara so rightly warns us. This is precisely the mistake Mr Constable makes—and I hope he will not take my comment ill—in his recent essay, *What does Natural Law Jurisprudence Offer?*[1] Mr Constable believes that, from a Thomist notion of natural law, based on the idea of 'order', there can be inferred the idea of an 'organic community', based on the idea of 'service', 'guided' I am quoting his words by 'some persons or groups of persons' having 'a clear insight into the nature of goodness'.

I can only register quite frankly and openly my dissent from such views, and declare that if these were the implications of natural law, personally I would find it impossible to accept them. If not indeed of Plato's Republic, Mr Contsable's 'organic community' seems to me to smack of that 'corporativist' idea against which no lesser authority than Professor Maritain has warned us in his admirable essay, *The Rights of Man and Natural Law*, where he denounced it as one of the 'temptations' deriving 'from old concepts formerly in favour in certain Christian circles'.[2]

Let us be quite chary in drawing conclusions from 'natural law' which might turn into a highly controversial political programme. Let us not forget that the 'organic theory of society' has in recent days been a welcome excuse for the suppression of individual freedom. Let us, above all, practice a healthy distrust of any 'persons or groups' who claim to have 'a clear insight into the nature of goodness'.

With these last two points, we have come to the crux of the problem. The ontological theory of natural law is a great and impressive construction. But it does not seem to take into sufficient account those aspects of natural law that have become the lasting inheritance of modern man. With its insistence on the objective notion of 'order' and law, it tends to disregard or to belittle the importance of the subjective notion of a claim and a right. In one word, it does not adequately stress that idea of 'natural rights' which has become part and parcel of modern civilisation.

[1] *Catholic U. L. Review* (1954), **4**, 1.
[2] Maritain, *the Rights of Man and Natural Law* (1944), pp. 54–5.

'We hold . . . that all men . . . are endowed by their Creator with certain unalienable Rights.' Americans, after all, have proclaimed this doctrine to the world, and have inserted it in the *Declaration of Independence*.

No doubt the 'ontologist' may point out that there is no 'right' without 'law', and that the very notion of a subjective claim presupposes that of an objective order. And he will be perfectly justified in doing so, and this is where the ontological argument is indeed unassailable. But I seriously doubt that he can find any clear assertion of that claim—of 'natural rights'—in his sources, whether in Plato or in St Thomas Aquinas. This claim is in fact a modern development of 'natural law', and for a recognition of 'natural rights' the time was not ripe either in classical days or in the Middle Ages.

The same reservation should be made, I believe, with regard to the 'clear insight into the nature of goodness', that is, to the authoritative interpretation of natural law which seems implied in the ontological position. Quite apart from the fact that an undue stress on the possibility of such authoritative interpretation runs the risk of converting natural law into a new kind of positivism, it is quite clear that such a notion can only be a further stumbling block to the modern. I sincerely hope that I will not be accused of conceding too much to some recent attacks on the revival of natural law as a cloak for the introduction of 'authoritarian systems'.[1] If those shafts are aimed at the Church, I would like to say that they miss the mark insofar as the *magisterium* of the Church, which Catholics accept in the interpretation of moral truths, is after all based itself on a free acceptance. But the fact remains that, if the recognition of a 'natural order of things' is linked to the idea of an authoritative interpretation through the Church or any given society, the revival of natural law will automatically rule out all those *qui foris sunt*, who do not belong to that society. Surely this is not what the conveners of this meeting had in mind. I propose to examine in my concluding lecture the possibilities of hope left for us in that revival.

(IV) VALUE JUDGMENTS AND NATURAL LAW

If both natural law as a technology and natural law as an ontology

---

[1] Such as can be found, for example, in Mr E. C. Gerhart's pamphlet, *American Liberty and Natural Law* (1952) and in his letter to the editor, *Canadian Bar Review* (1954), **32**, 477.

are open to objections and encounter difficulties, is there a way of presenting the case for natural law in a manner which might— even if it did not ensure general acceptance—at least make that notion less obnoxious to the modern world at large? To avoid misgivings, I might as well begin by saying that, if I borrow the name for the third kind of approach to natural law from the founder of utilitarianism, this should not be taken to mean that I am a follower of Bentham and pleading a merely utilitarian approach to our problem. It just happens that the word 'deontology' (τὸ δέον—that which is binding) seems to provide one of those convenient labels which must, however, always be used with necessary caution.

Can we agree, at least, on certain things that are binding? The problem is all here, in this very plain, simple question.

In order to develop my argument, I am going back first of all to the image of the 'bridge'—the bridge between 'fact' and 'value', between what *is* and what *ought to be*. This time I am taking my text from an author who, though not very widely known in Anglo-Saxon countries, has of late been the subject of some very admirable work here in America. He is a fellow-countryman of mine, and his name is dear to all Italians.

At the beginning of his *Scienza Nuova* Giambattista Vico has a remark which seems important for the problem we are discussing. This remark is put forward in the forms of two 'axioms' or *Degnità*—the fundamental exposition of principles by which Vico prefaces his study of history and philosophy. I shall quote them here in the English translation which has recently been made of his work by two American scholars.

Degnità CXI: The certitude of laws is an obscurity of judgment, backed only by authority, so that we find them harsh in application, yet are obliged to apply them by their certitude. In good Latin *certum* means 'particularised', or, as the schools say, 'individuated'; so that, in over-elegant Latin, *certum* and *commune* are opposed to each other.
Degnità CXIII: The truth of the laws is a certain light and splendour with which natural reason illuminates them; so that jurisconsults are often in the habit of saying *verum est* for *aequum est*:

I am quite ready to grant that the two passages I have quoted are far from being easy to interpret.[1] But, to put it briefly, Vico's

[1] In order better to illustrate Vico's conception of natural law and its relevance to the point here under discussion, I would like to quote from a recent and excellent book on the Italian philosopher by Dr A. R. Caponigri, of the University of Notre Dame: 'In its most immediate and concrete sense, the natural

idea seems to be that in every law one can find an element which he calls the *certum* (the element of authority), and an element which he calls the *verum* (the element of 'truth', which is discovered by 'reason'). *Certum* and *verum*, authority and reason, are the two facets of the law, two aspects of the same thing, two different angles from which all law can be considered. Sometimes the *certum* may obscure the *verum*, authority takes the place of judgment, and laws are obeyed only because of their 'certitude'. But there is no law which, illuminated by the light of reason, does not reveal an element of *verum*, the 'truth' which it contains, like a soft kernel within the hard shell of authority that enfolds it: though it may happen that this very authority is the value of the law, that 'certitude' is itself a valuable guarantee against the disrupting forces of anarchy, so as to justify the old Roman adage *dura lex sed lex*—which Vico would like to read: *lex dura est sed certa est.*

I believe that these ideas can shed some light on the problem which we are discussing, that they do constitute a new approach to the question of the bridge between *is* and *ought*, between facts and values. For indeed, insofar as every law is a compound of *certum* and *verum*, every law is in itself a bridge over that chasm— or at any rate an attempt at bridging it. For every law is no doubt a factual proposition, inasmuch as it is a particular authoritative statement. But it is also and at the same time—insofar as it aims at a particular end, and is not a senseless imposition—a statement about 'values'.

I have until now used, or tried to use, the word 'value' with the utmost discretion. As I am well aware of its invidious meaning, I have put that word under a safety belt of inverted commas. But now I find that I can do no better than use that word to

---

law is [to Vico] the mediation between the truth and the certitude, the concreteness and the universality of the law. . . . The "certum" and the "verum", which natural law seeks to mediate, are dimensions, not of single laws, but of the total process of law. . . . The natural law he understood to be, not that transcendent and unenacted normative law, allegedly implied in the concept of "human nature", but the movement of the process of the historical formation of the structures of positive law towards an immanent ideality . . . the universality of the natural law consists, not in the fact that in all times and in identical places identical positive law should prevail, but that in all the forms of positive law, despite the diversity of material circumstances which dictate the immediate force of the law, the same ideal principle is at work.' Caponigri, *Time and Idea. The Theory of History in Giambattista Vico* (1953), pp. 35, 68, 116.

describe what I have in mind. Perhaps I can give it force by an example.

Take the difference between the common law and continental law in the matter of testaments. Surely it does make a difference to the father of a family if, according to the common law, he is free to dispose of his entire estate or, according to the *Code Napoléon* and to the codes that have been modelled on it, he is not allowed to do so because a portion of his estate is reserved—'earmarked' as it were—for his offspring. But surely the difference between the two systems is not merely a difference of 'fact', a difference between the wording of the codes or the rules which courts will enforce in the different countries. Something else is at stake, as will be clearly shown by the reaction of any Latin *paterfamilias* when he is first told that an English father may disinherit his children and leave all his property to a charitable institution. Even though my Latin *paterfamilias* may not go so far as to say that such a practice would be against 'natural law', he would certainly have strong feelings about such a patent disregard of what he considers the unity of the family and the rightful expectations of children. Is it going too far to suggest that such an example as this clearly indicates that the law embodies certain 'values': in this particular case a particular notion of the comparative claims of family duty and individual freedom?

I have chosen my example at random. What I want considered is this idea: it is possible in each and every legal proposition to ascertain the 'value' it contains—even down to traffic regulations if you please, since there can be no doubt about the 'value' they protect, that of our own personal safety. I know full well the ambiguity of the word 'value' which I am using in this context; I would be quite willing to use a different word if I could think of a better one. My point is of far greater relevance, and far more controversial: for it amounts to nothing less than admitting that we have gone all this long way to find the ground of obligation of law without realising that this ground does not lie outside, but within the law itself, that it must be sought in the interplay of the *verum* and the *certum*, in the ideal principle which is at work in every law despite the material circumstances that engross it. For each and every law is indeed nothing other than a 'normative translation' of a particular value: we must try and break the shell in order to get to the kernel. And if a particular rule will not yield an answer to our quest, it is to the general system of which that rule is a part that we must turn, and we will no doubt find it.

L

Let me try to put this same argument in another way. I have already referred to Kelsen's 'pure theory of law', and I think we would all agree that Kelsen strives at a construction and interpretation of law entirely agnostic as far as 'values' are concerned. Every legal order can, according to Kelsen, be construed as a *Stufenbau*, a system of rules which derive their validity one from the other, until we come to the 'basic norm' which is the condition of validity of them all, and makes the whole system into a coherent pattern. When I think of Kelsen's pure theory of law I am always reminded of a passage in *Alice in Wonderland*, and of Alice's reply to the King of Hearts. 'At this moment the King, who had been for some time busily writing in his notebook, called out "Silence!" and read out from his book "Rule Forty-two. *All Persons more than a mile high to leave the Court*."—Everybody looked at Alice.—"*I'm* not a mile high," said Alice.—"You are," said the King.—"Nearly two miles high," added the Queen.— "Well, I shan't go, at any rate," said Alice: "besides, that's not a regular rule. You invented it just now."—"It's the oldest rule in the book," said the King.—"Then it ought to be Number One," said Alice.'

Briefly, the point I am trying to make is this. The ultimate ground of validity of the law, the *verum* of laws as distinct from their *certum*, the *Grundnorm* of Kelsen, the *Rule Number One* of Alice—they are not 'facts', but 'values'. I said in my little book on *Natural Law* that Kelsen's 'pure theory of law' can be used to show the Achilles' heel of positivism. I do not propose to repeat my argument here. But I would like to say that Kelsen's insistence on the purely hypothetical character of the *Grundnorm* can deceive nobody. Inasmuch as that hypothesis has to be endorsed by a fact, Kelsen's refined form of positivism shows its real face, the reduction of law to a mere expression of force—and even this is an assertion of 'value'. There have been indeed—and there always will be—political philosophies based on the assumption that force is the ultimate ground of obligation. But such philosophies, by the very fact that they glorify force, cannot avoid attributing to it an ethical value. Hobbes' *Leviathan* will free men from fear; indeed 'not renouncing' trumps can have its 'morality'. We have only to look around to convince ourselves that to a very large number of people might *is* right. But I wonder how many of us actually take the trouble to point out to such people the revealing admission contained in the use of the word 'right' in this context.

So much for the *verum* and the *certum* of the law and for the presence of a value judgment in every legal proposition. I have been very agreeably surprised to come across some interesting work lately done in this country on lines singularly akin to the one I have been indicating. I refer to Professor McDougal's programme of 'value clarification'. I believe as he does that there is a new and fascinating line of enquiry open to jurisprudence. My only difference with Professor McDougal is, that while he seems to think of the 'values' underlying a given legal proposition or a given legal order as 'preferences', as 'goals', as 'objects of decision', I would plead that they should also and foremost be considered and studied as 'grounds of obligation'. In fact, I believe that it is here that the notion of natural law as a 'deontology' can, if at all, find its justification: for the problem of natural law is to me essentially that of the intersection between the legal proposition and the value that underlies it, the ascertainment of the element of obligation that makes us feel we are obeying the law not merely because of its 'certitude'—to use Vico's expression again—but because of the element of 'truth' it contains, a truth carrying conviction. The difficulty of course is to persuade ourselves that such 'values' are 'objective qualities' in the law itself and not mere subjective or emotional reactions on our part, devoid of any universality.

To make this point more clear I am relying upon a quotation from a contemporary Oxford and (recently) Cambridge author, one of those writers with the rare gift of presenting deep thoughts gracefully as well as convincingly. In one of his essays on the Christian predicament which have won him a deserved reputation among all those who are seriously interested in religious and ethical problems, Professor C. S. Lewis has drawn attention to the importance of value judgments in education. *The Abolition of Man*[1] is really concerned with the study of literature, but I think that what he has to say is not without importance also in the field of jurisprudence.

Mr Lewis takes his start from the well-known story of Coleridge at the waterfall. 'You remember that there were two tourists present: that one called it "sublime" and the other "pretty", and that Coleridge mentally endorsed the first judgment and rejected the second with disgust.' According to Mr Lewis, the modern trend in literary criticism is to accept Coleridge's anecdote merely as an illustration of 'personal' or 'subjective' reactions. He quotes from an elementary textbook for English schoolboys where the

[1] Riddle Memorial Lectures, University of Durham (1943).

authors comment in the following way: 'When the man said *That is sublime*, he appeared to be making a remark about the waterfall. . . . Actually . . . he was not making a remark about the waterfall, but a remark about his own feelings. What he was saying was really *I have feelings associated in my mind with the word "sublime"*, or shortly, *I have sublime feelings*.'

Mr Lewis has no quarrel with what would seem to me the rather high expectations placed on the intelligence of schoolboys: his quarrel is with the philosophical position implied in such comment, a position which he believes is not only dangerous for schoolboys, but wrong for the teachers themselves. In fact, he believes that such a position—the modern position with regard not only to literary appreciation, but to all value judgments—constitutes a break with what has been for all times the normal approach to any assessment of what does and what does not deserve appreciation and approval:

Until quite modern times all teachers and even all men believed the universe to be such that certain emotional reactions on our part could be either congruous or incongruous to it—believed, in fact, that objects did not merely receive but could *merit*, our approval or disapproval, our reverence, or our contempt. The reason why Coleridge agreed with the tourist who called the cataract sublime and disagreed with the one who called it pretty was of course that he believed inanimate nature to be such that certain responses could be more 'just' or 'ordinate' or 'appropriate' to it than others. And he believed (correctly) that the tourist thought the same. The man who called the cataract sublime was not intending simply to describe his own emotions about it: he was also claiming that the object was one which *merited* those emotions. But for this claim there would be nothing to agree or disagree about. To disagree with *This is pretty*, if those words simply described the lady's feelings, would be absurd: if she had said *I feel sick* Coleridge would hardly have replied *No, I feel quite well*.

This rather lengthy quotation will, I hope, throw some light upon what I had in mind when speaking of 'values' as 'grounds of obligations', and of the problem of natural law as the problem of ascertaining where these grounds ultimately lie. For my part, I believe that in every human society, in fact in 'human nature' itself, there are certain ultimate standards or values which determine approval or disapproval, assent or dissent; and I believe that it is these same values that determine our judgment as to whether a law is 'just' or 'unjust': in other words—to use a very ancient language that seems perfectly appropriate at this point—whether we are bound in conscience to obey it or not. To ascertain such values may be thought a modest—or an immodest—undertaking. Yet I think that, failing all other ways, such an undertaking is well worth attempting, and may even in the end lead us to a much greater amount of agreement than we might expect. Personally, I am quite willing to accept Mr McDougal's 'tabulation' of the values which correspond to 'our present-day democratic preferences for a peaceful world'[1] as a very near approximation of the values I have in mind. Surely it is only his modesty as a field worker, his concern with a purely 'scientific' presentation of the case, that prevents Professor McDougal from seeing such values not only as resulting from our 'democractic preferences', but as corresponding for a very large part to what *semper et ubique* has been thought *bonum et aequum*. In fact, they are in many points reminiscent of what our benighted forbears would have called 'natural law'.

I shall devote the last part of this lecture to a number of grave and serious objections which I know can be made to my presentation of the case.

I can see my first objector addressing me, more or less, thus: 'You have, in your last lecture, expressed your misgivings about the ontological theory of natural law, a theory which purported to offer a rational justification of the ultimate values on which the obligation of the law depends. You now come forward and tell us about the existence of such values. If you do not think that they are demonstrable, does this mean that you ask us to accept them by faith?'

This is a current objection to natural law thinking. I referred at the beginning of these lectures to the discussion which has taken place in the *Canadian Bar Review* on the subject of natural law. I find that this sort of objection is the one which Professor Friedmann uses in his contribution to the discussion: a very formidable and closely knit argument against natural law.[2] Actually, Professor Friedmann had already worded that objection very briefly and clearly in the Preface to the first edition of his well-known book, *Legal Theory* (1944): 'Ultimate values must be believed, they cannot be proved'.

My answer to this objection would be that the alternative

---

[1] 'The Comparative Study of Law for Policy Purposes: Value Clarification as an Instrument of Democratic World Order', *Yale Law Journal*, 1952, **61**, 915, 916.
[2] *Canadian Bar Review* (1953), **31**, 1074.

between reason and faith is a wrong alternative. The answer can be provided in terms which are well known in the history of Christian thought. Surely the progress of the mind is twofold, and the *intellectus quaerens fidem* has its counterpart in the *fides quaerens intellectum*. Surely in making my reservations about the adequacy of the 'ontological argument' to meet the predicament of our time, I never intended ruling it out as one of the best and most pertinent ways for grounding 'natural law' on a rational basis. I suggest that we keep an open mind for all the arguments to be brought forward confirming our beliefs. To conceive of natural law as a deontology is not in any way to exclude the possibility of rational argumentation. We may agree on the result, and yet differ on the method: but what matters is the agreement. In fact, far from rejecting the old philosophy of 'the Right and the Good', we may well welcome its support and believe in our hearts of hearts that the time has come for a more charitable assessment of its merits. But why should we not be equally charitable about the help we may get from other quarters? Does not the sociologist, the anthropologist, the student of comparative jurisprudence —to mention only some aspects of the present 'scientific' trend which has in many eyes taken the place of old philosophy—also provide us at times with conclusions confirming our 'deontology'? If in the end we should find that our disagreements are smaller than we expected, is not this all we can ask in our present predicament? I shall let the matter rest here, since all I wanted to stress was merely the point that if 'ultimate values' are believed, there is no necessary exclusion of their being rationally argued.

Another objection I can well foresee: the objection of historical relativism. This is a strong objection, one which a man like myself, born and bred in the historical tradition of the Italian idealist school, cannot avoid being painfully aware of.

Certainly, it is very difficult not to be shaken by the doubt that our 'values' and 'value judgments' may not be historically conditioned, since they may change and actually have changed according to time and circumstances, and hence are relative to these and possess no absoluteness whatever. To this objection I would like to answer with the words of Professor Strauss in his remarkable book on *Natural Rights and History*, where, in the first chapter, he deals at length with the question of the relativity of values, and hence of natural law (or natural right, as he calls it with the terminology current on the Continent).

'One cannot understand the meaning of the attack on natural

right in the name of history before one has realised the utter irrelevance of this argument. . . . Some of the greatest natural right teachers have argued that, precisely if natural right is rational, its discovery presupposes the cultivation of reason; and therefore natural right will not be known universally. . . . In other words, by proving that there is no principle of justice that has not been denied somewhere or at some time, one has not yet proved that any given denial was justified or reasonable.'[1] Briefly, this is the main answer ready for the objections of the historical relativist.

I therefore turn to a third objection to the assertion of 'values', viz., that their claim to absoluteness is dangerous and can only lead to fanaticism or to pharisaism. This objection is very clearly worded in Professor Friedmann's contribution to the *Canadian Bar Review*. 'Since the days of the Greek philosophers,' he writes, 'hundreds of natural law philosophers, great and small, failed to establish values of natural law which, on closer analysis, do not assert one political faith or another. . . . It is an immortal merit of the "awesome influence" of Holmes and of those he inspired . . . who have discovered the inherent nebulousness or hypocrisy of formulas which, under the guise of natural law principles, advocate a particular political philosophy.'

So very serious an accusation may well induce us to watch our steps. But none are in a better position to face that accusation than we of the modern world, the members of a free and democratic society. Surely anyone professing belief in the existence of certain ultimate values constituting the ultimate ground of our allegiance to the law or the system of law under which we live, will be careful not to make this statement in any way justifying the accusation of fanaticism or hypocrisy. I think the answer to Professor Friedmann's objection is a profession of humility and sincerity on our part, as well as a better awareness of the principles that inspired the growth of our Western civilisation. 'I beseech ye, in the bowels of Christ, think that ye may be mistaken.' The words which Cromwell addressed to the Scots on the eve of the battle of Dunbar still echo in our heart, and we know that they have shaped our way of life and made a free society possible. But must the respect for other people's beliefs necessarily make ours insecure and irrelevant? Surely when an issue is really great, men must take sides; and they never hesitate to do so. Let me note a case which has remained deeply impressed in my memory.

Some years before the War—it must have been, I think, in the

[1] Strauss, *Natural Rights and History* (1953), p. 9.

middle thirties—the Oxford Union voted with a large majority a resolution to the effect that 'this House' would under no circumstances fight for its King and country. Boys will be boys, and perhaps those young men only thought at the time of causing some little scandal. But, in those years, such words were echoed round the world, and made capital of by Fascist and Nazi propaganda. Here was a good illustration of the decadence of Britain and British youth, soon to be conquered by the Master Race. Yet not many years had passed when that very youth was called upon to make the last stand, and I have little doubt that a large number of those same young men who had moved and voted that fateful resolution gave their lives for their King and their country. This is what I mean by knowing what the real values are, and by acting accordingly. I think we ought never to forget that the original meaning of 'martyr' is 'witness'.

Having re-examined the case for natural law my only conclusion is that the case still stands on its merits. I have left the door open for further discussion and also, if you like, for further definition. Should we really decide to draw up the list of 'ultimate values', I would for my part try to remember the old adage, *omnis definitio in jure periculosa*. But there is a final point. If my reading of historical evidence is correct, the doctrine of natural law has always represented a minimum of agreement. Such was the Roman theory of *jus naturale*, expressing the basic principle on which the different peoples and races composing the Roman commonwealth could be united by a common bond of law and human fellowship. Such was the medieval, Scholastic theory of *lex naturalis*: is there anything more gratifying about the theory than the fact of its being devised to bring together Christians and heathens? I need not remind you of the famous passage in St Thomas Aquinas[1] where he clearly asserts the Christian duty to respect the laws and the authority of the infidels, because 'divine law, which is a law of grace, does not abolish human law which is founded on natural reason'. But—perhaps most important of all for us who live in a divided world and are beginning to despair of the possibility of ever overcoming our divisions—such was the great historical significance of the revival of natural law that took place at the beginning of our era. After decades of bitter and fruitless controversy, suddenly the writers of opposite camps seem to discover the possibility of talking a common language. Hooker borrows wholesale from St Thomas, Grotius pays tribute to the great

[1] *S. Theol.*, 2a 2ae, 10, 10.

Spanish schoolmen. Natural law is here the indication that the age of 'ideological' strife has passed, and that an agreement has been reached on the matter of ultimate principles. We must keep this in mind in view of Professor Friedmann's accusation of intolerance. History shows that the recourse to natural law was the sign of an earnest desire for mutual understanding.

It is this desire for mutual understanding that I would plead if ever we attempt to list the 'ultimate values'. I would plead that we focus our attention on what unites us rather than on what separates us. Personally, I would recommend that we take into account all that has enriched the conscience of the modern man and goes to make his great, unparalleled heritage. Surely Christians have the right to stress the part which the Gospel—as a great Christian writer of my country once put it—has played in 'revealing man to man'. Of their Christian inheritance the Western nations may well be proud, for it has served them well in the course of their history. 'The closeness with which English law approaches the moral law'—writes Lord Justice Denning—'is, I believe, due to the fact that it has been moulded for centuries by judges who have been brought up in the Christian faith. The precepts of religion, consciously or unconsciously, have been their guide in the administration of justice.' No wonder that in England the bond of legal obligation is felt so strongly.

On the other hand I cannot help feeling that Christians ought at times to be reminded that smugness and pride are not Christian virtues. The values by which we live and on which our world rests are not exclusively Christian values. We ought to be aware that something has happened to the modern world, which, whether we like it or not, we have to take into account: what Maritain, always so sensitive to these problems, has called the 'secularisation' of Christian values. These secularised values have become the common coin, the accepted currency, of a composite and no longer entirely Christian society.

However composite and in itself divided, that society has a sufficiently marked physiognomy for us to recognise it as our own—and to cherish it. Why then should we be chary of proclaiming our faith in it and of inscribing its great principles on our banner? Many warning voices have lately reminded us of the dangers of the hour: one raised not so long ago by George F. Kennan, has not passed unnoticed, I can assure you.[1] Another

---

[1] I am referring to G. F. Kennan's address at a University of Notre Dame Convocation marking the dedication of the I. A. O'Shaughnessy Hall of

great American personality has admirably defined the predicament
of our time: Learned Hand on his eightieth birthday has expressed
better than I could ever hope to do, what I think are the hopes and
the fears of our generation:

Today we stand at bay, with all those conventions challenged that have
for so long saved us from 'the intolerable labour of thought'. The
slogans we live by: 'democracy', 'the Common Man', 'Natural Law',
'Inherent Rights of man', 'the Bill of Rights', 'the Constitution'—the
whole paraphernalia of our eighteenth-century inheritance—all must
now make good their claims against the furious repudiation of powerful
and relentless enemies. We are in the distressing position of all who find
their axioms doubted: axioms which, like all axioms, are so self-evident
that any show of dissidence outrages our morals, and paralyses our
minds. And we have responded as men generally respond to such
provocation: for the most part we seem able to think of nothing better
than repression; we seek to extirpate the heresies and wreak vengeance
on the heretics. . . . Happily there are a substantial number who see
that, not only when they were first announced, but as they still persist,
the doctrines that so frightened us constitute a faith, which we must
match with a faith, held with equal ardor and conviction. So we are
repeatedly assured, and rightly assured: but what we much less often
observe is that, in making use of our faith as a defence, we may be in
danger of destroying its foundation and abandoning its postulates.

These are wonderful words, which we might do well to remember. Perhaps it is not a question of high-sounding proclamations
after all, but merely of an awareness of our predicament and of a
firm resolve to face it with a brave heart but also with simple,
unassuming humility. It is no use inscribing such principles on our
banners unless we are prepared to undertake also the modest
everyday work which is required in order to make them living and
guiding. Above all we must be aware of the peril which Judge
Hand pointed out, lest in making recourse to our faith as a defence,
we destroy its foundations and abandon its postulates.

This, then, is the predicament in which we stand today, and
unless I am greatly mistaken, I think that it is this predicament
which our forbears used to call by a name, and by one name only:
the defence of 'natural law' against the forces that try to submerge
it. More fortunate than we are, many of them lived in days when
the conflict between natural and positive law, between reason and
force, between ideals and reality were less pronounced or apparent.

Liberal and Fine Arts, 15 May 1953. The address was rebroadcast by the
BBC Third Programme, and printed in The Listener, 16 July 1953, pp. 93–94.

Yet they clearly indicated the way to be followed in case that conflict should break out, the way, at any rate, which alone can ensure the respect of the basic values making life worth living. 'Natural law' still has something to teach us about the defence of these values at all levels of human existence, from the level of the single individual man to that of the world at large.

Actually, the predicament of the individual man is perhaps less terrible than is usually believed; for old Mother Conscience still does her job well, and surely men never lack a clear knowledge of right and wrong when they are cornered and have to make basic decisions. I have mentioned the story of the Oxford undergraduates; I would have many other poignant stories to tell from the dark recent days, of men who did not dodge the issue. Let us hope never to see such days again, never to have to withstand 'positive law' because of its blatant violation of 'natural justice'. Men bear witness by their deeds, whether they obey the laws or disobey them. When obedience is no longer 'for conscience' sake' then alone can we surmise that the twilight of 'values' has set in, and that the reign of force has taken the place of the rule of reason.

Far more serious and difficult is the predicament of those who are responsible for group, rather than for individual, decisions. Well may we pray for 'those who are in office', that their mind be clear and their judgment enlightened. This is how His Holiness Pius XII, in an address to the first Convention of Catholic Italian lawyers, outlined the rules that should guide a judge in his application of the law and in his attitude towards it:[1]

(1) With regard to any judgment, the principle must be that the judge cannot avoid the responsibility of his decision by attributing it entirely to the law or to the lawgiver. No doubt, the latter bears the main responsibility for the effect of the law. But the judge, in applying the law to the particular case, is a concurrent cause, and therefore shares the responsibility for those effects.

(2) The judge can never with any of his decisions oblige anyone to some action which is intrinsically immoral,—that is, contrary to the laws of God or the Church.

(3) He can in no way explicitly acknowledge and approve an unjust law, nor pronounce a penal sentence that may imply such an approval.

(4) Nevertheless, not any and every application of an unjust law implies such an acknowledgment and approval. There are cases when

[1] This address was printed in the volume *Diritto Naturale Vigente*, note 1 above, p. 155.

the judge can—and sometimes even must—let the unjust law have its course, when this is the only way to avoid a greater evil.

Except for the reference to 'the laws of God or the Church', I do not think that any decent man, even supposing he is a complete agnostic, would take exception to such rules. The difficulty lies in following them.

As for the predicament of the world at large, let us be perfectly clear that natural law is no cut and dried solution, no infallible cure for all our troubles. Here indeed the problem is not even that of a conflict between natural and positive law, but that of the absence of a legal order altogether. International law, as things stand today, is a good target for the shafts of the sceptic. But, as Professor Goodhart puts it very well, the weakness of international law is not due to the lack of enforcement, but 'to the absence of an international moral sense'. These words can only mean: that what matters is first to 'instaure' or restore the 'international moral sense'. The possibility of agreeing on the 'rules of the game' and of abiding by them will follow as a logical consequence. Surely this is where 'natural law' may have a word to say, especially if we take it, as I have tried to, as a minimum of agreement on principles.

A more apt conclusion to these lectures I could not find than by using the words with which the President of Notre Dame summarised the gist of a discussion which took place here not long ago, when representatives of different faiths and creeds met together to examine the same problem which we have met to reconsider now. If indeed it can be shown that there is some agreement not only between the different traditions of our Western world, but between the great cultures of the East and the West, then surely there is reason to believe that, as Father Hesburgh put it, natural law may provide that 'common ground where we can begin to draw all men, everywhere, together in a unity that reflects what is common to human beings as human beings'.

B

TWO QUESTIONS ABOUT LAW

This paper is about the relationship between legal and political theory. Its title is taken from a well-known passage at the beginning of Kant's *Rechtslehre*.

The question, what is law (*was ist Recht*), is a question that may well cause the legal theorist the same kind of embarrassment which the question, what is truth, causes the logician . . . Indeed, the legal theorist may succeed in laying down what pertains to the law (*quid sit iuris*), viz. what the laws say or have said at a given time and in a given country. But whether that which the laws prescribe is right, and the general principle according to which it is possible to know what is right and wrong (*iustum et iniustum*), this will certainly remain hidden from him unless he forsakes for a while his empirical premisses and turns to pure reason for the source of those judgments, in order to lay down the foundation of a possible positive legislation. In this search those existing laws may indeed furnish him with excellent guidance. But a purely empirical theory of law, like the wooden head in Phedrus' fable, is a head that may be beautiful, but alas! has no brains.[1]

I take it that Kant is here distinguishing between two possible questions that can be raised about law: the question of definition and the question of valuation. The question of definition is that of ascertaining what the law is at a given time and in a given country, of assessing, that is, the criteria by which we acknowledge certain rules to be 'laws' to the exclusion of others. This is what the

[1] I. Kant, *Metaphysische Anfangsgründe der Rechtslehre*, Einleitung, §B.

lawyers express with a phrase which is of current and almost daily use in their specialised language. Their concern is to determine what laws are 'valid'. The question of valuation, on the other hand, is that of deciding whether that which the laws prescribe is right or wrong. It is a question of assessing why laws are 'obligatory' or binding. Both definition and valuation are implied in Kant's 'transcendental deduction' of law, which purports to establish how law comes about, *wie ist Recht überhaupt möglich*. This is what Kant has in mind when he asserts the possibility of a 'construction of the concept of law as a pure notion *a priori*'. Kant's conception of law contains both a definition and a valuation. Law is 'the overall concept of the conditions, under which the free choice of an agent can be reconciled with the free choice of another according to a universal law of liberty'.

I now propose to examine the present state of legal theory in the light of the requirements laid down in Kant's prolegomena. I shall classify the different currents that carry the day into two main categories. The first is by far the most popular and the most acceptable to the professional lawyer. I shall call this category of legal thought by the name which has by now gained almost universal acceptance: Legal Positivism. As against the common features of Legal Positivism, I shall class the theories that oppose some or all of its tenets under the name of Natural Law theories.

It is not, however, an easy task to give a short and clear-cut definition of the sense in which the expression 'Legal Positivism' is used in contemporary legal literature. We spent a whole fortnight last year at a meeting we held in North Italy, trying to assess the basic features of the positivist approach.[1] Hart from Oxford was there, and Ross from Copenhagen, together with a small party of legal philosophers, old and young, from both Europe and America. All we could do was to draw up a detailed list of several possible characterisations. Among them, at any rate, there is one which, as Bobbio has rightly pointed out,[2] can be taken as a kind of shorthand definition of the main positivist contention. Positivism is the theory according to which there is no other law except 'positive law'. In order that this definition should not read tautologically, we must, however, add at once: it is the theory that

---

[1] See R. A. Falk and S. I. Shuman, 'The Bellagio Conference on Legal Positivism', in *Journal of Legal Education* (1961), **14**, no. 2, pp. 213–228 (Ital. trans. 'Un colloquio sul positivismo giuridico', in *Rivista di Diritto Civile*, no. 5, 1961).
[2] N. Bobbio, *Il positivismo giuridico*, Torino, 1961.

maintains that the only proper use of the word law is that of the lawyers, a theory that is polemically aimed against 'natural law', against any law that is not factually existing and empirically veri-fiable. If this be the case, there seems to be some further ground for classing all opposite theories of law, all theories that will not reduce law to positive law, under the general heading of Natural Law theories.

I have just said that there are many versions of Legal Positivism. Here again, by simplifying certain issues, I believe that these varieties can be reduced to three basic types.

(1) The first, and perhaps the best known type of Legal Positivism, is the one which I would be inclined to indicate by the name of *Imperativism*. It is the theory of law which we readily associate with the names of Austin, of Hobbes and perhaps, if we are familiar with medieval thought, with that of William of Ockham. According to this theory, a 'valid' law is the command of a 'sovereign' endorsed by the fact of habitual obedience.

(2) The second type of Legal Positivism is best known by the name by which its followers aim at differentiating themselves from the first and the third kind of positivism. *Realism* is the type of legal thinking which we in Europe most readily associate with America. Long before this school had a name, its basic assumption had been expressed by Holmes in his famous dictum, that law is the prophecy of what the Courts will do in fact. Law is here taken as a social phenomenon, as a decision or a process of authoritative decisions.

(3) The third type of Legal Positivism is the most refined and by far the most complex. It is the one that still dominates European legal thought, owing to the decisive and lasting influence of Kelsen. It styles itself with different names: I believe the most appropriate one is *Normativism*. According to this theory, law cannot properly be understood except as a set of normative propositions. The 'validity' of each norm hinges on the validity of other norms, and thus leads us back to a 'basic norm', to an 'ultimate rule of recognition' which qualifies every single norm by giving it relevance and connecting it into a system. Quite recently, Professor Hart has produced the ablest and most up-to-date defence of this kind of positivism in his book, *The Concept of Law*, which was published last spring at Oxford.

We must now ask ourselves what these different versions of

positivism have in common. Perhaps we will reach a clearer grasp of the issue if we distinguish the constructive from the destructive side of the positivist doctrine.

On the constructive side, the common and main characteristic of all three types of positivism is to provide us with some adequate means for determining what the law is at a given time and in a given country. From this point of view, positivism certainly contains an answer to the question *quid iuris*. Whether its followers link the existence of law to the location of sovereignty, or to a process of decisions, or to the recognition of a legal system, their aim is to construct a model that may be of use to the professional lawyer. They lay down the requirements which must be fulfilled for a law to be 'valid'. No doubt the positivists of the third type insist on a subtle distinction between 'validity' and 'effectiveness'. A law may be valid even though it is not, at least under certain circumstances, effective. But ultimately the validity of a law depends on its being part of a system, and this, in order to be positive, must also possess a certain degree of effectiveness. The issue is an issue of fact, an issue that can be solved by means of empirical verification.

On the destructive side, Legal Positivism is equally emphatic. To the legal positivist law is a kind of 'closed shop', a slice of experience which yields its own criteria of verification to the exclusion of all others. The extraneous, non-legal criteria which are thus excluded are manifold; the most notorious one is the moral one. To the positivist there is an unbridgeable chasm between the *is* and the *ought*, between fact and value. His banner is 'ethical neutrality'. 'The existence of law is one thing; its merit or demerit another. Whether it be or be not is one enquiry; whether it be or be not conformable to an assumed standard is a different enquiry. A law, which actually exists, is a law, though we happen to dislike it, or though it vary from the text, by which we regulate our approbation or disapprobation.'[1] Thus Austin in a famous passage which can well be taken as the basic text, if not actually as the manifesto, of Legal Positivism. This is also the point which has caused the greatest amount of scandal. Let us remark, for fairness sake, that the 'contention that it is in no sense a necessary truth that laws reproduce or satisfy certain demands of morality'[2] does not necessarily commit its authors to a profession of non-cognitivism in ethics. Among legal positivists, some are sceptics,

[1] J. Austin, *The Province of Jurisprudence Determined*, 1954 ed., p. 184.
[2] H. L. A. Hart, *The Concept of Law*, Oxford, 1961, p. 181.

some not. They tend to be so with us on the Continent; they do
not in English-speaking countries. Austin, as a utilitarian, can
hardly be called a relativist; I do not think Hart is one. Felix
Cohen, the Yale legal philosopher, wrote a whole book to prove
that law can be measured by ethical standards. Yet his basic
contention is couched in the sharpest possible words: 'Law is law,
whether it is good or bad, and only on the admission of this
platitude can a meaningful discussion of the goodness and badness
of law rest.'[1]

Now this is precisely the point where Natural Law takes issue
with Legal Positivism. As I have done with the latter, I shall use
the phrase 'natural law' merely as a shorthand device for indicating such notions of law which have a common denominator:
that of being attempts at bridging the chasm between the *is*
and the *ought*, at restoring the role of valuation in legal
experience. Their varieties are even greater than those of Legal
Positivism.[2]

(1) There is, first of all, a way of conceiving natural law which
deliberately calls itself *ontological*. It refuses the distinction between
the *is* and the *ought* on the ground that there is a fundamental
relation of being and oughtness. It postulates the conception of an
'order of reality' of which human, positive laws are but a part and
from which alone they derive their validity. As Hart has seen very
well, 'the clearest, perhaps, because it is the most extreme, form of
expression of this point of view, is associated with the Thomist
tradition'.[3]

(2) There is, secondly, a way of conceiving natural law which I
would call *technological*. It maintains that it is possible to elaborate the criteria by which law can be both determined and judged
by referring to the 'purpose' of law itself, or to the 'nature of
things', or to the 'typological situations' of man in society. A
good example of this kind of natural law is the *ius naturale* of the

---

[1] F. S. Cohen, *Ethical Systems and Legal Ideals*, 1959 ed., p. 15.

[2] For shortness sake I shall use the typology which I have proposed and
developed elsewhere ('The case for natural law re-examined', see above,
pp. 119–72, and 'Le Droit Naturel', in the vol. with the same title published
by the Institut de Philosophie Politique, *Annales de Philosophie Politique*
III, Paris 1959, pp. 147–57) and which only in part corresponds to the much
more satisfactory and critically defendable typification proposed by Erik Wolf
in the conclusion of his admirable book, *Das Problem der Naturrechtslehre*,
2nd ed., Karlsruhe, 1959.

[3] Hart, op. cit., p. 152.

M

Romans. One of its most convinced and convincing advocates today is Professor Fuller of Harvard.

(3) Third, I would put a notion of natural law which probably hardly deserves that name at all. I shall call it *deontological*. This way of thinking contents itself with the assertion that there are certain principles or values related to law, and that these principles are relevant to its existence.

These three varieties of Natural Law have in common only one point: that they subordinate the question of knowing what the laws have said or say at a given time and in a given place, to that of knowing whether what they say is right or wrong, *iustum vel iniustum*. They thus tend to dissolve the problem of the validity of law into that of its obligatoriness. They provide us with a valuation of law which purports to be a definition.

The time has now come for examining in what sense, if at all, the different theories of law which I have tried to categorise also answer the overall question which Kant raised, that of explaining how law comes about, *wie ist Recht überhaupt möglich*.

To take Legal Positivism first, I have already said that there is no doubt in my mind that it provides an answer to the question *quid iuris*. But it does so at the cost of reducing law to a fact, and this is bound to produce some logical difficulties. To be sure, normativism alone, among the three types of positivism, seems to do justice to the peculiar character of that fact, thus leaving the door open to further enquiry. To say that laws are norms is to stress that they are, first and foremost, ought-propositions. Their oughtness—the normativist maintains—does not depend on a fact, but on the oughtness of other norms; and only in the last resort is the oughtness or validity of the legal order in need of an ultimate factual implementation. No one better than the normativist is aware of how disturbingly the language of law is akin to the language of morals. He makes no bones of the fact that words such as 'right', 'duty', 'obligation' are used in the law in a prescriptive as well as in a descriptive fashion. Clearly, there is a puzzle here that deserves investigation.

On the other hand, Natural Law puts the problem of *iustum et iniustum* first: but there are great differences in the consequences which its different versions would like us to draw from the primacy of valuation over definition. The ontological notion of natural law brushes aside the problem of bad laws by denying that they are laws: but surely this is merely a verbal expedient for saying that they are not obligatory. Nor does the expedient stop here. In talking, as some ontologists do, of a 'continuity of law', they overlook the difference in meaning of the word law in such expressions as the 'laws of nature', the 'laws of the State' and the 'laws of morals'. In order to conceive of these different laws as normative or ought-propositions it will be necessary to postulate the existence of a divine Creator who has allotted to each creature its part. The 'laws of nature' do no more than describe the 'order of reality'. God alone can prescribe them. Orthodox Thomism on the whole is much more coherent than many of its modern, secularised versions.

The same faulty logic can be detected in the technological argument. The 'nature of things' is unable of itself to yield a normative proposition. The contrary impression derives from overlooking the fact, that the 'thing', whose very 'nature' is said to be normative, is already qualified by a particular purpose. The moment we talk of a purpose, we talk of a choice; and a choice can only take place on a deontological, not on a technological level.

We are thus left with our main problem unsolved; the question of how law comes about still faces and baffles us. The positivist's answer is to sacrifice the *ought* to the *is*; the natural lawyer's to sacrifice the *is* to the *ought*; surely the problem is to explain how law can express both an *is* and an *ought*, how it can be both a fact and an ought-proposition. I believe that there is an element of truth on both sides, and that the final word is not so much a matter for legal as for political theory.

To begin with, that law is a fact is something which the political theorist can hardly be expected to question; the laws are there, good and bad, as patterns of human behaviour. The student of politics would certainly agree with the positivist lawyer in saying that even bad laws are laws, though he would point out that it is precisely here that the problem begins: should bad laws be obeyed or resisted? I have just said that of the three types of positivism, the 'normativist' version seems to me the most important and promising. I think the time has come to do it full justice. Not without some Continental pride, I am thinking of the startling advance which legal science has made with us thanks to the normativist method. Legal science is, and cannot but be, 'formal' and 'ethically neutral'. In Professor Hart's words, 'the analysis or study of meanings of legal concepts is an important study to be distinguished from (though in no way hostile to) historical enquiries, sociological enquries, and the critical appraisal of law

in terms of morals, social aims, functions etc.'[1] But this is not the
only, nor the main, contribution of normativism to legal theory.
It is this kind of approach that has enabled us (to quote Hart
again) to realise 'that a legal system is a 'closed logical system' in
which correct decisions can de deduced from predetermined legal
rules by logical means alone'.[2] I would like to add that, so
conceived, normativism seems to me to provide an ideal ground
for one of the most interesting recent explorations in legal
philosophy: I mean the use of logic in law, or, as the word now
goes, the nature of Deontic Logic. This kind of research is being
actively pursued here at Yale, where it can boast of the pioneer
work of Hohfeld. I have it on Mr Anderson's authority that those
who engage in it do not propose to offer support for any particular
system, but 'to test its internal consistency, to verify its logical
adequacy to its declared purpose, and to isolate and clarify the
assumptions on which it rests'.[3] Perhaps I may be allowed to
point out that, except for the use of less sharpened tools, this is
not unlike what legal theory has tried to do with us in the last
hundred years. In it lie the justification and the limits of Legal
Positivism.

Yet these limits must be taken into account, and they are clearly
apparent if we place ourselves from the standpoint of political
theory. I am well aware that what I am going to say could be said
much more precisely and pertinently in strict philosophical
language. The question is, after all, how can normative propositions be derived from purely factual statements. As Hare puts it
in his by now almost classical little book (but Hume and Kant, if
I am not mistaken, had said the same thing long before him), 'no
imperative conclusion can be validly drawn from a set of premises
which does not contain at least one imperative'.[4] How can the
positivist speak of an *ought*—of 'rights', and 'duties', and 'obligations'—if his premise is simply an account that a legal system
exists and that it has a certain amount of effectiveness? In the
plain language of the man in the street, why is it that we experience
law not only as compulsory, but also as binding? Surely the
imperative mood in which many (though not all) rules of law are

---

[1] Hart, op. cit., p. 253.
[2] Hart, ibid.
[3] A. R. Anderson, *Logic, Norms and Roles*, 1961 (mimeogr.): significantly
enough, Mr Anderson borrows these words from Church's *Introduction to
Mathematical Logic*.
[4] R. M. Hare, *The Language of Morals*, Oxford, 1952, p. 28.

couched can be shown to be merely a delusion. Can those rules not be couched equally well in the indicative mood, or at any rate in the form of hypothetical imperatives? There is no rule in the law that says: 'do not wilfully commit murder'. The rule is, rather, 'if you wilfully commit murder you will be hanged'. Even the short and peremptory command which I read every day when I cross the street: 'Don't walk!' sounds to me very much like a hypothetical imperative: 'if you cross when the lights are red you will be run over by a bus or fined by a policeman'. I may quite well choose to cross the red lights if I don't mind paying the fine or if I am in the vein of committing suicide. Whence, the command? Whence, the obligation? These are the questions which, with Socrates, the political theorist candidly asks, or should ask. He wants to know both what the laws are and what makes them binding.

The question, I know full well, is as old as political theory. But let me stress the fact that I am raising it here from a strictly legal and political angle. I am not concerned with the problem of turning hypothetical into categorical imperatives. I shall leave this task to the moral philosopher. In the two examples above, the issue is clear enough: both the punishment of murder and the use of traffic lights aim at protecting human life, the highest of all earthly values. My point is that the obligatoriness of laws does not only derive from the moral duty which they may or may not express, but from another and concurrent principle of validation. I am speaking of 'positive', 'national' laws, of such laws that are valid at a given time and in a given country: laws that are set to us by some human authority. They are the rules which we single out among innumerable other rules according to criteria which are not unlike those which the positivist offers. Behind Kelsen's 'basic norm', behind Hart's 'rules of recognition' there looms a social and political reality which, by common usage, we call by a name, ambiguous if you like, and yet pertinent. Can it be the case, that by assessing what we mean by the State we might get a clearer grasp of what we mean by the law; can political philosophy help in the completion of legal theory?

Alas! sad tidings have lately reached our ears on this respect. Miss Murdoch, the Oxford philosopher and novelist, has recently remarked that 'whereas moral philosophy survives by the skin of its teeth, political philosophy has almost perished'.[1] Surely, as far

[1] I. Murdoch, 'A House of Theory', in the coll. vol. *Conviction*, London, 1958, p. 224.

at any rate as my country and the United States are concerned, political philosophy has not succumbed to the onslaught of linguistic analysis only. There is one further reason for this state of affairs. It is the immense popularity of the new 'science' of politics. That science has little use for the old classic theory of the 'State'. It rejects the very notion 'among the intellectual amusements of the past'. It is interested only in 'the raw material of government'.[1] That raw material is the brute fact of power.

If only political scientists could agree on the definition of power!

The concept of power [writes Professor Dahl] is as ancient and ubiquitous as any that social theory can boast. If [this assertion] needed any documentation, one could set up an endless parade of great names from Plato and Aristotle through Machiavelli and Hobbes to Pareto and Weber to demonstrate that a large number of seminal social theorists have devoted a great deal of attention to power and the phenomena associated with it. Doubtless it would be easy to show, too, how the word and its synonyms are everywhere embedded in the language of civilised peoples, often in subtly different ways: power, influence, control, pouvoir, puissance, Macht, Herrschaft, Gewalt, imperium, potestas, auctoritas, potentia etc.[2]

I submit that we can hope to unravel the problem of the State only by unravelling the different meanings of the words that have just been so generously and yet so indiscriminately lavished upon us. I am old-fashioned enough to believe with Rousseau that a power which we are forced to obey is something different from a power which we are obliged to acknowledge. We must find different names for the two. I submit that such time-honoured words as 'might' and 'authority' can serve very well for that purpose.

Yet not even this distinction helps us to do away with all our difficulties. Let us suppose that a policeman arrests a notorious offender at the point of his gun. Is this an exercise of might, or an exercise of authority, or of both? Surely the policeman has force on his side, since he carries the gun; but his force is something different from that of an ordinary gunman. He has the authority too, but this authority is not properly his, of him as a man, but of his office. In between the level of might and that of authority, could there not be an intermediate level, a third dimension as it were, where might is no longer pure might and is not yet authority? Certainly we do not speak of the 'might' of the policeman. But

[1] A. F. Bentley, *The Process of Government*, 1948 ed., p. 263 and ch. VI.
[2] R. A. Dahl, 'The Concept of Power', in *Behavioral Science* (1957), **2**, no. 3.

neither do we speak, in this context at any rate, of his 'authority'. We speak of his 'power'. And if we look more closely into the case, we shall find that we speak of the power of the policeman in the same way as we speak of the power of the 'State'. Both are made possible by the existence of laws. They are 'creations' of the law. They are, indeed, legal fictions.

Please do not misunderstand my words. I do not mean to say that the man who actually dons the policeman's uniform is a fiction. Neither do I mean to say that there is no 'social reality' behind the State. What I mean is that the power which both exert is something different from either might or authority. In my view, power is the legal exercise of force or might; authority is legitimate power.

I shall now try to lay down as briefly as I can the main contention of this paper. I believe that legal considerations have an important contribution to make to political theory, and that in turn political theory can be of some help for the understanding of law, for an answer to the two Kantian questions. To take my first point first, I believe that political science is wrong in neglecting the study of law, in overlooking the difference between might and power. If its purpose, so we are told, is to assess 'who gets what, where and how', I cannot see how it can do this without first knowing what the law is in a given place and at a given moment. It may well be true that, as the saying goes, he who pays the piper calls the tune; but the tune is of some importance, were it only because people dance to it. More seriously, we must not only know who the 'bosses' are; we must know who are the 'officials' in a given society, in 'whose name' they issue commands, what gives them 'authority'. To do this we must first of all assess the structure of power in the form which it takes as an institutionalised legal order. It is this legal order which the lawyer conceptualises and personifies in the State. If the concept of the State is to make any sense, it must refer to something different from, and infinitely more complex than a mere 'pattern of identifications, demands and expectations'.[1] The concept of the State is a legal, not a sociological concept.

But this personification of the legal order in the State also explains why the whole question of what law is hinges on whether we take the State to be a fact or a value. If the monopoly of power in the modern State is merely a fact, then the whole structure of normative propositions that centre around it is merely a set of

[1] Lasswell and Kaplan, *Power and Society*, 1957 ed., p. 181.

hypothetical imperatives, of rules concerning the use of force *if* and *when* the State so disposes. In that case, the 'bad man's' notion of law is correct: laws do not entail any proper sort of obligation. In order that power be binding, in order that laws should be true ought-propositions and not mere descriptions about the use of force, we must add to the mere fact of the existence of the State a value-clause, we must 'invest' its commands with a particular halo and perhaps even conceive the basic norm as a categorical imperative. We must, in other words, be able to speak not only of the power of the State, but of its authority.

This, I believe, is what Max Weber had in mind when he spoke of the 'legitimation' of power. And since I have quoted an author who should not be suspect to political scientists, I shall take from him, too, the following words which link up with my earlier argument and provide me with the best conclusion. 'Natural Law', Weber wrote, 'is the specific and only consistent type of legitimacy of a legal order which can remain, once religious revelation and the authoritarian sacredness of a tradition and its bearers have lost their force'.[1] A natural law of this kind would seem to meet the requirements of what I have called a purely deontological approach to the problem of law. But it also comes very near, if I am not mistaken, to what the modern analysts would call 'decisions of principle'. I wholeheartedly agree with those among them who have the courage to say that such principles are not meaningless nor such decisions necessarily irrational.[2] After all, as far as laws and politics are concerned, we make such decisions incessantly, in that 'plebiscite of every day' which, in Renan's admirable phrase, alone constitutes a nation. Are we not, by such decisions, bearing witness to the obligatoriness of laws, and at the same time contributing to their existence? To be sure, this is not the 'bad man's' notion of law, but that of the good citizen. But alas, as even Aristotle had to admit, it is only in a truly good State that we can hope to find such truly good citizens. Perhaps it is true, after all, that *iustitia fundamentum regnorum*.

---

[1] *Max Weber on Law in Economy and Society*, Ed. M. Rheinstein, Harvard U.P., 1954, p. 288.
[2] R. Wollheim, 'Philosophie Analytique et Pensée Politique', in *Revue Française de Science Politique* (1961), XI, no. 2.

C

A CORE OF GOOD SENSE: REFLECTIONS
ON HART'S THEORY OF NATURAL LAW

(1) A number of years ago, while I was still at Oxford, Mr Hart told me that he had been giving some thought to natural law and had come to the conclusion that there was at least one law which could be called 'natural' and whose existence could be demonstrated by rational arguments: it was the 'right of every man to freedom'.[1] I answered by relating Voltaire's reaction to the miracle of St Denis: on hearing the legend that the decapitated protector of Paris rose up and picking up his head made the rounds of the city, Voltaire remarked, 'Well, it is only the first step that costs'.

Like St Denis, Mr Hart has gone a long way since that first step. His recent book, *The Concept of Law*,[2] contains a chapter on natural law which is of great interest to me, for it represents a remarkable effort on the part of an avowed positivist to recognise the merits of that ancient and venerable notion which I myself have tried to clarify many years ago.[3] In the struggle between the defenders of natural law and the defenders of legal positivism the work of Hart is an important turn of events. It would seem that in recent years both sides have shown a willingness, if not to sign a treaty of peace, at least to admit the possibility of co-existence. But Mr Hart goes further. To recognise, as he does, a 'core of good sense' in the idea of natural law is to show an

[1] H. L. A. Hart, 'Are there any Natural Rights?', *The Philosophical Review*, vol. LXIV, no. 2, April 1955.
[2] Oxford University Press, 1961.
[3] *Natural Law* (1951).

understanding that goes beyond tolerance.[1]

The possibility of admitting that, at least on different planes, there is a basis for both positions is a relatively recent acquisition. I shall not cite the solutions proposed by defenders of natural law, of whom I am one, because I have treated this theme elsewhere.[2] I prefer to summarise the views of positivists, since it is among them that we find Mr Hart.

(2) Mr N. Bobbio, who still maintained not long ago that the notion of natural law is meaningless and contradictory,[3] has come to recognise more and more explicitly the 'historical function' of this superannuated concept in the defence of certain values against the organised force of those in power.[4] He has done more. In a detailed analysis of the various meanings of the terms 'natural law' and 'legal positivism', he has brought out with surprising clarity the true dimensions of the difference between them and exposed the often crude misunderstandings which nurture that difference.[5] Here I shall merely recall his three versions of legal positivism: as a method, as a theory, and as an ideology. As a method, or better, as a way of considering law, positivism is closely bound up with legal science and the work of jurists. As a theory it corresponds to the modern concept of the statist character of law. Finally, as an ideology, positivism implies the attribution of moral value to positive law. It is expressed in the phrase: *Gesetz ist Gesetz* (law is law), and its corollary is a rigid theory of obedience.

If these distinctions are accepted, the only kind of positivism which seems to me to have its papers in order is the first, for it is evident that whoever pursues the science and not the philosophy of law is required to limit himself to the facts, to the rules actually in force in the place and time in which he lives. Furthermore it is

[1] It surprises me that this aspect of Mr Hart's legal philosophy has not yet been subjected to detailed discussion. I know only two authors (and I learned of them from Mr Hart himself) who have alluded to it in their reviews of *The Concept of Law*, M. J. T. Noonan in the *Natural Law Forum*, vol. 7, 1962, and M. M. C. Singer in *The Journal of Philosophy*, vol. LX, no. 8, April 1963.
[2] 'Two questions about law', See above, pp. 173–84, and 'Legality and Legitimacy', *The Review of Metaphysics*, vol. XVI, no. 4, June 1963.
[3] N. Bobbio, 'Quelques arguments contre le droit naturel', in the volume *Le Droit naturel (Annales de Philosophie politique*, III, Paris, 1959).
[4] N. Bobbio, *Locke e il diritto naturale* (University course), Turin, 1963, p. 75.
[5] N. Bobbio, 'Sul positivismo giuridico' (*Rivista di Filosofia*, vol. LII, no. 1, 1961), and, Giusnaturalismo e positivismo giuridico' (*Rivista di Diritto civile*, a. VIII, no. 6, 1962).

to its rigorous 'neutrality', its careful avoidance of value judgements, and its presentation of a faithful picture of the positive juridical order that the modern science of law is indebted for the success of which it is justly proud. As far as the second and third types of positivism are concerned, both seem to me to be open to criticism. As a reflection of a particular historical situation, the success of legal positivism as a theory is bound up with a contingent fact, the fact that the modern State has assumed a monopoly of law and the making of law. This concept also runs into serious difficulties when it tries to explain the juridical character of a law that is not from the State, such as canon law or international law. Finally, legal positivism as an ideology ends up as a simple inversion of natural law, if not as a theory of natural law in its own right. To affirm the moral duty of obeying laws is exactly what natural law theories have always proposed. The only difference between the two ideologies is the way in which they present the obligation of obedience. Those who oppose natural law to positive law see obedience as conditioned and limited, while those who conceive positive law as an end in itself find no such limits. One ideology deserves another. There will always be those who refuse to accept the maxim, *Gesetz ist Gesetz*, and who will prefer to obey God rather than men.

I find that Mr Bobbio's distinctions lead to two important results. On the one hand they show us the basis of positivist theory as a foundation and even as a condition of legal science. On the other hand they also—in the author's own opinion—make it possible to safeguard certain positions of natural law theory with respect to the criticism of positive law and to the problem of justice. It seems clear to me in any case that the principal argument of positivism against natural law is a speculative one: it is moral relativism, according to which natural law is only one ideology among others. In particular the theory of natural law would be but one way of justifying certain values (which may vary endlessly) through recourse to a supposed 'nature' of things or of men.[1] It is indeed a fact, as I have pointed out elsewhere,[2] that the

---

[1] N. Bobbio, 'Giusnaturalismo e positivismo giuridico'. The thesis that 'natural law is not a morality or an ideology of justice but a theory of morality . . . a way of founding morality (any morality)' has been taken up by Bobbio in his latest course (*Locke e il diritto naturale*, 1963). It was the object of a report presented at the recent International Congress of Philosophy in Mexico City.

[2] 'Two questions about law', see above p. 173.

majority of *our* positivists are also sceptics. But if they oppose the universal pretensions of natural law, they do not deny the need behind it. It is therefore essential, as Eisenmann has pointed out,[1] to distinguish the different aspects of the problem of law as seen from the point of view of 'description', 'casuistry', and 'legislation'. For my part I would add the points of view of obligation and obedience. However that may be, it is evident that only by admitting these different levels can one conceive the possible coexistence of the two rival theses. I find confirmation of this in a recent article by an author who is certainly not suspect of softness toward natural law, Mr Alf Ross, the eminent representative of the Scandinavian school.[2]

(3) Mr Ross categorically rejects the notion of natural law. His scepticism and moral relativism lead him to view the pretensions of natural law in a most unfavourable light.[3] At the same time he repudiates the normative concept of law so dear to the heart of the positivist. For him law is but a fact to be studied and described in purely empirical terms. The scientific study of law must be purged of the last vestige of 'metaphysical' and *a priori* language, such as duty, obligation, and especially validity: for the notion of validity, implying as it does the obligatory character of law and the duty of obedience, cannot be reduced to empirical observation and so has no place in a truly positivist doctrine. But it is precisely for this reason that the stubborn defender of natural law (Ross therefore admits that there are such) has no quarrel to pick with the positivist nor the latter with the former. It is evident that since the question of the validity of a certain juridical order is a question of values, and since natural law is invoked precisely for the sake of giving such an order validity or obligatory force:

there can be no reason for the philosophy of natural law to deny the positivist thesis, and for not recognising that a juridical order is a social fact capable of being described in purely empirical terms without any reference to the problem of validity. The defender of natural law is concerned with the question of knowing if a certain effective order also

[1] Ch. Eisenmann, 'Le juriste et le droit naturel', in the volume cited, *Le Droit naturel*, 1959.
[2] A. Ross, 'Validity and the Conflict between Legal Positivism and Natural Law', taken from the *Revista Juridica de Buenos Aires*, IV, 1961.
[3] A. Ross, *On Law and Justice*, University of California Press, 1959, chs. 10 and 11.

obliges its subjects from a purely moral point of view. But before he can answer this question he must know that a certain order effectively exists and what its contents are. Thus the question of validity necessarily presupposes the positivist thesis, namely that the existence of a juridical order can be verified and described independently of every moral idea or of natural law.[1]

Again I have the impression that the theses of natural law emerge relatively unscathed from the test to which they have been subjected. Not only does Ross explicitly admit the possible coexistence of two points of view concerning law, but he is also forced to resort to extreme scepticism and relativism in order to deny the natural law any merit. He does it precisely to be able to deny any intrinsic validity to the positive order and thus escape what Bobbio calls the third type of positivism. He even denounces the traces of this kind of natural law in a concept of law like that of Kelsen.[2] Nevertheless he sees nothing to prevent a philosopher of law from proposing the problem of the validity of the juridical order (the problem whose solution is denied to the jurist) and to find its solution (or believe he finds it) in a natural law which expresses the 'universally valid principles governing the life of man in society'. What Ross wants to show is not that in doing so the philosopher will venture into a path without issue, but that there are two entirely different problems here, two ways of reasoning about law of which only one, that of positivism, is within the competence of the jurist.

In spite of their differences, Bobbio and Ross have this in common in their views of legal positivism: it is a theory which excludes natural law from consideration while leaving place for it in questions of value on which the theory of law does not have to pronounce but which can be the object of a different study. Now it was precisely under this aspect that I myself proposed a timid defence of natural law several years ago, to try to save at least the idea of it in the sense of a 'deontology', as the critical determination of values which inspire, sustain, and confirm the juridical order.[3] Certainly this was minimal, not calculated to satisfy the strict proponent of the natural law who maintains that there is a law 'which flows from the nature of things'. Let me say frankly that the proponents of natural law and not the positivists are

[1] A. Ross, 'Validity and the Conflict', etc., pp. 64–66.
[2] ibid. pp. 78–82.
[3] A. P. d Entrèves, 'Le droit naturel', in the volume cited of *Le Droit Naturel*, 1959.

the ones who insist on the maximum with the greatest intransigence. They want the full admission of the 'ontological' notion of natural law: there exists an eternal and immutable law which can be the object of our knowledge. The positive law is valid only to the extent that it respects the natural law and is based on morality. As Mr Hart[1] has observed, the clearest and most coherent expression of this point of view is still the proposition of St Thomas: *lex iniusta non est lex; omnis lex humanitus posita in tantum habet de ratione legis, in quantum a lege naturae derivatur* (an unjust law is not law; any humanly enacted law has the character of law to the extent that it is derived from the law of nature).[2] There is no question here of abstaining from a judgment of value in order to know the law, as with Mr Bobbio, nor of seeing, as Mr Ross would have it, that the juridical order is a social fact describable in purely empirical terms. Judgment of fact and judgment of value are inseparable for the intransigent proponent of natural law. He is required to deny the character of law to any positive law that contradicts the natural law. This is the stumbling block to any rapprochement between natural law and positivism.

(4) Let us now look at the original and unusual solution proposed by Mr Hart. We may begin by pointing out that he is not in agreement with those who like Bobbio and Ross see a necessary connection or at least an elective affinity between moral relativism and legal positivism. He observes that the founders of English positivism such as Bentham and Austin were not relativists in morals.[3] In his case, therefore, we may look for a positivism which does not rule out the knowledge of moral principles, either in general or in connection with legal problems. In fact, Hart's definition of positivism is very simple, and very different from those we have seen proposed by Bobbio and Ross. 'Here we shall take Legal Positivism to mean the simple contention that it is in no sense a necessary truth that laws reproduce or satisfy certain demands of morality, though in fact they have often done so.'[4] The positivist, therefore, cannot accept the thesis of the classical doctrine of natural law on this key point, but it does not follow

[1] H. L. A. Hart, *The Concept of Law*, p. 152.
[2] *Summa Theologica*, 1a, 2 ac, q. 95, art. 2.
[3] op. cit. p. 253.
[4] ibid. pp. 180–181; 'Positivism and the Separation of Law and Morals', *Harvard Law Review*, vol. 71, no. 4, February 1958.

that while affirming the separation of law and morality one ought to overlook that this doctrine may 'contain elementary truths of importance'.

Modern criticism of natural law—to summarise Hart—can all be brought back to the familiar distinction between 'descriptive' and 'prescriptive' propositions, between judgments of fact and judgments of value. The very expression, natural law, illustrates the difference in meaning which the word *law* can assume as a description of a factual condition and as a prescription of conduct or of order. In its prescriptive acceptation the idea of natural law is not necessarily linked to belief in a personal God who has 'ordered' the laws of nature. The very fact that its hold is ndependent of both divine and human authority ought to lead us to inquire if in spite of every-thing this idea does not contribute to a better understand-ing of both law and morality. There is certainly no question of reviving the whole teleological view of nature on which the classical doctrine of natural law was founded and which was used to transform into prescriptions what was in fact only a description of the normal development of things. But there is no need to postulate with Aristotle or St Thomas the existence of an end proper to man and constituting his 'good' in order to account for the fact that there is a sense in speaking, as one com-monly does, of the proper end of all animate existence, namely, that of survival, *perseverare in esse suo*. Hobbes and Hume were satisfied with this 'very attenuated version' of natural law, and according to Hart it justifies natural law even today.[1] If we are concerned with societies organised for survival and not with a 'suicide club', we have a perfect right to ask,

whether, among these social arrangements, there are some which may illuminatingly be ranked as natural laws discoverable by reason, and what their relation is to human law and morality. To raise this or any other question concerning *how* men should live together, we must assume that their aim, generally speaking, is to live. From this point the argument is a simple one. Reflection on some very obvious general-isations—indeed truisms—concerning human nature and the world in which men live, show that as long as these hold good, there are certain rules of conduct which any social organisation must contain if it is to be viable.[2]

[1] *The Concept of Law*, pp. 182–187.
[2] ibid. p. 188.

(5) I have tried to give a faithful summary of Hart's reasoning, and I think I have shown how far he has gone along the path I spoke of at the beginning of this article. He speaks of 'universally recognised principles of conduct which have a basis in elementary truths concerning human beings, their natural environment, and aims'. These principles 'may be considered the *minimum content* of Natural Law, in contrast with the more grandiose and more challengeable constructions which have often been proffered under that name'.[1]

Hart then goes on to 'consider, in the form of five truisms, the salient characteristics of human nature upon which this modest but important minimum rests'. I shall not go into detail but merely mention these truisms as observations of a contingent but undeniable situation. (a) Men are not exoskeletal creatures but are very vulnerable, and it is therefore necessary to protect human life. (b) In spite of differences among them, men are ultimately reduced to a certain equality. This is not the case among nations, and that is why international law has a precarious existence. (c) They are neither angels nor devils, and they may therefore be required to tolerate, support, and respect one another. (d) Their resources and goods are limited. There must be, therefore, some kind of safeguards for goods and some allowances for exchange of goods. (e) Their intelligence and will are weak. It is thus necessary to promote voluntary co-operation among them within a coercive framework of predetermined sanctions. These five truisms are the reason why law and morals include a specific content. That is to say, they disclose 'the core of good sense in the doctrine of Natural Law'. Here also is the reason why the definition of law in purely formal terms 'has proved so inadequate'.[2] Except in the sense that we shall examine soon, 'the positivist thesis that "law may have any content" ' is unacceptable to Hart, 'for it is a truth of some importance that for the adequate description not only of law but of many other social institutions, a place must be reserved, besides definitions and ordinary statements of fact, for a third category of statements: those the truth of which is contingent on human beings and the world they live in retaining the salient characteristics which they have'.[3]

Hart therefore proposes a modernised version of Hobbes and Hume. He says as much, with a sincerity that does him credit,

[1] ibid. p. 189.
[2] ibid. p. 194.
[3] ibid. p. 195.

and the fact gives us a useful guide. I imagine the questions I am going to ask him differ little from questions proposed long ago to the two authors who inspired him. My first question is: what value does this natural law have as a normative proposition; what obligation does it carry with it? My second question is: How is this natural law related to positive law, and to what extent can positive law avoid taking its requirements into account? It is hardly necessary to add that these two questions are closely related.

(6) To answer the first question I think we should make the most of a remark that Hart glides over casually but which is of capital importance; namely, that the relationship between the natural facts enumerated above and the 'content' of legal and moral regulations is a 'rational' one, not a relationship of causality. Psychology, sociology, and other sciences deal with the *causes* for which certain rules flow necessarily from a given social situation, but they do not treat the existence of these rules as depending on a choice, on a conscious resolve on the part of those who enact them. Only the 'truisms' of the natural law give us the *reasons* why, given the end of survival, 'law and morals should include a specific content'.[1] If I am not mistaken, this is how Hart seeks to bridge the gap between fact and value, to transform the natural law from a descriptive proposition to a normative one:

The general form of the argument [he says] is simply that without such a content laws and morals could not forward the minimum purpose of survival which men have in associating with each other. In the absence of this content men, as they are, would have no reason for obeying voluntarily any rules; and without a minimum of co-operation given voluntarily by those who find that it is in their interest to submit to and maintain the rules, coercion of others who would not voluntarily conform would be impossible.[2]

Is this a convincing reason? Has Hart really succeeded in bridging the gap between fact and value, between the *is* and the *ought*, a task deemed impossible by analytical philosophy following the celebrated judgment of Hume? Sir Isaiah Berlin clearly alludes to this as an achievement of Hart's reinterpretation of

[1] ibid. p. 254.
[2] ibid. p. 189.

N

natural law.[1] Nevertheless if is not difficult—and Hart admits it himself—to see the value judgment implicit in what is at first presented as a simple observation of fact, namely in the proposition that the aim of all human association is survival. We have a repetition here of Hobbes' own case. Hobbes too seems to deduce from an observation of fact (the state of nature as *bellum omnium contra omnes*) the precept, the 'general rule of reason', *pax est quaerenda, bellum vitandum*, and all the rules which follow from it.[2] But in fact he interposes a value judgment between the observation and the prescription, the judgment that the conservation and defence of human life are a good thing.[3] Besides, it is enough to read the famous text in chapter XIII of *Leviathan* where he contrasts the benefits of the civil state with the state of nature, to be convinced that Hobbes had a very well-established and clearly defined table of values. But the resemblance to Hobbes does not stop here. It is also revealed in Hart's notion of reason. If he insists on the 'mediatory' function of reason, it is because he looks upon the task of reason as not to establish values but to deduce 'conclusions' from 'theorems' (as Hobbes put it), and to 'find' the rules of morality, not to prove them (as Hume would say).[4] This is, if you will, a purely formal and nominalistic concept of reason. The classical proponent of the natural law will find it deficient. For my part I do not find it so. It seems quite enough for the natural law to give 'good reasons'.[5] A statement from Hume seems to summarise better than any commentary the thesis of Hart, to which I have no difficulty in subscribing: 'Tho' the rules of justice be *artificial*, they are not *arbitrary*. Nor is the expression improper to call them *Laws of Nature*; if by natural we understand what is common to any species, or even if we confine it to mean what is inseparable from the species.'[6]

(7) Let us now proceed to the obligations which flow from the natural law as a normative proposition. I have just cited Hart as

---

[1] I. Berlin, 'Does Political Theory still Exist?' in the volume, *Philosophy, Politics and Society*, 2nd series, Ed. P. Laslett and W. G. Runciman, Oxford, 1962, p. 27. Sir Isaiah also emphasises the 'kernel of truth' contained in the old *a priori* doctrines of natural law.

[2] T. Hobbes, *De Cive*, ch. III, no. 32; *Leviathan*, ch. 17.

[3] N. Bobbio, Quelques arguments, etc. pp. 148–185.

[4] D. Hume, *A Treatise on Human Nature*, bk. III, pt. I, sect. 1.

[5] I borrow this expression from A. C. Garnett, 'Good Reasons in Ethics: A Revised Conception of Natural Law', *Mind*, vol. LXIX, no. 275, July 1960.

[6] D. Hume, op. cit., bk. III, pt. II, sect. 1.

saying that it is the specific content furnished by natural law which assures the voluntary obedience of men to positive law. Clearly then this voluntary obedience is an essential feature of law and the obligatory character of law is not derived exclusively from the coercive force which it possesses. I cannot repeat in detail Hart's discussion of the problem of obligation.[1] He starts from an analysis of language and arrives at the important observation that the very notion of obligation implies 'the existence of a rule; yet it is not always the case that where rules exist the standard of behaviour required by them is conceived of in terms of obligation.'[2] Another distinction must be introduced—Hart constantly insists on it—between the 'internal' and 'external' aspect of rules of conduct.[3] This distinction has nothing to do with psychology or the personal feelings of those who observe the rules.[4] It depends on the point of view from which the rules are considered. To the observer who does not accept them himself, the rules will be mere regularities in the behaviour of men. But to a 'member of the group which accepts and uses them as guides to conduct' the rules appear in the correlative terms of duty and law, as the 'basis' or 'reason' for behaving in a certain way.[5]

This distinction throws considerable light on the problem of natural law and the obligations which flow from it. To this distinction Hart returns when he speaks of natural law as the content of positive laws, without which men, as they are, would have no reason to obey voluntarily. Certainly that content does not reduce exclusively to the simple rules enunciated in the truisms. The reasons for voluntary obedience are complex. They constitute what Hart calls the accepted morality in a given society, and it can happen that the morality accepted by a dominant group implies the isolation or oppression of another group, as in slavery or racism.[6] But it is none the less true, says Hart, that for a system of rules to be imposed by force on one group, there must be others in sufficient numbers who accept it voluntarily. 'Without their vol-

[1] H. L. A. Hart, 'Legal and Moral Obligation', in the volume, *Essays in Moral Philosophy*, ed. A. I. Melden, Seattle, 1958; *The Concept of Law*, passim.
[2] *The Concept of Law*, p. 83.
[3] H. L. A. Hart, *Definition and Theory in Jurisprudence—an inaugural lecture*, Oxford, 1953; *The Concept of Law*, passim; 'Scandinavian Realism', *The Cambridge Law Journal*, November 1959.
[4] *The Concept of Law*, p. 56.
[5] ibid. pp. 86–88; 'Legal and Moral Obligation', p. 90.
[6] *The Concept of Law*, p. 196.

untary co-operation, thus creating *authority*, the coercive power of law and government cannot be established.'[1]

Hence a society with law contains those who look upon its rules from the internal point of view as accepted standards of behaviour . . . But it also comprises those upon whom, either because they are malefactors or mere helpless victims of the system, these legal standards have to be imposed by force or threat of force; they are concerned with the rules merely as a source of possible punishment. The balance between these two components will be determined by many different factors. If the system is fair and caters genuinely to the vital interests of all those from whom it demands obedience, it may gain and retain the allegiance of most for most of the time, and will accordingly be stable. On the other hand it may be a narrow and exclusive system run in the interests of the dominant group, and it may be made continually more repressive and unstable with the latent threat of upheaval. Between these two extremes various combinations of these attitudes to law are to be found, often in the same individual.[2]

Let us notice the light which this relationship between law and morality throws on the political scene. We should like to know to what extent law and morality condition each other. On the one hand Hart seems to admit that positive law is closely linked to a specific content indicated by natural law. On the other hand he maintains, as we have seen, 'that it is in no sense a necessary truth that laws reproduce or satisfy certain demands of morality'. This is the fundamental dogma of legal positivism, and he accepts it. We must therefore look further into this point, my second question: what is the relationship between positive and natural law, and to what extent may the former ignore the latter?

(8) To understand Hart we must again turn to other ideas on which the solution of our problem depends, the most important of which is the notion of validity. Hart treats it amply, and I shall recall here only what seems essential to our question. For Hart, if I understand him correctly, the notion of validity goes beyond the existential or factual judgment of the type: law is the system of rules which are in fact observed in a certain place and at a certain time. It is rather a 'normative' judgment which supposes a criterion or 'rule of recognition', which in turn allows us to declare that a particular rule corresponds to a given system of which it forms a part and that one can and ought to make use of it to

[1] ibid. p. 196.
[2] ibid. p. 197.

qualify certain behaviour as relevant from the legal point of view.[1] We find here again the distinction that Hart favours between the internal and external approach to a legal system. We also find traces of the profound influence of Kelsen on Hart's thought. This criterion of qualification is an essentially formal one for Hart as it is for Kelsen. It is furnished not by the content of a particular rule itself but by reference to another rule.[2] It is only in determining the 'rule of recognition' that the question of fact reappears. On this point Hart rejects Kelsen's 'basic norm' (*Grundnorm*). He affirms very clearly that the problem of determining the criterion of validity of the legal order is an 'empirical, though complex, question of fact', not of hypothesis.[3] What does this question of fact boil down to? Simply to the acceptance on the part of those who obey and apply the rules as 'valid':[4]

There are therefore two minimum conditions necessary and sufficient for the existence of a legal system. On the one hand those rules of behaviour which are valid according to the system's ultimate criteria of validity must be generally obeyed, and, on the other hand, its rules of recognition specifying the criteria of legal validity and its rules of change and adjudication must be effectively accepted as common public standards of official behaviour by its officials.[5]

With this elucidation of the notion of validity let us return to the principles of the natural law, or of morality in general, and their relation to positive or 'valid' law. To this problem Hart devotes the last section of the chapter we have been examining, a section entitled 'Legal validity and resistance to law'.[6] The title itself shows that Hart considers the problem important. He cites recent cases contesting the validity of positive law in the name of natural law. The question of resistance is not ordinarily among those collected in treatises on legal theory, but in spite of such difficulties Hart does not hesitate for a moment to draw the logical conclusions from his rigorously positivist point of view. His notion of validity, as we have seen, implies two criteria and no others: the formal criterion of the legal qualification of one rule by another, and the criterion of fact, of the existence of an

[1] This thesis is already contained in the essay, *Definition and Theory in Jurisprudence* of 1953. Hart has refined it a great deal since then.
[2] *The Concept of Law*, p. 103.
[3] ibid. p. 245.
[4] ibid. p. 99.
[5] ibid. p. 113.
[6] ibid. pp. 203–207.

ultimate rule of recognition. It follows that the validity of a particular rule cannot depend in any way on its content, on its conformity to the principles of natural law or morality, a criterion exterior to the system. Hart realises that to accept the thesis of the subordination of positive law to natural law means to abandon or at least to constrict to the point of total transformation the notion of validity generally accepted by those who deal with positive law, a very broad notion which recognises the validity of any rule which satisfies the criteria established by the particular legal order under study.

Let us observe, however, that Hart appeals more to practical considerations than to logical argument in support of his thesis. He disagrees with Kelsen's view 'that it is logically impossible to regard a particular rule of law as valid and at the same time to accept, as morally binding, a moral rule forbidding the behaviour required by the legal rule'.[1] He merely asks the question: 'What then of the practical merits of the narrower concept of law in moral deliberation? In what way is it better, when faced with morally iniquitous demands, to think "This is in no sense law" rather than "This is law but too iniquitous to obey or apply"?'[2] In Hart's eyes it is the merit of the positivists such as Austin, Gray and Kelsen to have seen clearly that the second proposition is the correct one. Even Kelsen's noted expression, 'the rules of law can have any content whatsoever', is explained and justified in this sense. The positivists would never deny that morality and law are related. They merely want to guard against confusing legal validity and moral obligation.[3] Hart absolves them from all transgression into what Bobbio calls positivism as ideology. They could never be found guilty of confusing the question of validity with that of obedience. It is this kind of positivism, Bobbio's positivism as method, that Hart espouses. I have already expressed my own opinion that positivism in this sense seems to me to be the very condition of legal science. To profess it is a sign of clear thinking and intellectual honesty on the part of the jurist.

(9) I must nevertheless add that I fail to see this as the end of the story. It seems to me that in spite of the clarity of his treatment Hart may have unwittingly become bogged down on an impassable road. Is it perhaps because he has ventured too far along the way

[1] ibid. p. 246.
[2] ibid. p. 205.
[3] *Positivism and the Separation of Law and Morals*, passim.

of the natural law? The first step is not always the one that costs the most. I see two difficulties in Hart's reasoning, and I shall close this long discussion by asking him to clarify them.

My first difficulty arises not from a disagreement with Hart but from a desire to determine the precise role and place of natural law as he conceives them with respect to law on the one hand and morality on the other. We have just learned that the validity of a legal norm does not depend in any way on its equity or iniquity, its moral value or lack of it. On the other hand Hart tells us that natural law constitutes a minimum content of any legal order, that it contains the elementary principles which men must respect as long as men are what they are and propose to set up a viable society. Are we to conclude that natural law is a central and privileged sphere of morality distinguished by its sacred and inviolable character? It may readily be admitted that a society founded on evil laws may lack that voluntary co-operation of which Hart speaks; but the system might still maintain itself, at least for a time, by force. Furthermore we know that the most viable of systems must be prepared to have recourse to force. A suitable dose of morality must be imposed on those who do not welcome it. What dosage and what conditions is a question which Hart has recently discussed, with as much logic as good sense.[1] Finally we know, and again it is Hart who says it, 'that neither the law nor the accepted morality of societies need extend their minimal protections and benefits to all within their scope, and often they have not done so.'[2]

This last point perplexes me, even though I follow Hart's reasoning. What happens if the forced imposition of the so-called morality of a group which has seized power is in flagrant violation not only with the morality of the oppressed group but even with the minimal conditions imposed by the natural law for the very existence of a legal order; if, in other words, the contradiction reaches the point of violating the 'minimum protection for persons, property, and promises' which are, in Hart's own view, the 'indispensable features' of law and hence of the legal order?[3] If a despot, for example, were to order the death of all his subjects, or the confiscation of all their goods, or their reduction to slavery, could we still maintain that while these laws are evil they are still laws? Or must we concede that natural law represents, so to

[1] H. L. A. Hart, *Law, Liberty, and Morality*, Stanford University Press, 1963.
[2] *The Concept of Law*, p. 196.
[3] ibid. p. 195.

speak, the borderline of evil, the frontier beyond which iniquity gains the upper hand and destroys law itself? I must say that I cannot see the exact line of demarcation between natural law and morality, and I think that on this point Mr Hart owes us a further explanation.

On the other hand the place of natural law is just as unclear to me from the point of view of law proper. Mr Hart's expression, 'natural law', I am fully aware, is used in an objective, not a subjective sense. At least that is my impression from reading his work. The question of 'natural right' or rights in the subjective sense, which was the topic of his first essay of 1955, has been relegated to silence in *The Concept of Law*. Nevertheless we might at least ask to what extent he would be disposed to recognise the existence of natural rights, once he has admitted the existence of a natural law. It is clear that for him the existence of right in the objective sense has its logical counterpart in the existence of subjective rights. An entire section of his book is devoted to an examination of the powers which law creates and confers in a given situation.[1] Does the existence of natural law create powers, faculties, rights for the individual, rights which would in some way constitute a defence against 'the organised force of those who hold power'—to use Bobbio's expression? Does it set up a limit to the action of the State, a guarantee against arbitrary power? Anyone who has thought through the history of natural law must agree that it is exactly on this point that the modern notion of natural rights differs from the classical doctrine of natural law, and in current usage the term natural rights is by now no longer associated to the notion of an objective order of universally valid truths. Since the question of natural rights comes up here in connection with the problem of obedience, it should be considered from that angle. I therefore go on to my second difficulty, which, I repeat, is not so much of a difficulty as a desire for clarification of the courageous and unusual position which Mr Hart has found it necessary to take on the subject of obedience and resistance.

---

[1] I cannot enter here into the details of the fundamental distinction, which Hart develops fully, between 'primary rules' which impose obligations and 'secondary rules' which confer powers. This distinction has been severely criticised, from the point of view of positive English law, by L. J. Cohen in his review, 'The Concept of Law', *Mind*, vol. LXXI, no. 283, July 1962. What is important here is that Hart thinks that law as a whole cannot be understood except as the combination of these two kinds of rules. (*The Concept of Law*, p. 237.)

(10) For those who like myself believe that the central problem of all legal philosophy is the problem of obligation, it is certainly gratifying to see this old problem restored to honour and placed at the very centre of recent debate.[1] Hart tells us expressly that to accept the positivist thesis is not to deny that there is a problem concerning obedience. Specifically he says that the certification of the positive validity of a rule by no means constitutes a demand that it be obeyed.[2] I shall only ask: to whom is the invitation addressed, the invitation to refuse obedience to a law recognised as juridically valid but morally iniquitous? I imagine that it could be addressed to the subjects of a State, to those who belong to a particular legal order, to the members of a social group whose acceptance, as we have seen, is the ultimate condition for the validity of the system. In that case it would be an appeal to resistance or insurrection, an invitation to act in such a way that the system will collapse. This would be the phenomenon which Hart describes under various aspects as pathology of the legal order. A system in which obedience begins to bend is a system in which the criterion of validity has become, or is about to become, blurred and useless.[3]

But this invitation could also be extended—as the Englishman Hart is well aware—to the officials, the magistrates and judges who explain and interpret the law, who have the task of deciding case for case what the valid rule is. Hart likes to compare the declaration of the judge, 'It is the law', to that of the umpire who says 'Goal', or anyone who marks up a point when applying the rules of a game.[4] What puzzles me is this: what does the judge do, and what would Hart have him do, in the case of an 'evil law'? I suppose he would have to say: I admit that this law is valid according to the established order, but I refuse to apply it in the name of a higher and holier cause. I suppose he could do even more: jam the machinery of the established order, offer his resignation, suffer for the cause. The judge can go farther than the

---

[1] The thesis of Isaiah Berlin in the article cited, 'Does Political Theory still Exist?' is that the question, 'Why obey?' is always the essential question of political philosophy. Only a few years ago the generally accepted opinion at Oxford was that there was no sense in asking questions of this kind.

[2] *The Concept of Law*, p. 206.

[3] ibid. pp. 114–115.

[4] This is also the key notion Hart uses to refute the 'realist' ideas of the American or Scandinavian kind and to defend the 'normative' concept of law as a system of rules: the judge does not 'make' law, he determines and applies it.

simple citizen toward aggravating the pathology of the system and making it irreparable. What puzzles me is not that Hart asks the hypothetical judge to be a hero—we all knew real ones during the Resistance—but that he asks him to say that a law is valid when he clearly does not consider it so, since he refuses to apply it. I fail to see the distinction between his refusing to 'declare' the law and saying that it is not valid. In refusing is he not recurring to a criterion of validity that is above the system? This is precisely what the defenders of natural law have always done, and Hart has opened the door—perhaps imprudently—to one of their strongest arguments.

At this point the reader may be ready to ask if my observations are to be taken as approval or criticism. I dare hope that their sense is clear with regard to Mr Hart's book and the idea of the natural law that it espouses. I find the book remarkable from every point of view. I am attracted above all by the fact that it revives the discussion of all the traditional problems not only of the philosophy of law but also of political philosophy. It reflects the present disenchantment with the ideal of 'neutrality' which has dominated our studies too long, as well as the desire to restore reason, or at least 'good reasons', to the field of moral science.[1] What Hart has written about natural law should be compared with what Hannah Arendt recently wrote concerning the Nazi laws which 'went against nature'.[2] Unfortunately Rousseau's famous dictum about the legislator who 'must feel that he is in a position to change, so to speak, human nature', has found too many followers for two centuries, not only among politicians but also among jurists.[3] It is good to find someone saying openly what we have always felt, that human nature does not change easily and that it has a way of taking revenge.

I fear, however, that in stirring up what had become the calm coexistence of positivism and natural law, Hart will draw fire from both sides. I strongly doubt that the Continental positivist, for whom positivism is closely bound up with moral relativism, will embrace without flinching Hart's restoration of natural law as a minimum of incontestable truth, modest as it is. On the

[1] I. Berlin insists on these two points in the fine article I have already cited. See especially pp. 17 and 33 for a concise criticism of the irrationalism of the 'ideologies' and of the fetish of *Wertfreiheit*.
[2] H. Arendt, *Eichmann in Jerusalem; a Report on the Banality of Evil*, New York, 1963, ch. VIII.
[3] J. J. Rousseau, *Social Contract*, bk. II, ch. vii.

other hand I do not believe that the logical proponent of natural law can be content with what Hart offers him. Not only will he reject the purely formal and nominalistic concept of reason of which I spoke, but he will have his foot in the door to make further demands. Why should natural law be limited to the question of survival? If the conservation of life is good, it is because there is a 'good life', the Aristotelian would say, or, the Thomist would add, because natural life is the means of assuring eternal life. The barriers are down, and all the values which have appealed in turn to natural law will find support once more, each with its exclusive pretensions.

I have already stated why I find Hart's interpretation of natural law completely plausible. As Hart reminds us, the wisdom of Hobbes and Hume was to 'have been willing to lower their sights', and this expression seems apt here also. The art of the happy medium is a difficult one, and it is perhaps this very English art which led Hart not only to find good common sense in natural law but also to put such a generous share of it into the composition of his book.

INDEX